Imagining Nature
Blake's Environmental Poetics

In *Imagining Nature* Kevin Hutchings combines insights garnered from literary history, poststructuralist theory, and the emerging field of ecological literary studies. He considers William Blake's illuminated poetry in the context of the eighteenth-century model of "nature's economy," a conceptual paradigm that prefigured modern-day ecological insights, describing all earthly entities as integrated parts of a dynamic, interactive system. Hutchings details Blake's sympathy for – and important suspicions concerning – the burgeoning contemporary fascination with such things as environmental ethics, animal rights, and the various fields of scientific naturalism.

By focusing on Blake's concern for the relationship between nature and ideology (including the politics of class, gender, and religion) Hutchings avoids the sentimentalism and misanthropic pitfalls all too often associated with environmental commentary. He articulates a distinctively Blakean perspective on current debates in literary theory and eco-criticism and argues that while Blake's peculiar humanism and profound emphasis upon spiritual concerns have led the majority of his readers to regard his work as patently anti-natural, such a view distorts the central political and aesthetic concerns of Blake's corpus. By showing that Blake's apparent hostility toward the natural world is actually a key aspect of his famous critique of institutionalized authority, Hutchings presents Blake's work as an example of "green Romanticism" in its most sophisticated and socially responsive form.

KEVIN HUTCHINGS is assistant professor in the English Department, University of Northern British Columbia.

Imagining Nature

Blake's Environmental Poetics

KEVIN HUTCHINGS

McGill-Queen's University Press
Montreal & Kingston · London · Ithaca

Legal deposit third quarter 2002
Bibliothèque nationale du Québec

Printed in Canada on acid-free paper that is 100%
ancient forest free (100% post-consumer recycled)
and processed chlorine free.

This book has been published with the help of a grant
from the Humanities and Social Sciences Federation
of Canada, using funds provided by the Social Sciences
and Humanities Research Council of Canada. Publication
has also been supported by a grant from the University
of Northern British Columbia.

McGill-Queen's University Press acknowledges
the financial support of the Government of Canada
through the Book Publishing Industry Development
Program (BPIDP) for its publishing activities. We also
acknowledge the support of the Canada Council for
the Arts for our publishing program.

**National Library of Canada Cataloguing
in Publication Data**

Hutchings, Kevin D. (Kevin Douglas), 1960–
   Imagining nature: Blake's environmental poetics
   Includes bibliographical references and index.
   ISBN 0-7735-2342-1
   1. Blake, William, 1757–1827 – Criticism
   and interpretation. 2. Nature in literature.
   3. Environmentalism in literature. I. Title.
   PR4148.N3H88 2002   821.7   C2001-904260-4

Typeset in Palatino 10/12
by Caractéra inc., Quebec City

For my parents

Contents

Figures

Selected specimens of Blake's visual art have been reproduced in this study by kind permission of the owners, including plates from the following illuminated works: *The Book of Thel* (Copy J, Houghton Library, Harvard University); *Europe: A Prophecy* (Copy B, Glasgow University Library); *Milton* (Copy C, New York Public Library); and *Jerusalem* (Copy E; Yale Centre for British Art). In my discussions of Blake's illuminations, plate numbers follow the order established in these versions of the poems, all of which are reproduced in full colour by the William Blake Trust and Princeton University Press (see bibliography for details). Where appropriate or necessary, I have indicated in parentheses the corresponding plate number from David Erdman's edition of *The Complete Poetry and Prose of William Blake*. Two of Blake's watercolours have also been reproduced here by kind permission of the Tate Gallery, London: "Newton" and "The Wood of the Self-Murderers: The Harpies and the Suicides."

Explanation of Notes

All references to Blake's writing are to David V. Erdman's edition of *The Complete Poetry and Prose of William Blake*. In my parenthetical citations I refer first to plate and line numbers (for example, 34:24–6) and second, for ease of reference, to the page number where the citation occurs in the Erdman edition (for example, E134). In my citations I also make use of the following abbreviations, where necessary, to signify individual works:

AI	"Auguries of Innocence"
BT	*The Book of Thel*
BU	*The Book of Urizen*
DC	*A Descriptive Catalogue*
FZ	*The Four Zoas*
J	*Jerusalem*
M	*Milton*
MHH	*The Marriage of Heaven and Hell*
NNR	"There is No Natural Religion"
SIE	*Songs of Innocence and of Experience*
VDA	*Visions of the Daughters of Albion*
VLJ	"A Vision of the Last Judgement"
E	David V. Erdman, ed. *The Complete Poetry and Prose of William Blake*
B	G.E. Bentley, Jr. *Blake Records*

Acknowledgments

Since the inception of this book, and throughout the various stages of its production, I have received a great deal of assistance. The dedicated help and support of my students, teachers, colleagues, friends, and family have made the process of research and writing distinctly enjoyable and rewarding.

The opportunity to study and celebrate William Blake's poetry and art over an extended period of years comes as a great privilege, one I continue to be keenly aware of and deeply thankful for. Where I have read Blake's work against the critical grain, I have tried to do so in the spirit of "Mental Fight," acknowledging the poet's own dictum that opposition is true friendship. At the end of the day, I can only hope that I have done at least some interpretive justice to the poetry and art that have so enriched my intellectual life.

This book has been published with the help of a grant from the Humanities and Social Sciences Federation of Canada, using funds provided by the Social Sciences and Humanities Research Council of Canada. Its publication has also been supported by a generous grant from my home institution, the University of Northern British Columbia. The research and writing processes were aided immensely by fellowship support provided by McMaster University and the Social Sciences and Humanities Research Council of Canada.

An abridged version of chapter 2 first appeared as "'Every Thing that Lives': Anthropocentrism, Ecology, and *The Book of Thel*" (*The Wordsworth Circle* 28, no. 3 [1997]: 166–77). I would like to thank James C. McKusick, the issue's guest editor, for valuable advice on improving the article. As I write this acknowledgment, an abridged portion of chapter 3, entitled "William Blake and 'The Nature of Infinity': Milton's Environmental Poetics," is in press at the journal *Nineteenth-Century Contexts*. I am grateful to *Nineteenth-Century Contexts* and Taylor & Francis for permission to reprint this material; and I thank the journal's two anonymous readers, each of whom provided me with helpful scholarly criticism.

Versions and portions of the arguments contained herein were presented at meetings of the North American Society for the Study of Romanticism (held at Boston College in 1996, McMaster University in 1997, and Dalhousie University in 1999), the Northeast Modern Language Association (Towson University, 1998), the American Conference on Romanticism (University of California at Santa Barbara, 1998), and the British Association for Romantic Studies (University of Leeds, 1997; and Keele University, 1999). I would like to thank the panelists and audience members who, at each of these meetings, helped me to fine-tune my thinking by offering me constructive criticism and helpful advice; and I gratefully acknowledge the financial assistance provided by Mrs Marion Northcott Schweitzer, whose McMaster University travel bursaries made my conference participation possible on more than one occasion.

For kind permission to reproduce the designs and paintings featured in this book, I would like to thank the Glasgow University Library, Houghton Library, New York Public Library, Tate Gallery, and the Yale Centre for British Art.

This book grew out of work originally conducted for my doctoral thesis, which I defended at McMaster University in September of 1998. I would like to thank Maroussia Ahmed, Donald C. Goellnicht, Brian John, Mark S. Lussier, William Alejandro Martin, William McConnell, Corene McKay, Fiona E. McNeill, and Tilottama Rajan for written or verbal input. The anonymous readers for McGill-Queen's University Press and the Humanities and Social Sciences Federation of Canada offered detailed commentary that helped me to hone my insights, and I am grateful for their attentive work on my behalf. Hearty thanks are also due to the people at McGill-Queen's University Press, especially Philip Cerecone, Joan McGilvray, Brenda Prince, Claire Gigantes, and Filomena Falocco, whose professional and cordial attention to this project has made its publication a most pleasurable experience. I owe my most profound debt of scholarly gratitude to David L. Clark, whose devoted pedagogy, energetic and ongoing critical dialogue, and unflagging moral support have been invaluable sources of aid and inspiration throughout the course of my work on this book. Finally, I must thank my partner, Lisa Dickson, who has listened repeatedly and patiently not only to every argument that has found its way into this book but to all the dross as well.

Imagining Nature

Introduction:
"Green Romanticism"
and Blake Studies

If, in the process of "recovering" nature, Marxism or any other political movement ignores the violence and ideological complexity of nature as a cultural concept, it will only recover a nature imbued with those ideologies which have helped provoke present crises. In short there is a danger that much reactionary thought will return on the backs of nature and of those who rightly recognize ecological politics as of the utmost urgency. Of course there are obvious and fundamental distinctions which can help prevent that – between human nature and the nature that is destroyed by human culture; between the ecological and the ideological conceptions of nature. But ... they are distinctions which the concept itself traditionally slides across and between.

(Dollimore 115)

NATURE AND IDEOLOGY

I have chosen for my epigraph a quotation from Jonathan Dollimore's *Sexual Dissidence* (1991) because it so concisely summarizes the central issues at stake in this study. Following the lead of such prominent "Green Romanticists" as Jonathan Bate and Karl Kroeber, I am concerned with what Dollimore loosely refers to as the critical "process of 'recovering' nature." At the same time, however, I am aware of the impossibility of this task, for any attempt at such "recovery" presupposes that nature's non-human essence can indeed be made available to human understanding. Hence while my research has been motivated in part by my desire to catch a respectful glimpse of nature's irreducible otherness, its ultimate aim involves not the "recovery" of nature but the more humble task of re-evaluating nature's status as a cultural concept. In particular, by examining the major *uses* to which nature has been put in the work of William Blake and some of his most important precursors, contemporaries, and critics, I hope tentatively to delineate an alternative, distinctively Blakean view of the relationship between humanity and nature, a view that productively challenges the traditional Western notion that humans should exercise a hierarchical and narrowly anthropocentric "dominion" over the entire non-human portion of creation.[1]

Given his reputation as one of nature's most prominent English literary antagonists, my focus on Blake may seem strangely problematic in this context. In chapter 1, therefore, I shall examine the critical assumptions that have underpinned the establishment of Blake's paradoxical reputation as an anti-natural Romantic author. For the moment, suffice it to say that Blake's centrality to this study stems from my conviction that he, perhaps more profoundly than any other poet in English literature, was aware of "the violence and ideological complexity of nature as a cultural concept" (Dollimore 1991, 115). Among other things, Blake's critical obsession with the unholy triumvirate of "Bacon & Newton & Locke" (J 54:17; E203) expresses his awareness that even the most rigorous Enlightenment philosophy and science – whose methods of inquiry challenged the central tenets of the earlier theological episteme by attempting to formulate a disinterested, "objective" view of nature – cannot be trusted to liberate the natural world from its colonization by anthropomorphic systems of thought.

Blake's suspicion of contemporary concepts of nature is well founded, for although Enlightenment science inaugurated a powerful critique of theological "mystery" (and so potently challenged the political authority of Blake's most detested institution, "Priesthood" [MHH 11; E38]), its ostensible objectivity dangerously disguised the ideological assumptions supporting its practice. As Michel Foucault has pointed out, "the subject in the discourse of eighteenth-century naturalists becomes exclusively a subject *looking* according to a grid of perceptions, and *noting* according to a code" (1991, 56–7). In other words, naturalism's "grid of perceptions" and quasi-legal "code" of notation function a priori to construct the natural object, inevitably causing it to conform somewhat to the scientist's all-too-human expectations. Hence when the discourse of Enlightenment naturalism claims to speak *of* non-human phenomena, it actually *orders* them. Like all discursive activity, in short, naturalism can never undertake merely a neutral mediation of its objects of study, despite its various claims to the contrary.[2]

Indeed, by privileging a taxonomy concerned to transcribe and categorize objects and their constituent elements largely in terms of quantifiable properties, scientific naturalism renders possible the mathematical manipulation of natural objects according to their human utility, ultimately enabling the things of nature to be valued and appropriated as resources, the so-called "raw materials" of industrialist manufacture. I shall examine Blake's attitude towards industrialism and the instrumentalization of nature later in this study. For the moment, I would emphasize that although eighteenth-century naturalism often entailed a thoroughly human, self-interested construction and consumption of nature, it was able effectively to hide this crucial fact; for the celebrated authority of science rested not on the fallible names of its individual practitioners but on "an anonymous and coherent conceptual system of established *truths* and methods of *verification*" (Foucault 1977b, 126; emphasis added). From Blake's iconoclastic standpoint, what makes thinkers like Bacon, Newton, and Locke so perniciously dangerous is their scientific ability to disguise the extent to which their own "discourses 'constitute' the truths they claim to discover and transmit" (Bové 1990, 56). In this sense, nature itself appears to authorize the findings of a distinctively human and human-centred scientific practice.

Like all cultural productions, however, the heterogeneous discourse of Enlightenment naturalism arose under particular historical conditions and in the context of specific strategies of government. Hence when Francis Bacon remarks in *The Dignity and Advancement of Learning* (1623) that "the *inquisition* of truth" is the scientist's "whole object" (4:296), we should attend most carefully to his words; for the observations, descriptions, and "facts" comprising the indefinite discourse of eighteenth-century empiricism were derived from techniques of inquiry associated with the Inquisition itself. Indeed, as Foucault remarks, the all-encompassing knowledge of empirical naturalism – which played an important role in the economic and political conquest of the western world – is inseparable from the Inquisition's all-encompassing "politico-juridical, administrative and criminal, religious and lay, investigation" (1995, 226). In early seventeenth-century England, for example, there existed a palpable connection between the inquisitorial techniques supporting anti-witchcraft legislation and the investigative procedures of scientific inquiry; it is no mere coincidence that the rhetoric and methodologies of Bacon's seminal writings often smack of courtroom legalism and the interrogative practices associated with contemporary witch trials.[3] Although subsequent practitioners of naturalism, by refining their investigative procedures, gradually dissociated scientific discourse from such explicitly juridical contexts (Dreyfus and Rabirow 1992, 162), the enabling connections between naturalism and inquisitorial politics were too fundamental to be completely severed.

Indeed, one may be tempted tentatively to hypothesize a correlation between early Baconian models of nature's inquisition and the rise of "panoptic" modes of social surveillance at the end of the eighteenth century. Consider, for example, Bacon's description in *The New Atlantis* (1624) of the relationship between animal experimentation (in the context of the public menagerie) and the scientific study of human bodies. In his utopian community of Bensalem, Bacon envisions "parks and inclosures of all sorts of beasts and birds, which we use not only for view or rareness, but likewise for dissections and trials; that thereby we may take light what may be wrought upon the body of man" (3:184). By observing animal bodies and behaviours in the wake of their experimental manipulation, Bacon argues, the scientist will establish models and methods for the effective manipulation of *human* bodies. While Bacon does not exactly correlate the social surveillance of animal and human bodies here, his reference to "the body of man" certainly establishes a similar objectification of the two. This objectification is especially interesting in light of Foucault's suggestion that Jeremy Bentham's idealized prison, the "Panopticon," may have been inspired by Le Vaux's menagerie at Versailles. Like the Panopticon, this menagerie had at its centre a one-room, windowed, octagonal pavilion from within which an authorized observer could comfortably gaze upon the differently categorized animal occupants of a series of surrounding cages (Foucault 1995, 203). Hence, one might argue, the royal naturalist's penetrating gaze – which could encompass virtually all the mundane individual and social behaviours of its non-human objects – adumbrates an effective model for the intervention of a pervasive, instrumentalist governmentality in the human social world, a mechanism of rationalized surveillance "defining power relations in terms of the everyday life" of human populations (ibid., 205).

Whether or not this tentative correlation between naturalistic observation and human social surveillance holds true, there can be little doubt that the developing theories and methods of objective science carried profound ramifications with regard to their potential for overt political appropriation. During the eighteenth century, numerous thinkers invoked Newton's concepts of natural law to support established or emerging models of governmental authority, metaphorizing such things as monarchs, magistrates, and police forces as gravitational centres regulating, as if naturally, the orbital movements of subordinate social bodies and the populace at large.[4] And later, in the early nineteenth century, key concepts from the burgeoning field of biology began metaphorically to be applied in political theory: "organism, function, life thus engender social organization, social function, the life of words and languages" (Foucault 1991, 57). Like concepts derived from Enlightenment physical science, the assumptions of biological naturalism were increasingly applied to all areas of society, where, crucially, they acquired a status approximating that of revealed truth.

In recent years, the science of ecology has been involved, to a certain extent, in a continuation of this historical trend. Just as Bacon's science rejected explanatory models and principles having "relation clearly to the nature of man rather than to the nature of the universe" (1623, 4:57), ecological science, to quote Sueellen Campbell, attempts to describe the way the nonhuman world "exists apart from us and our languages" (1996, 133). As the latest authoritative discourse on nature and natural process, twentieth-century ecology offers insights that many people accept as objective descriptions of nature's authentic mode of existence. But if the discourse of ecology, like Baconian science, promises something like a non-anthropomorphic view of the natural world, it does so with a crucial difference: it attacks the Baconian assumption that nature's value lies primarily in its human utility. Drawing in part on sophisticated models derived from cybernetic theory, scientific ecology decentres humanity by positing axiomatically "that every organism is unique but that all organisms and environments are essentially interdependent" (Kroeber 1994, 23). In other words, ecology focuses both on individual particulars and holistic systems without necessarily privileging either term in this complex equation. While I do not wish to belittle the importance of this double focus (which, as we shall see, has an important analogue in the eighteenth-century discourse of "nature's economy"), I would point out once again that a related dynamic characterizes the operation of a certain historical mode of governmentality. As Foucault has demonstrated, panoptic political rationality effectively produces "both individualization and totalization" (1988, 85). This double focus of governmental surveillance is evident, for example, in the all-important institution of the police. On the one hand, police supervision "seeks ideally to reach the most elementary particle, the most passing phenomenon of the social body" (Foucault 1995, 214). At this level, the *individual* human, internalizing his or her own social surveillance, is constituted as a self-governing subject. On the other hand (and inextricably related to this constitution of individual subjectivity), the police functions to ensure a holistic totalization of the state: "Men and things are envisioned as to their relationships: men's coexistence on a territory; their relationships as to property; what they produce; what is exchanged on the market" (ibid. 1988, 79). In brief, a crucial similarity between the ecological and governmental models I have been discussing involves the constitution of the individual entity in the context of a communal totality, whether this totality is conceived in terms of the earthly biosphere or the political state. In either case, the individual must be conceptualized in terms of the *functions* it performs in the context of the greater community: individuality is tolerable to the extent that it does not disrupt the order constituting the systemic "whole." At the point of disruption, should this occur, the individual must either be contained within, or expelled from, the larger order; or its deviant behaviour must be instrumentally modified to conform to what is authoritatively perceived as its proper, holistically integrated mode of being.

While analogous models of the relationship between particulars and wholes can be found in both the discourses of ecology and political rationality, there is a fundamental difference between each discourse – a difference that guarantees their ultimate non-coincidence. Simply stated, ecology focuses primarily on the objects and processes of nature, while the object of governmental rationality is the human subject in community. The objection will thus arise that my analytic sketch conflates the *separate* realms of nature and culture. To a certain extent, this objection is entirely valid; for ecology, as an aspect of biological study, is ultimately a "hard" or empirical science, while political history belongs conceptually to the "softer" anthropocentric complex of discourses we refer to as the human sciences. To revisit my epigraph, then, there are "obvious and fundamental distinctions ... between the ecological and the ideological conceptions of nature"; but, as Dollimore quickly adds, "they are distinctions which the concept traditionally slides across and between" (1991, 115) – as, for example, when the scientific insights of ecology are invoked to support ethical propositions or calls for environmental legislation. While I do not wish to deny the separate "reality" of the non-human domain, I would emphasize once again that the alterity, or otherness, of this domain, far from being available to human apprehension, must ultimately be approached through language and the social discourses organizing its conventional usage. To conceive the things of nature *discursively*, then, is to acknowledge the practice we inevitably impose upon them, to bear in mind that "it is in this practice that the events of discourse find the principle of their regularity" (Foucault 1972, 229). Hence an ideologically aware ecological criticism must not only relentlessly question the regulative uses to which nature is put in society; it must also reflect on its *own* status as a discursive practice. Crucially, moreover, ecological criticism must embody an awareness that nature's "meanings" are always produced in social contexts involving competing claims for definitive mastery. In analysing nature, therefore, one inevitably analyses not only non-human objects and processes but human power relations, of whose configuration nature inevitably becomes a major sign or symptom.

ECOLOGY, CRITICISM, AND ROMANTIC LITERATURE

The notion that nature is a discursive construct – that nature embodies, on a conceptual level, the inescapable politics of human practice – is hardly new to Romantic studies; it shows up forcefully in the work of numerous critics of the "New Historicist" stamp. Alan Liu, for example, argues succinctly that there is "no nature except as it is constituted by acts of political definition made possible by particular forms of government" (1989, 104). Liu's concern for the *politics* of nature's representation in Romantic literature is, for reasons I have been discussing, an important one. In the eyes of some of the most prominent advocates of Romantic ecocriticism (or "green Romanticism"), however, such insights have generated a great deal of angry counter-polemic. Thus, Jonathan Bate responds to Liu's comments on nature by exclaiming that "'Nature' is a term that needs to be contested, not rejected. It is profoundly unhelpful to say '*There is no nature*' at a time when our most urgent need is to address and redress the consequences of human civilization's insatiable desire to consume the products of the earth. We are confronted for the first time in history with the possibility of there being no part of the earth left untouched by man" (1991, 56). There can be little doubt that Bate is addressing an important issue here. If nature as such does not exist, then upon what basis – what literal ground – may an effective environmental politics be established and deployed? For Bate, criticism such as Liu's is not only self-defeating; it is symptomatic of the ecological crisis itself.

The main problem with Bate's critique of Liu, I would argue, is that it is based largely on rhetorical misprision, a deliberate misreading of what Liu actually says. By claiming in the above-quoted passage that Liu says "there is no nature" (rather than what he does say: "there is no nature *except* ..."), Bate trades rigorous logic for rhetorical and polemical affect. He can thus go on apocalyptically to prophesy, in a tone of profound indignation, that "when there have been a few more accidents at nuclear power stations, when there are no more rainforests, and when every wilderness has been ravaged for its mineral resources, then let us say '*There is no nature*'" (ibid.). Unfortunately, Bate's critique – or dismissal – of Liu sacrifices the ecocritical project that *potentially* inhabits Liu's criticism: a project of questioning established *definitions* of nature, the modes of government that produce and support them, their material consequences for biospheric and cultural diversity, and the possibility of formulating a practical, politically informed theory of socio-ecological transformation.

Another prominent Romantic ecocritic, Karl Kroeber, objects to discursive or ideological views of nature on ostensibly historicist grounds. Although he sarcastically agrees that England's Romantic poets "would not wish to contradict the current critical banality that 'nature' is a social construct,"[5] Kroeber argues that these poets "would regard the assertion as question-begging ... , because they believed that human consciousness (and the social constructs made possible by it) is a result of natural processes" (1994, 17). With this strangely tautological and syllogistic reading of Romanticism (nature is discursive, but discourse is natural; therefore nature is natural), Kroeber joins Bate in dismissing the potentially important environmental insights of discourse theory – despite the fact that the "natural processes" to which he refers are by no means transcendental "givens."

The idealistic desire to transcend nature's troublesome discursivity is most apparent in Bate's defensive analysis of the Wordsworthian pastoral. The purpose of the eight book of *The Prelude*, Bate asserts, "is not so much to show shepherds as they are but rather to bring forward an image of human greatness, to express faith in the perfectibility of mankind once institutions and hierarchies are removed and we are free, enfranchised, and in an unmediated, unalienated relationship with nature" (1991, 29). With these words, Bate paints a utopian picture that is unquestionably attractive; but it is a picture that betrays the naivety of his ecocritical project. Significantly, he provides no concrete models for the attainment of such a deinstitutionalized, non-hierarchical social relationship with nature. He seems to assume, rather, that a certain kind of pastoral literature, "properly" (that is, uncritically) read, will be sufficient to inaugurate such a relationship. Furthermore, by taking seriously the tantalizing possibility of attaining an "unmediated, unalienated" human relationship with nature, Bate effaces the importance of language, which structures all poetic representations of nature, indeed all subjective views of the natural world.

My purpose in this argument is not to reject the insights of critics like Bate and Kroeber outright (as they have tended to do, for example, with the theoretical insights of critics like Liu, Jerome McGann, Marjorie Levinson, and Marilyn Butler). While acknowledging the importance of their pioneering work in green Romanticism, I wish, rather, to question the efficacy of the dichotomy Bate and Kroeber construct between ecological criticism and other modes of critical inquiry. Such dichotomization, implicit in many of the passages I have quoted, becomes dramatically apparent in Kroeber's general assessment of critical approaches other than those explicitly devoted to an environmentalist agenda. "Like the engineers and planners developing top-secret star-war systems of mass destruction," he warns, "high tech literary theorists enter into debates with themselves far too abstract to be connected with specific and immediate realities of injustice, poverty, and devastation of the natural environment" (1994, 40). Kroeber's concern for the political relevance of academic criticism is certainly admirable and worthy of emulation; but his aligning his critical opponents with the producers of atomic weaponry is questionable, if only because it betrays his own failure openly to acknowledge any personal responsibility for the social and environmental problems he identifies. (Have none of Kroeber's tax dollars supported the American military complex?) This is a significant critical omission. As William Howarth observes, an ecocriticism that "insists on an Us-Them dichotomy ... cannot be self-scrutinizing, only adversarial. Since ecology studies the relations between species and habitats, ecocriticism must see its complicity in what it attacks" (1996, 69).

An ecological criticism that cannot be self-scrutinizing runs the risk of naively celebrating all initiatives that encourage the perceived enhancement of green and wild spaces, while condemning all actions that seem to oppose such a program. In studies concerned with the historical antecedents of ecological thought, such prejudices might potentially lead to various kinds of critical myopia. In the history of English forest management, for example, England's forest policies, whether tending to legislate widespread consumption of forest products *or* the natural conservation of afforested areas, have always been inextricably tied to the politics of the moment. The view of the forest as a natural resource to be exploited for the sake of profit played an obvious role in the consolidation of English capitalism and imperialist rule (Schama 1996, 154). But, as Simon Schama has demonstrated, the contrasting image of the forest as a natural greenwood retreat to be preserved and protected was no less ideological and discursive, since it tended to represent nature as the site of a highly conservative social renovation (as in the Robin Hood myths or the ritual of the royal hunt) (ibid., 135–55). Indeed, because the twentieth-century conservation movement has important historical roots in the juridical practice of "afforestation" for the sake of the royal hunt, today's ecological activist, Robert Pogue Harrison remarks, "cannot help but be a monarchist of sorts" (1992, 69).

In seventeenth-century England, John Evelyn, recognizing that English deforestation had reached epidemical proportions, advocated the need for legislated afforestation "for the preservation of our *Woods*" (1664, 108). While Evelyn's insights make him something of a proto-environmentalist, his desire to subject such forests as Dean and Sherwood to protective enclosure carried potentially oppressive socio-political ramifications. For Evelyn, the common inhabitants of England's forests were "not generally so *civil*, and reasonable, as might be wished; and therefore to design a solid *Improvement* in such places, his *Majesty* must assert his *power*, with a firme and high Resolution to *Reduce* these men to their due *Obedience*, and to a necessity of submitting to their *own*, and the *publick* utility" (112–13). Clearly, for Evelyn, the preservation of England's forests necessarily entailed a judicious curtailing of the freedoms traditionally available to lower-class forest dwellers. And while his proposed solution to the associated problem of "due *Obedience*" involved getting these people "well *Tenanted*, by long *Terms*, and easie *Rents*" (112), such philanthropic treatment of local populations was not commonly practised in the early history of English forest preservation.

Indeed, during the eighteenth century, the legislated preservation of forest habitats often carried apalling consequences for local populations. As E.P. Thompson has argued at length, the famous English Forest Laws, which controlled such activities as hunting, fishing, and the cutting of wood, turf, and heath, tended to threaten the economy, crops, and traditional agrarian rights of the labouring people living in or near the forests (1975b, 49, 64). After 1691, violations of these laws could result in punishments ranging from fines of twenty to thirty pounds, to a year in prison, to seven years' transportation – imprisonment and transportation being meted out, predictably, almost solely to the poor (59–60). Understandably, the common "forest farmers bitterly resented the increasing number of parks created by royal or ministerial favour" (110). Indeed, the laws designed to protect wild animals such as deer from overhunting ultimately backfired, as poachers united into highly organized companies to kill deer not only for venison but for mere retribution against the legislators and enforcing officers of the contemporary "conservation" movement (64). While we have no concrete record suggesting that William Blake held an opinion on these matters, the poachers' reactionary and environmentally destructive behaviour exemplifies the general Blakean proposition that law in fact creates the conditions of its own transgression. At any rate, the social hardships caused by England's early legislative efforts to preserve rural forests were so profound that the Reverend Will Waterson, vicar of Winkfield, wrote in his "Reading Book" (ca. 1727–56) that "*Liberty* and *Forest Laws* are incompatible" (quoted in Thompson 1975b, 49). One is tempted to ask whether Blake was thinking of the well-known injustices surrounding contemporary anti-hunting legislation when, in *Jerusalem*, he celebrated "Hunting" as one of the "Sources of Life in Eternity" (38:31; E185).

The point I wish to emphasize with this brief historical sketch – inspired largely by Thompson's painstaking Marxist historicism – is that human concerns for the protection of "material nature" cannot be separated from questions of social discourse and political authority. To appreciate the complexity of the issues surrounding what we now refer to as environmental preservation, an informed and responsible ecocriticism must be open to the insights of a wide range of critical approaches, which can help its practitioners reflect upon the far-reaching consequences of their own ideologically motivated theories and practices. Indeed, if an important aspect of the science of ecology is the notion that all things are complexly interrelated, then to be closed to other viewpoints is to be strangely anti-ecological.

And yet, like those Marxist critics who argue that all human problems will be resolved by a widespread embrace of Marxist doctrine, there are some ecological critics who would have us believe that all modes of critique should be made subordinate to ecological concerns. For example, Warwick Fox goes so far as to imply that the concerns of the "deep ecology" movement "well and truly *subsume* the concerns of those movements that have restricted their focus to a more egalitarian human society" (Salleh 1995, 82–3). While such an assertion is certainly problematic, its basic reasoning is not entirely unsound: "Human survival and the survival of nature are ... co-ordinate with one another" (Bate 1991, 34), because "it is on the health of the natural world that all ideologies, all societies, and all cultures ultimately depend" (Kroeber 1994, 66). These are forceful and important claims. It is necessary to note, however, that their logic is not unassailable. For example, the practice of capitalism (as opposed, perhaps, to its theory) depends not on the benevolent treatment of nature but on the existence of an ecologically harmful consumer society; for capitalist growth requires the continuing and accelerated exploitation of the earth's natural resources to supply a largely created consumer demand. William Blake was certainly aware of this kind of problem. In his epic poem *Jerusalem*, for instance, he declares that "the Kingdoms of the World & all their glory ... *grew* on Desolation" (98:51; E258; emphasis added). Such oxymoronic, life-negating *growth* partakes of the approach to life that French ecological philosopher Michel Serres attributes to the human "parasite" (1992, 9–10) – an approach wherein, by single-mindedly consolidating our own self-interest, we condemn to death the biospheric host that supports us.

Given the complexity of the issues surrounding environmentalist discourse, how do we begin to construct an ecological politics that can both address its attendant social conflicts and self-reflexively negotiate inevitable complicities with the problems it seeks to resolve?

In my own experience, the best and most succinctly articulated solution to this question comes from ecocritic David Mazel. Extrapolating from Edward Said's politically motivated critique of western Orientalism, Mazel formulates an approach to environmentalism that is worth representing here at length (the embedded quotations are Said's): "Rather than treating environmentalism as a conceptually 'pure' and unproblematic *resistance to* power, a resistance based upon an objective and disinterested organization of knowledge, I suggest we analyze it as just one of many potential modes for *exercising* power, as a particular 'style,' both political and epistemological, 'for dominating, restructuring, and having authority' (1996, 3) over the real territories and lives that the [concept of] environment displaces and for which it is invoked as a representation" (144). Mazel's theoretically sophisticated approach to environmental politics, by acknowledging the interimplication of environmentalism and the exercise of power, offers the possibility of formulating an ecological criticism that is truly self-reflexive, a criticism that builds upon the insights of other modes of critical analysis rather than rejecting them. Moreover, by acknowledging the discursive aspect of nature – its status as a cultural *idea* embodying human assumptions, desires, and politics – as well as the importance of "real territories and lives," Mazel's critique tempers the unwitting idealism that can plague less analytical valorizations of nature's materiality. This double emphasis on the discursive *and* the "real" provides the ground for a dialectic that aims at altering destructive human discursive practices while acknowledging the materiality – and attempting to respect the profound alterity or unknowability – of non-human nature. As I shall demonstrate in the ensuing discussion, Blake's poetic references to nature often partake of such a dialectical impulse.

BLAKE'S POETICS AND THE POLITICS OF NATURE

In much of Blake's visionary poetry, representations of nature and natural objects embody a sense of doubleness, evincing tension between what we might see as the poet's desire to imagine the things of nature in ideal and infinite terms (i.e., as extra-cultural "givens," unbounded and uncontaminated by human intervention), and his darker, more sober understanding of their inescapable discursivity. A particularly interesting example of such doubleness occurs in Blake's depiction of "Bath" in *Jerusalem*. When Blake introduces Bath by praising it as the "healing City!" (40:1; E187) in early, unfinished versions of the poem,[6] he is gesturing towards its healing waters, the most celebrated aspect of Bath's geography. In his *Practical Dissertation on Bath Waters* (1707), for example, one Dr Oliver promised potential patrons that the waters of Bath, taken both internally and externally, could cure *any* disease, even including the smallpox (Neale 1976, 39). It is in this "natural" sense that Bath is Blake's "mild Physician of Eternity," a "mysterious power / Whose springs are unsearchable & knowledg infinite" (41:1–2; E188). Since Blake was deeply offended by "mystery," his reference to Bath's "mysterious power" might be read as a subtle indictment.[7] However, his association of its natural springs with the privileged visionary concepts of eternity and infinity also suggests his willingness, at one level, to value the things of nature in the highest of terms.

But Blake was ultimately dissatisfied with this positive introductory portrayal of Bath. In the only "finished" version of *Jerusalem*, Copy E, Blake rearranges the plates, so that Bath is introduced into the text not as a representative of eternity and infinity but as "Legions ... the physician and / The poisoner: the best and worst in Heaven and Hell" (37:1–2; E183). Blake's repositioning of this passage may be interpreted in two ways. First, Bath's ambivalent, oppositional characterization gestures towards the age-old idea that the line distinguishing the therapeutic from the poisonous or good from evil in nature is imperceptibly narrow (at times perhaps even indistinguishable), necessitating, for its attempted negotiation, the most rigorous care. We see this kind of oppositional dynamic, for example, in the following passage from Shakespeare's *Romeo and Juliet*:

> O, mickle is the powerful grace that lies
> In plants, herbs, stones, and their true qualities;
> For naught so vile that on the earth doth live
> But to the earth some special good doth give;
> Nor aught so good but, strained from that fair use,
> Revolts from true birth, stumbling on abuse.
> Virtue itself turns vice, being misapplied,
> And vice sometime's by action dignified. (1969, 2.3.15–22)

Although Blake's portrait of Bath as "physician and / ... poisoner" likely plays with this notion that nature itself embodies both good and evil, a second, social reading of Bath's characterization is potentially more fruitful. Indeed, as Shakespeare's reference to the *application* of virtue and vice might suggest, the potential goodness or evil that may arise from the things of nature depends to a great extent on human appropriations of the natural. Bath, as Blake characterizes it on plate 37, is certainly subject to incursions from the human social realm: its identification as "Legions" (a demon Christ exorcises from a man in Mark 5:9) likely concerns "its status as a spa, a place of social ostentation and fortune-hunting as pictured in eighteenth- and nineteenth-century novels" (Paley 1983, 206–7). Undoubtedly, Bath's reputation as a seasonal resort for gambling, drinking, revelling, and illicit sex was already well established at the turn of the eighteenth century. As the anonymous author of *A Step to the Bath* (1700) described it, the resort was "a Valley of Pleasure, yet a sink of Iniquity" (quoted in Neale 1976, 39). By gesturing on plate 37 towards Bath's *human* history, Blake emphasizes the ways that a potentially "healing" natural phenomenon can become "poisonous" as a result of its human appropriation. This is the sense, perhaps, in which we might read Blake's statement that "the voice of Bath, [is] faint as the voice of the Dead in the House of Death" (39:44; E187). Appropriated by the deathly voice of human social discourse, Bath's own "natural" voice – and the excessive "knowledg infinite" (41:2; E188) that might, in its articulation, have unsettled a destructive human epistemology – all but disappears.

Another interesting example of the doubleness of Blake's vision of nature occurs in *Jerusalem* on the plate following the interpolated one discussed above. Under the influence of an ideology which supports "Swelld & bloated General Forms," "The wine of the Spirit & the vineyards of the Holy-One. / ... *turn into* poisonous stupor & deadly intoxication: / That they may be condemnd by Law & the Lamb of God be slain!" (38:19, 28–30; E185; emphasis added). In this passage, the vineyards and the wine, representing, on the earthly level, nature and its productions, have themselves undergone no ontological change. They have merely been reconceptualized, ideologically altered so that they come to signify "stupor & deadly intoxication" rather than the more benign Spirit and holiness which, as we shall see in chapter 1, animates all Blakean "life." This change is part of Blake's critique of orthodox religion, whose discursive economy, upheld by its own institutionalized "Law," imposes erroneous moral signification upon a natural world whose prior "innocence" is suggested by its association with Christ, "the Lamb of God."

But these examples of the human misappropriation of a pristine nature are ultimately problematic. Bath, even in its positive valuation as the site of healing springs, is also already a "City," a distinctively human construct. On the level of Blake's epic mythology, moreover, Bath is a human being – one of the "friends" of the giant Albion. As for the vineyards of plate 38, these *belong to* the "Holy-One" and so, from the human standpoint, are implicated in the institutional structures through which humans attempt socially to apprehend God. Thus, although we may catch tantalizing glimpses of the innocence of purely "natural" entities in Blake's writing, we must ultimately concede the impossibility of such innocence and understand that Blake's poetic gestures toward it represent nothing more than fleeting, albeit important, expressions of idealistic desire.

The discursivity of Blakean nature – nature's inescapable implication in the human systems of power that organize the constitution and circulation of knowledge – becomes especially apparent on plate 43 of *Jerusalem*, where we witness the "congenerat[ion]" of nature itself. The political context of nature's congeneration is particularly telling. Prior to this event, we are told that Luvah, "Albions Spectre" (J 60:2; E209), "strove to gain dominion over Albion / They strove together above the Body where Vala was inclosd" (43:61–2; E192). As the positioning of Albion and Luvah "above" Vala's "inclosd" body would suggest, the goal of this mutual striving is ownership of the passive, objectified Vala, the goddess of Nature herself. That Vala is the object of contention here is further suggested by the remarks that the bitter Albion makes to Luvah in the wake of the latter's victory over him: "Go and Die the Death of Man, *for* Vala the sweet wanderer" (43:66; emphasis added). Subsequently, Luvah and Vala flee from Albion's presence:

And as they fled in folding fires & thunders of the deep:
Vala shrunk in like the dark sea that leaves its slimy banks.
And from her bosom Luvah fell far as the east and west.
And the vast form of Nature like a serpent rolld between,
Whether of Jerusalems or Valas ruins congenerated we know not …
(J 43:77–81; E192–3)

I shall examine the intricate politics of Albion's relationship to Luvah, Jerusalem, and Vala in my discussion of *Jerusalem* in chapter 4. For the moment, it will suffice to point out the most important implication of this passage, which portrays something akin to the birth of "Nature" in Blake's mythology: Nature is "congenerated" out of "ruins" resulting from the struggles for political "dominion" (such as the one we witness between Albion and Luvah) that contextualize Albion's fall. Although Blake chooses to leave us uncertain whether nature arises from "Jerusalems *or* Valas ruins," we can be relatively certain of one thing: "the vast form of Nature" is, for Blake, the very *product* of power relations.

Blake's representation of nature as discursive production is crucial to an understanding of his sexual politics, for, in much of his writing, nature and femininity are closely related. We see the inescapable inter-implication of nature and patriarchal politics, for example, in the deceptively simple text and designs of *The Book of Thel*. In this work,

as I shall demonstrate in chapter 2, Thel's subjectivity and view of
nature are organized in such a way that she inevitably experiences
and evaluates the creatures of the Vales of Har, including herself, in
terms of an oppressive discourse of androcentric instrumentalism.
Thel's abandonment of her sister-shepherds in the opening lines of
the poem implies, I will argue, an intuitive act of rebellion against
these discursive parameters; and her desire to attain an existence she
characterizes as "gentle" (she obsessively repeats the word four times
in 1:12–13; E3) suggests her underlying awareness that Har's patriar-
chal pastoralism involves an unacceptable discursive violence. Rather
than seeing Thel as an Innocent soul who fails ultimately to make the
necessary transition through Experience *en route* to "organized Inno-
cence" (the traditional dialectical reading of the poem), I will delineate
Thel's new-found critical understanding that the natural "Innocence"
of Har is *already* "Organized" by its patriarchal inscription, an inscrip-
tion that complicates the seemingly anti-atomistic proposition, artic-
ulated by Har's non-human entities, that "every thing that lives, /
Lives not alone, nor for itself" (BT 3:26–7; E5).

In chapter 4 I shall continue my examination of nature and sexual
politics in Blake's *œuvre* by discussing in detail the relationship
between Vala and nature in *Jerusalem*; for Blake's critics, following the
example of the fallen Albion and his sons, often mistakenly identify
Vala as nature "herself." For the moment, it will suffice to point out
that Blake does indeed figure materiality in feminine terms when he
speaks of such things as "Time & Spaces womb" (J 85:28; E244). This
metaphor of nature's womb has a long, illustrious, and critically prob-
lematic history in English letters. We witness a famous literary and
theological usage of it in *Paradise Lost* (1674), where Milton constructs
his Chaos as a realm of "embryon atoms" and "pregnant causes" –
"The womb of nature and perhaps her grave" (1992, 2.900. 913, 911).
By sending his Son into the non-place of Chaos, Milton's masculine
God actualizes the latent reproductive potential of this realm, replac-
ing its ostensibly feminine "anarchy" and "confusion" (2.896–7) with
a hierarchically organized, androcentric order of creation.

Earlier in the century, Francis Bacon had already transposed this
theological metaphor into a naturalist register, arguing that the scien-
tist, by "penetrat[ing] into the inner and further recesses of nature,"
might discover in nature's very "womb ... many secrets of excellent
use" (1860, 4:50, 100).[8] In Bacon's commentary, the potent God of mas-
culine theology gives way to the less mysterious but no less potent
male scientist, who, through ceaseless experimentation on nature's
feminized body, helps to restore order to – and male domination over –
postlapsarian nature. For his own part, Blake reproduces the gendered

language and logic of Miltonic and Baconian cosmology most force-fully in a notorious aphorism from *The Marriage of Heaven and Hell*: "Where man is not nature is barren" (10:69; E38). This "Proverb of Hell" suggests that "man," far from being a product of nature's womb, is that which brings nature itself to life. In one economical utterance, it seems, Blake reduces the female (and feminine nature) to her repro-ductive role and then denies the vitality of this role by locating the principle of "life" in "man." Clearly, such a proposition has both sexist and anti-natural implications.[9]

And yet, to quote Mark S. Lussier, we should not *over*emphasize the importance of this one hellish proverb, for "Blake's stance to nature did not crystallize into such a single vision" (1996, 398). While it can be problematic to read Blake's *œuvre* synchronically, it would be unwise to ignore developments or changes in his usage of indi-vidual complex figures like that of nature's "womb." While this womb in *The Marriage of Heaven and Hell* requires, for its fruitfulness, the presence of "man" or humanity, a far different story emerges in certain designs and passages from *Jerusalem*. In the design to plate 8 (see figure 1), for example, we witness the social outcome of a mode of thought that reduces the female to her biological (i.e., "natural") role in sexual reproduction. Here, Blake depicts a naked female bound by a harness to the moon, symbolizing the twenty-eight days of her menstrual cycle. According to Minna Doskow's essentialist reading of the design, this "fallen female" is "condemned to the never-changing repetition of the simply physical, ever waxing and waning, ever the same, for imagination is absent" (1982b, 48–9). I would argue, on the contrary, that "imagination is absent" here only insofar as society essentializes the female *as* "the simply physical," relegating her to the subordinate term in a dualistic conception of the relationship between soul and body, humanity and nature, ideality and materiality. By exposing these dichotomies as cultural constructs rather than accepting them as natural "givens,"[10] one can understand the extent to which discourses of nature (and not nature itself) are responsible for the female enslavement Blake depicts in this design.

Indeed, nature's "barrenness" in *Jerusalem*, rather than resulting from man's absence, often arises as an explicit consequence of his discursive activity. On plate 30, for example, Albion's essentializing of Vala – his reductive identification of her as "Nature Mother of all!" – plays a key role in *causing* "Albion the high Cliff of the Atlantic [to] become a *barren* Land" (30:9, 16; E176; emphasis added). Later in the poem, moreover, in a much more explicit invocation of the womb metaphor, Blake depicts the appalling consequence of a social econ-omy in which the female must internalize a male-centred regime of

1   *Jerusalem*, plate 8
Yale Center for British Art, Paul Mellon Collection

"Moral Law" (69:35; E223): "all the Males combined into One Male & every one / Became a ravening eating Cancer growing in the Female" (69:1–2; E223).

Here, it is clearly male presence (and not absence, as in the aphorism from *The Marriage of Heaven and Hell*) that renders nature's life-giving womb barren. As David L. Clark remarks of this passage, it "would be hard to imagine a more gruesome warning against the dangers of the consolidation of power in the hands of men" (1994, 187). In chapter 4 I shall discuss in detail *Jerusalem's* depiction of the relationship between nature and patriarchal politics in an attempt to clarify the poem's critique of an androcentric governmentality that figures nature as passively feminine.

Like gender politics, the question of class plays an important role in *Jerusalem's* critique of contemporary appropriations of nature. From Blake's perspective, one of the most important of these appropriations was carried out by Newton and his followers; for the principles of mechanical materialism enabled many of the industrial revolution's technological innovations, causing among other things an unfortunate transformation of labour and labour relations:

> And all the Arts of Life. they changd into the Arts of Death in Albion.
> The hour-glass contemnd because its simple workmanship.
> Was like the workmanship of the plowman, & the water wheel,
> That raises water into cisterns: broken & burnd with fire:
> Because its workmanship. was like the workmanship of the shepherd.
> And in their stead, intricate wheels invented, wheel without wheel:
> To perplex youth in their outgoings, & to bind to labours in Albion
> Of day & night the myriads of eternity that they may grind
> And polish brass & iron hour after hour laborious task!
> Kept ignorant of its use, that they might spend the days of wisdom
> In sorrowful drudgery, to obtain a scanty pittance of bread:
> In ignorance to view a small portion & think that All,
> And call it Demonstration: blind to all the simple rules of life.
> (65:16–28; E216)

As critics have often noted, Blake's reference here to the invention of "intricate wheels ... wheel without wheel" is an invocation of Enlightenment science, whose cosmology rejected the mysterious teleological causation informing pre-scientific understandings of organic process in favour of an empirically engaged mechanistic model of physical cause and effect. I shall examine different aspects of this paradigm shift closely in chapters 1 and 3. The important things to note at this point are the passage's most obvious socio-political concerns: the

eradication of "simple workmanship" and the subsequent enslave-
ment of a class of workers who are bound to industrial "labours
in Albion."

A brief look into the early history of modern scientific discourse
suggests that these two aspects of the industrial revolution are more
complexly related than we might at first realize. In Part 4 of his
Discourse on Method (1636), for example, René Descartes argued that,
by investigating both the forces of bodies and "the different crafts of
our artisans," humans could become "the masters and possessors of
nature" (Descartes 1955, 119). Later in the same century, in his *Plus
Ultra* (1668), one of Bacon's prominent English defenders, Joseph
Glanville, advised his readers similarly that "the *Empire* of *Man* over
inferior Creatures" might be obtained by understanding and appro-
priating "those things which have been found out by *illiterate Trades-
men*" (Glanville 1688, 188).[11] In the passage I've just quoted from
Jerusalem we see precisely this kind of appropriation at work as the
principles informing the construction of such things as the non-
industrial "water wheel, / That raises water into cisterns" are
exploited to invent the "intricate wheels" of capitalist technology. By
turning the principles of "simple workmanship" against the very
artisans who formulated them, the capitalist beneficiaries of science
demonstrated that Glanville's "empire of man over inferior crea-
tures" refers not universally to humankind's empire over nature but
to the power an élite class of men exercises over less-privileged mem-
bers of the human race. To quote Foucault's discussion of the forms
and limits of discursive appropriation, such a social dynamic neces-
sitates our asking a couple of important questions. First, "What indi-
viduals, what groups or classes have access to a particular kind of
discourse?" And second, "How is the relationship institutionalized
between the discourse, speakers and its destined audience?" (1991,
60). Far from having *access* to Enlightenment discourses on nature,
the artisan in Blake's poetry becomes, like the things of nature them-
selves, an *object* of these discourses; and his or her knowledge, appro-
priated by institutionalized science and industry, is used to produce
and enslave a whole class of "inferior" labourers under the burgeon-
ing "empire of man." For those of us who have reaped the innumer-
able benefits wrought by empirical science (including profound
innovations in medicine, food production, transportation, communi-
cation, and so on), Blake's emphasis upon this negative aspect of the
Enlightenment's historical legacy may seem somewhat unfair or even
myopic, the splenetic complaint of an eccentric craftsman marginal-
ized by the rise of a progressive technological industrialism.

But an adequate understanding of Blake's poetic philosophy nevertheless necessitates a closer examination of this part of his social critique, for in the passage we have been considering Blake makes explicit the wider social consequences of mechanical industrialism. Performing the same specialized task "hour after hour," Blake's worker follows Bacon's prescription that "the labours and industries of men" should be "distributed and then combined. For then only will men begin to know their strength, when instead of great numbers doing all the same things, one shall take charge of one thing and another of another" (Bacon 1860, 4:102). This seemingly ideal and progressive distribution of specialized labour falters, however, when it is put into practice: the worker becomes alienated from the final product of his or her labour, "kept ignorant," Blake says, "of its use." By the late eighteenth century, even Adam Smith, the great champion of *laissez-faire* economics, came to understand this problem. In *The Wealth of Nations* (1776), Smith observes that the "man whose whole life is spent in performing a few simple operations ... has no occasion to exert his understanding, or to exercise his invention ... He naturally loses, therefore, the habit of such exertion, and generally becomes as stupid and ignorant as it is possible for a human creature to become" (Smith 1937, 734–5).[12] It is perhaps in this sense that Blake's industrial worker, who "spend[s] the days of wisdom / In sorrowful drudgery," dwells "In ignorance," becoming "blind to all the simple rules of life." Such a life of bondage may seem "unnatural," but it is, like the machines at which the worker performs his or her labour, a material byproduct of the Enlightenment's scientific view of nature. In short, if the universe operates causally, like a machine of "intricate wheels," then mechanized industry – at least from within this paradigm – can hardly be said to be an aberration. On the contrary, as Blake the craftsman knew only too well, capitalist industrialism appropriated mechanistic models of nature in a manner that tended inadvertently to "naturalize" class oppression, turning the skilled artisan into an automaton, a mere instrument of industrialist mass production.

In the lines directly following his poetic denunciation of natural mechanism and capitalist industry in *Jerusalem*, Blake's narrator addresses Vala, informing her that a "battle rages round thy tender limbs" (65:29; E216). Insofar as Vala symbolizes nature, her "limbs" can be seen to represent the natural resources or raw materials necessary to capitalist manufacture. Since these resources – these parts or "limbs" of nature's body – are scarce and finite, a perpetual "battle" must be fought amongst industrialized nations for their control or possession. This exigency of capitalism necessitates further exploitation of the working class, as its able-bodied men are forcibly conscripted for the waging of corporeal warfare:

> We were carried away in thousands from London; & in tens
> Of thousands from Westminster & Marybone in ships closd up:
> Chaind hand & foot, compelld to fight under the iron whips
> Of our captains; fearing our officers more than the enemy.
> (65:33–6; E216–17)

Just as "the workmanship of the plowman" (65:18) is appropriated for use by an industry that ultimately negates this workmanship, turning "the Arts of Life … into the Arts of Death" (65:16), the ploughman himself is "Compelld to leave the plow" (65:48) to "defend" in battle this same industry. The consequences of such a state of affairs are devastating not only for the enslaved and violated worker-turned-soldier and his dependents but for the earth's domesticated and wild landscapes as well; for geographical areas comprising the "corn fields," the "warbling brook," and the "mirtle tree" are transformed into a capitalist battlefield blown by "the winds of desolation" (65:48–50).

According to Blake's logic, this grim scenario is the legacy of a scientific discourse (mechanistic materialism) whose knowledge, supported by the methodology of rational "Demonstration" (65:28), promises a view of nature that is "objective" and extra-discursive. Because of his commitment to political change, Blake was highly suspicious of his own (or anyone else's) desire to see nature in such terms. But this suspicion does not mean that Blake was an intemperate anti-materialist or ultra-idealist who ultimately detested the natural world. On the contrary, as I will argue throughout this study, Blake was aware of the political *and* environmental dangers of reifying nature as the locus of what Neil Evernden critically labels "the *material* given." For, like Evernden, Blake knew that an understanding of nature as "everything-but-us" "lends an aura of objectivity and permanence to the understanding of nature as norm" (1992, 23). And it is in this normative or regulatory sense that institutions deploy the concept of nature to "naturalize" their existence as institutions, placing their authority "beyond criticism" in "the realm of the absolute" (24). For Blake, the champion of intersubjective "Mental Fight" (M 1:13; E95), any mode of political absolutism, any foreclosure of dialogue, is dangerous indeed. And since contemporary Deistical science was beginning to see external nature in terms of an "economy" of interdependent entities and processes – a model whose emphasis on relationality was thought to carry profound ethical implications – Blake might be forgiven, perhaps even congratulated, for his reticence to celebrate "material nature" too quickly.

WILLIAM BLAKE AND NATURE'S ECONOMY

In the design to plate 22 of *Jerusalem* (see figure 2), Blake's iconography points towards two distinct modes of cosmology. At the bottom of the plate, "Three Immense Wheels" of mechanism (18:8; E163), partially submerged "in the Deep" (18:43), turn against each other in efficient causal fashion (suggesting the physical principle that for every action there is an equal and opposite reaction). Like the atom so often associated with Newton, each individual wheel is an entirely self-contained unit, exercising influence on other wheels only by way of external compulsion. These are the dark and "intricate wheels" of capitalist industry, which, as we have seen, compel artisans in Blake's poetry to perform slave labour and "to fight under ... iron whips" (65:16–51; E216–17). Since compulsion (a remarkably common word and concept in Blake's canon) constitutes their mode of relations, Blake refers to these cosmic wheels as "Iron Wheels of War" (22:34; E168). Above these Newtonian wheels, however, Blake depicts four hovering, cursively joined angels, white "Cherubim" whose interlocking wings comprise Blake's weave of "Forgiveness" (22:35). Although these human forms are integral entities, they co-exist each with the other in peaceful and harmonious community. Indeed, the posture in which Blake depicts these figures (conjoined at both upper and lower extremities) suggests that they are engaged in his highest ideal of internal or emanational relations, wherein "Embraces are Cominglings: from the Head even to the Feet" (69:43; E223). This fourfold community of angels symbolizes the organic and holistic (rather than mechanistic and atomistic) mode of relations that, as we shall see in chapter 1, distinguishes Blake's privileged model of cosmos and nature.

With the rise of the Romantic movement at the end of the eighteenth century, many European poets and philosophers began to deploy holistic models of nature to combat the atomism characterizing the physical and much of the biological sciences. Indeed, in his ground-breaking study *Nature's Economy: A History of Ecological Ideas*, Donald Worster argues that the "Romantic approach to nature was fundamentally ecological," because "it was concerned with relation, interdependence, and holism" (1995, 58). Since the concept of "ecology" was not introduced until 1869 (when the term was coined by

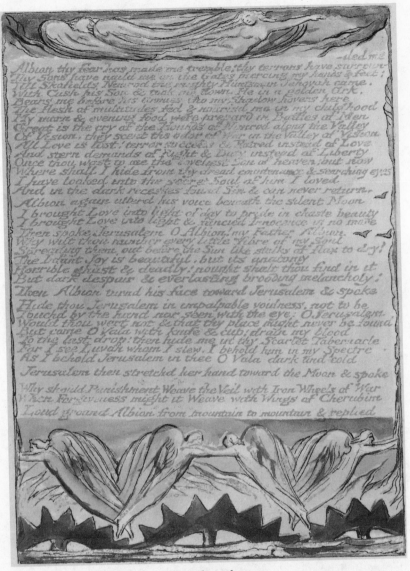

2   *Jerusalem*, plate 22
Yale Center for British Art, Paul Mellon Collection

Charles Darwin's most prominent German disciple, Ernst Haeckel), the Romantics did not know about "ecology" per se; however, they were aware of the analogous concept of "nature's economy," "a point of view that sought to describe all of the living organisms of the earth as an interacting whole" (x). Indeed, the eighteenth-century concept of nature's economy informed, and likely helped to inspire, the Romantic response to Enlightenment science (whose contrastingly reductionist methodology emphasized nature as an aggregate of individual particles or atomic units). Despite its attractiveness, however, the concept of nature's economy must be approached with critical caution, for, like its descendant "ecology," it is complex, ambivalent, and by no means immune to the vagaries of discourse.

"Economy" and "ecology" are related both conceptually and etymologically. The root of each term is the Greek *oikos*, which originally referred to the daily operations and maintenance of the human household (192). It is not uncommon for ecological critics to valorize the *oikos* as "dwelling place," or "home," seeking in this concept an attractive alternative to the antithetical notion that earthly nature is a potential enemy needing to be dominated and exploited in the service of humanity. But the idea of the *oikos*, considered historically, is by no means as innocent as it might otherwise seem. Pointing out, for example, that the word "pharaoh" means "great house," Janet Biehl reminds us that the grandest *oikos* ever constructed – ancient Egypt – was a thoroughly hierarchical, patriarchal theocracy (1991, 146). Indeed, the Greek word for "economy," *oikonomia*, signifies precisely the idea of house mastery (Howarth 1996, 73). In the eighteenth century, this idea of mastery, which clearly informed such concepts as "political economy" and "domestic economy," haunted the notion of "nature's economy" as well. In *The Book of Thel*, as I shall demonstrate in chapter 2, Blake depicts a "natural economy" whose holistic emphasis on relationality and interdependence sometimes disguises and indeed naturalizes an *oikos* whose underlying order is thoroughly patriarchal, defining its relations in terms of a masculinist instrumentalism which exploits nature and femininity to further its own self-interested ends.

It is important to note that the more recent concept of ecology does not entirely escape this problem of mastery. As Evernden has pointed out, ecology actually incorporates two seemingly incommensurable models of natural dynamics: the idea, on the one hand, of nature as a battlefield, upon which species and entities compete violently to assure their own survival, and, on the other hand, the more benign notion of nature as the site of an holistic, communal interdependence of all entities (1992, 9). In Charles Darwin's theory of evolution, these seemingly opposed impulses in fact comprise the thesis and antithesis of a dialectic in which the nightmare vision of a nature red in tooth and claw is balanced somewhat by Darwin's important, albeit lesser-known, emphasis upon biosocial cooperation between and among entities.[13] Because of this conceptual ambivalence, the discourse of ecology can be appropriated to naturalize the diametrically opposed ideologies of environmentalist activism, which aims to defend nature's specific diversity and relationality, *and* mainstream capitalism, which ensures its own prosperity by manipulating and exploiting nature both as primary resource and ultimate repository of human "waste" products. Although Blake is a product of pre-Darwinian times, his work contains insights that prefigure Evernden's understanding of "the perils of looking to ecology for social instruction" (ibid., 10); for it emphasizes, in its representation of the exclusive and exploitative drive of the atomistic "Selfhood," on the one hand, and the inclusive thrust of communal love and "mutual interchange" between entities, on the other, the ways that opposing ideologies can appropriate ecological concepts (or their historical analogues) to justify positions that are apparently incompatible.

For his own part, Blake is chary of overemphasizing either "self-centred" or "communal" positions, which find respective analogues in his poetic depictions of the conflict between "atomistic" and "holistic" views of the world. Significantly, as we shall see in chapter 3, Blake correlates the Satanic "Selfhood" with Newtonian physical science, basing his critique of Satanic self-interest in part on an understanding of the social and quasi-legal implications of Newtonian atomism. In an oft-quoted passage from a letter to George Cumberland (12 April 1827), Blake articulates his opposition to atomism in patently political terms: "I know too well that a great majority of Englishmen are fond of The Indefinite which they Measure by Newtons Doctrine of the Fluxions of an Atom. A Thing that does not Exist. These are Politicians & think that Republican Art is Inimical to their Atom. For a Line or Lineament is not formed by Chance a Line is a Line in its Minutest Subdivision[s] Strait or Crooked It is Itself & Not Intermeasurable with or by any Thing Else" (E783). According to Blake's logic, atomism negates the difference or particularity that "Republican Art" celebrates and attempts to guarantee. Blake was aware, to quote Charles Taylor, that atomism "tended towards homogeneity in that seemingly qualitatively distinct things were to be explained as alternative constructions out of the same basic constituents or basic principles" (1975, 10). Thus, the atom tends by its very definition to destroy particularity – that which the "Line[s]" and "Lineaments" separating particular entities guarantee – by reducing all entities to the same ostensibly common denominator. In this sense, the "truth" of the atom becomes *the* elementary truth, and, much more danger-ously, its priesthood of élite scientific interpreters becomes truth's oracle. Transposed into the wider social world, the theoretical homo-geneity of atomism tends, in Blake's view, to shore up the authority of "Politicians" by supporting a theoretical "state of Agreement," a false social holism or communal consensus "to which I for One do not Agree" (E783).[14] For Blake, atomism is an ideologically charged lie, a false "Doctrine" based on the notion of a purely mathematical entity "that does not Exist" but that takes on a palpable existence precisely because of the very real social and material consequences of its *theoretical* privileging.[15] Against this purely ideological entity, Blake asserts his own particularity – the experiential "I for One[ness]" that underpins his desire to refuse what he perceived as the homogenizing impulses of his era.

Perhaps the most powerful instance of Blake's critique of atomistic philosophy occurs in *Jerusalem*, where the poet differentiates the "Infant Joy" from "its anatomy":

The Infant Joy is beautiful, but its anatomy
Horrible ghast & deadly! nought shalt thou find in it
But dark despair & everlasting brooding melancholy! (22:22–4; E167)

Simply put, "The Infant Joy is beautiful" because it is holistic: Joy is a processive gestalt that organizes the complexity of the infant's experience or physiological and psychological makeup. Conversely, "anatomy" implies a "cutting up" (Luke Wilson 1987, 92) – here an act of philosophical dissection designed to reveal and systematize the component parts that together constitute the child's being. According to the terms of Blake's poetic critique, such an act is thoroughly misguided, for the component parts of Infant Joy are, like atoms themselves, non-existent (non-existent because joy is pre-cisely gestalt and therefore not reducible). Like Wordsworth, who in "The Tables Turned" (1798) condemns the atomism of a "med-dling intellect" that "murder[s] to dissect" (1967, ll. 26, 28), Blake believes that such reductive analysis results in a violent death: what he calls, perhaps echoing his poetic contemporary, "murder by ana-lyzing" (J 91:26; E251). Negating the gestalt that defines and indeed names the child, "anatomy" transforms the Infant Joy from a "beautiful" dynamic entity into an inanimate object that is "Horrible ghast & deadly."

Jerusalem contains numerous passages that oppose this kind of reductionism. Mid-way through this epic poem we are told, for example, that

> the voices of the Living Creatures were heard in the clouds of heaven
> Crying: Compell the Reasoner to Demonstrate with unhewn Demonstrations
> Let the Indefinite be explored. (55:55–7; E205)

The "Indefinite" in this passage refers to scientific methodology, the atomism that in Blake's thought erroneously attempts to abstract elementary constituents from the contexts that define the being of entities like the "Infant Joy." This abstractive process (and accompanying "objective" analysis) constitutes, one might say, the reductiveness of the *hewn* Demonstration. By advocating the need for "*un*hewn Demonstrations" – in which minute particulars remain contextually intact – the significantly "Living Creatures," or *zoa*, attempt to inaugurate a critique of atomistic epistemology. In other words, these creatures criticize the "Indefinite" method of abstraction from the standpoint of "life" conceived holistically, as an irreducible network of integral particulars co-existing in complex interrelationship. By "Compell[ing] the Reasoner to Demonstrate with *unhewn* Demonstrations," the Living Creatures would force him to compare the "deadly" results of his habitual anatomy (J 22:23; E167) with those obtained through a more inclusive or holistic methodology. Thus, the former "Indefinite" method of reasoning would "be explored" and its reductive life-negating tendencies "Demonstrate[d]." For it is not "Demonstration" itself that is necessarily the problem for Blake. To quote Brian John, Blake "attacked not reason, science, or the senses per se, but their misuse" (1974, 24–5). The "Living Creatures" deploy "unhewn Demonstration" in order relentlessly to oppose the "hewn Demonstration" of philosophical atomism, for this latter mode or "misuse" of reason threatens to negate their own identities as whole, *living* creatures.

Just prior to this call for "unhewn Demonstrations," Blake depicts a scene of labour that offers a practical alternative to the problem of atomistic reductionism, an alternative demonstrating the extent to which "holistic conceptions of nature necessarily lead to close attention to the individuality of the elements constituting the total system" (Kroeber 1994, 14):

> Labour well the Minute Particulars, attend to the Little-ones:
> And those who are in misery cannot remain so long
> If we do but our duty: labour well the teeming Earth. (55:51–3; E205)

In this passage, the labourers of the furrow strive to establish a balanced relationship with the whole order (the "teeming Earth" that is their field of labour) as well as with the myriad parts (the "Minute Particulars" or "Little-ones") that comprise that order. The labourers accomplish this balancing act not by focusing on the relatively abstract whole but by "attend[ing] to the Little-ones" – the most proximate and accessible forms they encounter in their everyday working practices. Such an act prevents "misery" in "the Little-ones" who comprise "the teeming Earth," thus affirming both particulars *and* the whole order in which they have their existence. This attention to and affirmation of particularity (which Blake opposes to the homogeneous reductionism of atomistic demonstration) generates a familial bond between the labourers and the earth, a sense of communion implicit in the workers' realization that they and the land that sustains them are "One Family!" (55:46).

Blake highlights this sense of familial connection in his poetic depiction of the workers' sympathetic identification with the land. Attending closely to the individual clods by sitting "down within / The plowed furrow" itself, the workers realize that the clods are "weeping" as a result of their having been cut by the plough (55:42–3). This insight causes the compassionate workers themselves to weep; hence, they resume their ploughing "in tears" (55:54). These reciprocal tears signify an "unhewn," holistic identification between labourer and land, suggesting that the workers have begun to cultivate a profound awareness of the minutely particular consequences of their work. And it is this awareness that inculcates in the workers a sense of "duty," an ethically motivated obligation to "labour well the teeming Earth." Thus, to a certain extent, Blake's understanding of the human relationship to the land might be said to anticipate the "land ethic" famously articulated by the American environmentalist Aldo Leopold, whose naturalist philosophy "treats the good of the biotic *community* as the ultimate measure of the value of individual organisms or species, and of the rightness or wrongness of human actions" (Mary Anne Warren 1992, 186).

I shall examine Blake's "environmental ethic" in some detail in chapter 1. For the moment, it is necessary to point out that the holism implicit in the workers' realization that they and the earth are "One Family" is by no means entirely laudatory in Blake's poetic mythos. Indeed, while such holistic identification suggests an expansive and thus positive sense of communal sympathy, it is also accompanied in Blake's dialectic by significant perils to the integrity of selfhood. Consider, for example, a passage from the subsequent plate, wherein Blake, elaborating on the metaphor of the plough, writes

> Of that Eternal Man
> And of the cradled Infancy in his bowels of compassion:
> Who fell beneath his instruments of husbandry & became
> Subservient to the clods of the furrow! the cattle and even
> The emmet and earth-Worm are his superiors & his lords.
> (J 56:33–7; E206)

If the "compassion" the workers feel for the "Minute Particulars" of the "teeming Earth" is taken too far, Blake warns us, the self – a "Minute Particular" in its own right – disappears. Identifying *too* closely with the things of the earth, in other words, the human worker falls beneath his or her own "instruments of husbandry," becoming "One" with the earth by returning to "Non-Entitys dark wild / Where dwells the Spectre of Albion: destroyer of Definite Form" (56:16–17). It is in this sense, perhaps, that the human being becomes "Subservient" to the natural environment: the "clod," as clod, remains a *whole* entity, while the human form, returning to dust by having been "Plowed in among the Dead" (57:14; E207), gives up its life, becoming a mere *part* of the clod's constitution. In the "Ode to a Nightingale" (1819), John Keats's speaker gains a similar insight as his "dull brain perplexes and retards" in the process of his becoming one with the bird who inspires his song (Keats 1988, ll. 34–5). Like Blake, Keats was also wary of too close an identification with the natural world, calling this overly sympathetic mode of communion an "easeful Death" (l. 52).

In the design for plate 33 of *Jerusalem* (see figure 3), Blake's iconography further emphasizes the perils of such sympathetic confusion of human and non-human identities. Here, the human ploughman stares intently at the earth he is ploughing, while the strangely humanized animals drawing the plough gaze up towards the heavens. The pained expression on the ploughman's downward-looking face adumbrates his "Subservien[ce] to the clods of the furrow," while the contemplative expressions on the animals' upward-looking faces suggest their contrasting "transcendence" of natural necessity in intellectual activity. That this design represents a confusion of human and animal identity is apparent in the fact that the ploughman and plough animals have identical bearded faces. In this design, as in the poetry, Blake uses the figures of the plough and earth to emphasize the consequence of a conceptual mode of being that courts heteronomy, the loss of ability to engage in such crucial Blakean activities as "Mental Fight" (M 1:13; E95) and "Self-examination" (M 40:37; E142). Since conscious self-possession is necessary to the recognition of political oppression, the temptation to identify "holistically" with the

Turning his back to the Divine Vision. his Spectrous
Chaos before his face appeard: an Unformed Memory

Then spoke the Spectrous Chaos to Albion darkning cold
From the back & loins where dwell the Spectrous Dead

I am your Rational Power O Albion & that Human Form
You call Divine, is but a Worm seventy inches long
That creeps forth in a night & is dried in the morning sun
In fortuitous concourse of memorys accumulated & lost
It plows the Earth in its own conceit. it overwhelms the Hills
Beneath its winding labyrinths. till a stone of the brook
Stops it in midst of its pride among its hills & rivers
Battersea & Chelsea mourn. London & Canterbury tremble
Their place shall not be found as the wind passes over
The ancient Cities of the Earth remove as a traveller,
And shall Albions Cities remain when I pass over them
With my deluge of forgotten remembrances over the tablet

So spoke the Spectre to Albion. he is the Great Selfhood
Satan: Worshipd as God by the Mighty Ones of the Earth
Having a white Dot calld a Center from which branches out
A Circle in continual gyrations. this became a Heart
From which sprang numerous branches varying their motions
Producing many Heads three or seven or ten. & hands & feet
Innumerable at will of the unfortunate contemplator
Who becomes his food such is the way of the Devouring Power

And this is the cause of the appearance in the frowning Chaos
Albions Emanation which he had hidden in Jealousy
Appeard now in the frowning Chaos prolific upon the Chaos
Reflecting back to Albion in Sexual Reasoning Hermaphroditic

Albion spoke. Who art thou that appearest in gloomy pomp
Involving the Divine Vision in colours of autumn ripeness
I never saw thee till this time. nor beheld life abstracted
Nor darkness immingled with light on my furrowd field
Whence camest thou! who art thou O loveliest? the Divine Vision
Is as nothing before thee. faded is all life and joy

Vala replied in clouds of tears Albions garment embracing

I was a City & a Temple built by Albions Children
I was a Garden planted with beauty I allured on hill & valley
The River of Life to flow against my walls & among my trees
Vala was Albions Bride & Wife in great Eternity
The loveliest of the daughters of Eternity when in day-break
I emanated from Luvah over the Towers of Jerusalem
And in her Courts among her little Children offering up
The Sacrifice of fanatic love: why loved I Jerusalem
Why was I one with her embracing in the Vision of Jesus
Wherefore did I loving create love, which never yet
Immingled God & Man, when thou & I, hid the Divine Vision
In cloud of secret gloom which behold involve me round about
Know me now Albion, look upon me I alone am Beauty
The Imaginative Human Form is but a breathing of Vala
I breathe him forth into the Heaven from my secret Cave
Born of the Woman to obey the Woman O Albion the mighty
For the Divine appearance is Brotherhood, but I am Love

3   *Jerusalem*, plate 33
Yale Center for British Art, Paul Mellon Collection

earthly environment is as dangerous, in Blake's view, as the temptation to assert an absolutely autonomous "atomistic" Selfhood. To this extent, even the "unhewn Demonstration" of holistic methodology carries potentially perilous consequences.

In chapter 4 I shall develop this argument by discussing the tension in *Milton* and *Jerusalem* between heteronomy and autonomy, especially as it is articulated in the complex network of associations comprising the relationship between Albion and the organic Polypus. I shall argue, in short, that the fallen Albion and the Polypus symbolize, respectively, pathological agency (an excessive privileging of an autonomous self conceived as unconnected with greater whole communities) and pathological communion (an excessive privileging of an organic or systemic "wholeness," whereby individual subjects are unwittingly absorbed into a heteronomous system in which they exist in an undifferentiated state of "soft affections without Thought" [M 24:38; E120]). Arguably, Blake invents the monstrous, organic Polypus to prophesy the frightening result of an extreme primitivism advocating an unproblematic "return" to a "natural" state of harmonious earthly coexistence. In Blake's view, the result of such a return to nature is an abdication of the critical faculty, leaving the subject open to, and powerless to oppose, the kinds of violent discursive inscription that we shall see at play in *The Book of Thel*. And yet in Blake's mythology an overt rejection of nature is equally harmful, stemming, as I shall argue in chapter 3, from modes of perception exercised by a Satanic Selfhood, which Blake explicitly associates in both *Milton* and *Jerusalem* with ecological devastation. According to Blake, one must develop a Selfhood in order to pass the totalizing Polypus (M 35:19–22; E135) *en route* to Eternity; but one must also "annihilate" the Selfhood in order to escape the anti-relational violence of Albion-Satan's egocentric or solipsistic regime. In short, it is in the attainment of a balanced relationship between self and not-self that one may develop a healthy sympathy for the things of the earth without violating the integrity or minute particularity of one's own determinate form or identity.

Blake achieves this balance, on the one hand, by focusing on individual rather than systemic integrity (Ault 1974, 30). There can be little doubt that this ultimate privileging of parts over wholes is politically motivated: Blake would certainly agree with John S. Dryzek's warning to environmental philosophers that the advocation of too close an identification with nature, as in the case of deep ecology's prescribed "willing immersion" in a larger, ecosystemic "Self," is "surely the essence of totalitarianism" (1995, 105). In Blake's view, a "holism" giving primacy to the whole over the part is potentially tyrannous, for when parts of a system are considered primarily in terms of their relationship to the greater system or whole, they are necessarily instrumentalized, as their perceived function in the grand scheme of things becomes their most important defining attribute. As we have seen, the danger of such instrumentalization involves the question of politics and interpretation: the particular group or institution (in Blakean terms, "Priesthood" [MHH 11; E38]) that society licenses to interpret the nature of the "whole" system will necessarily be in a position to dictate the proper role or function of each constituent part of that system. Indeed, this is precisely the role played by Bacon's élite men of science in *The New Atlantis* (1624). In the utopian community of Bensalem, politics takes the form of scientific administration, and decisions are made "for the good of the whole by the scientists, whose judgment was to be trusted implicitly, for they alone possessed the secrets of nature" (Merchant 1980, 180). In our own day, one should note, William Ophuls has advocated the creation of a similar élite, in this case a special class of "ecological guardians" whose superior scientific and ethical wisdom would direct the production of policy and legislation designed to guarantee the environmental sustainability of all human praxis (Quigley 1995, 180). Blake forestalls the tyranny potentially implicit in such modes of priesthood by privileging in his poetic philosophy the concept of "Infinity," which denies not only the knowability of a final whole but its very existence, thus frustrating any effort to determine the instrumental role of minute particulars within the grand order of things.[16] Ultimately, however, Blake is unable or unwilling to do away with the cosmological notion of a final whole. Thus, he attempts idealistically to imagine a holistic order in which the whole and its parts coexist "in perfect harmony" (J 34:21; E180).

Blake imagines such "harmony" by differentiating true wholes, or "General Forms," from their fraudulent counterparts, repeatedly making such a distinction in *Jerusalem*. As Los declares,

> Swelld & bloated General Forms, [are] repugnant to the Divine-
> Humanity, who is the Only General and Universal Form
> To which all Lineaments tend & seek with love & sympathy
> All broad and general principles belong to benevolence
> Who protects minute particulars, every one in their own identity.
> (38:19–23; E185)

Blake represents the worship of false wholes or general forms in terms of physical pathology: the "Swelld & bloated" condition of such forms signifies their unhealthy consumption or subsumption of minute particulars. The Divine-Humanity, on the other hand, does not consume or subsume particulars in a pathological totalitarian manner but incorporates them in such a way that they are "protect[ed] ... every one in their own identity."

I shall examine the major ethical and environmental implications of Blake's organic human cosmology in the next chapter. At this point, I will consider Blake's poetic representation of the relationship between the constituent parts and the grand whole that together comprise his peculiar vision of the cosmos. As Christ tells Albion in *Jerusalem*,

> Mutual in one anothers love and wrath all renewing
> We live as One Man; for contracting our infinite senses
> We behold multitude; or expanding: we behold as one,
> As One Man all the Universal Family; and that One Man
> We call Jesus the Christ: and he in us, and we in him,
> Live in perfect harmony in Eden the land of life. (34:16–21; E180)

Here we see that Christ is Blake's ultimate, unified whole: He is the singular "One Man," but he contains within his vast form a "multitude" of determinate particulars. In Blake's mythology, such holism is not totalitarian in nature, for Blake's all-encompassing Christ is himself a *part* of each integral or whole form he incorporates: not only are "we in him"; he is also somehow "in us." Such a cosmological ideal suggests an infinitude of interrelated parts and wholes leading not to hierarchical tyranny but to what Blake imagines as an egalitarian mode of "perfect harmony."

Blake's organic cosmology can offer green Romanticists and other literary ecocritics an interesting critical vantage point from which to consider the manifold implications of a contemporary concept of nature – "nature's economy" – that sought to describe all earthly entities as integral and interdependent parts of a dynamic, interactive system or whole. But can his cosmology ultimately underpin an ethic of respect for non-human creatures and the natural terrains they inhabit? Given Blake's unabashed anthropocentrism, one might be tempted to answer all too quickly in the negative. Indeed, Blake's insistent focus on the divine human form has played a central role in consolidating the prevailing critical perception that he is in fact nature's Romantic adversary. An ecocritical study of Blake's work – a study that wishes to consider Blake's art and poetry from within the context of a history of ecological thought – cannot proceed without facing the charge of Blake's supposed enmity towards nature. Hence it is to a consideration of this problem that we must now turn.

1 William Blake and the Natural World

Nature has no Outline:
but Imagination has. Nature has no Tune: But Imagination has!
Nature has no Supernatural & dissolves: Imagination is Eternity.

Nature is Imagination itself.

(Blake E270, E702)

THE CRITICAL LEGACY:
BLAKE, NATURE, AND SINGLE VISION

Although William Blake's attitude towards nature is equivocal and contradictory, as my epigraphs should plainly suggest, it has become a widely accepted critical commonplace that Blake is in fact nature's poetic adversary. For various reasons, critics have tended to privilege those significant aspects of Blake's writing that emphasize his idealist suspicion of material nature in lieu of his many declarations of respect for, and awe in the face of, the non-human world. Admittedly, this critical tendency has had its important dissenters. Writing in 1839, for example, one of Blake's earliest typescript editors, J.J. Garth Wilkinson, saw in Blake's mature poetry a tendency "toward Pantheism, or natural spiritualism"; Wilkinson chastised the poet for developing an excessive love of nature, a fondness that ostensibly caused Blake to mistake "the forms Truth, for the Truth itself" (xviii). Much more recently, in a sophisticated 1946 study entitled *William Blake: The Politics of Vision*, Mark Schorer pointed towards a "discrepancy in Blake's attitude toward the material universe," examining Blake's contrasting laudatory and condemnatory representations of nature as aspects of "the most enduring and the most extensive conflict in his personality and poetry" (1959, 6). But Schorer's convincing reading of a non-unified and self-contradictory Blake was almost immediately eclipsed by Northrop Frye's monumental study of Blake's *œuvre*, *Fearful Symmetry* (1947). Frye, positing in Blake's thought the presence of "a unified scheme" and "a permanent structure of ideas" (1970, 14), paints Blakean nature in the most emphatic Hobbesian colours: there is "nothing outside man worthy of respect," Frye would have Blake tell us, because "Nature is miserably cruel, wasteful, purposeless, chaotic and half dead." From the Blakean standpoint constructed by Frye, nature is quite simply "there for us to transform" (39); otherwise, as Frye remarks casually, it is "all very well to abuse nature" (40). With Wilkinson's and Schorer's interpretations all but forgotten in the wake of Frye's important intervention in Blake criticism, critics like David Riede could declare over three decades later that Blake "rejected nature utterly" (1978, 7) and do so almost without raising a critical eyebrow among scholars in the field.[1] Indeed, although Blake studies have witnessed profound changes in methodology and viewpoint since the publication of *Fearful Symmetry*, the view of Blake as nature's English Romantic adversary has become so well entrenched that even the poet's most recent and sympathetic biographer, Peter Ackroyd, is able to argue authoritatively that Blake "despised" the material world, regarding nature as "no more than the Mundane Shell or Vegetative Universe that was the vesture of Satan" (1995, 257, 328).

One of the most ubiquitous practices critics employ to uphold the construction of an unforgivingly idealistic anti-natural Blake is the citation of the poet's marginalia, which are commonly quoted as rhetorical *coups de grâce* proving beyond doubt that Blake was unequivocally hostile to the natural world. But for a number of reasons, this usage of Blake's marginal annotations is critically problematic. First, Blake's marginal commentary on nature itself lacks internal consistency. In his annotations to Wordsworth's 1815 collection of *Poems*, for example, Blake roundly condemns Wordsworth as the "Natural Man," explaining that Wordsworth "is at Enmity with God" (E665). Yet in annotating Swedenborg's declaration that "all the grandest and purest Truths of Heaven must needs seem obscure and perplexing to the Natural Man," Blake responds most furiously with "Lies & Priestcraft Truth is Nature" (E609). Clearly, as these conflicting examples indicate, if critics are to use Blake's annotations to support the thesis of his hostility towards nature (and its human corollary, the "Natural Man"), they must do so in a questionably selective manner. More important (and this is my second point), in using annotations to support critical readings of Blake's poetical works, critics fail to theorize annotations generically *as* annotations, forgetting that such jottings are not necessarily positions but more often polemical *reactions*. Such confrontational writings, produced spontaneously in the heat of particular interpretive moments, must be considered carefully in their specific performative contexts before they can be safely transposed to support general readings of Blake's philosophy or particular readings of his poetry; for the poetry, in contrast to the marginalia, is composed and published with great thought, care, and labour.

All too often, moreover, Blake's readers fail to give the annotations the close readings they demand and require. More than any of his writings, Blake's annotations to Wordsworth's poetry have been cited to support the overly simplistic claim that Blake is merely articulating, in his response to Wordsworth, a sense of disdain for material nature and its philosophical champions. Frye, for instance, cites Blake's 1814 annotation to *The Recluse* in direct preface to his claim, cited above, that Blakean nature is a site of Hobbesian warfare. Wordsworth writes:

> How exquisitely the individual Mind
> (And the progressive powers perhaps no less
> Of the whole species) to the external World
> Is fitted. – & how exquisitely too,
> Theme this but little heard of among Men
> The external World is fitted to the Mind.
> (*The Recluse*, lines 63–8, quoted in Blake 1988, E666–7)

Blake's celebrated response to this passage is "You shall not bring me down to believe such fitting & fitted I know better & Please your Lordship" (E666–7). Frye's influential claims aside, there is much more happening in this attack on Wordsworth than a straightforward Blakean critique of nature's shortcomings. For one thing, we must take into account the class-based hostility that might be motivating the response of the often derided and relatively impoverished working-class poet to the widely read and publically acclaimed utterances of England's future Laureate.[2] At the very least, such conflict would help to account for Blake's derisive and dismissive phrase "& Please your Lordship." Furthermore, as we shall see in the pages ahead, Blake was in all likelihood offended by the passivity implicit in Wordsworth's depiction of human-nature relations. In the passage above, for instance, Wordsworth argues that humanity and nature are "fitted" to one another, a process occurring through the agency of a mysterious unnamed force or entity (hence, perhaps, Wordsworth's use of the passive voice). Blake, who despises mystery, declaring in his annotations to Lavater that "Active Evil is better than Passive Good" (E592), could easily have found the doctrine of a "wise passiveness" to be the most offensive aspect of Wordsworth's seeming worship of nature. To attribute Blake's rancour against Wordsworth merely to his hostility towards the natural world itself (and not to perceived problems inhabiting Wordsworth's philosophical approach to that world) is to efface the complexity of Blake's response to the poetic doctrines of one of England's most renowned Romantic poets.

Since it is almost impossible to decipher how much of Blake's marginal response to Wordsworth is philosophically doctrinal and how much merely splenetic and reactionary, it is worth considering at this juncture another of Blake's famous annotations to the great poet. When Wordsworth praises the "Influence of Natural Objects / In calling forth and strengthening the Imagination / in Boyhood and early Youth," Blake responds with the often-quoted objection: "Natural Objects always did & now do Weaken deaden & obliterate Imagination in Me" (E665). Many of Blake's readers have accepted this remark as gospel, often using it to support the critical construction of a Blake whose philosophy is purely and transcendentally "Imaginative." It is important to note, however, that some of Blake's contemporaries were unwilling to take the poet at his word when he claimed thus to abhor nature and natural objects. Consider, for example, the following remarks of Benjamin Heath Malkin, Blake's earliest contemporary commentator. In *A Father's Memoirs of His Child* (1806), Malkin writes that Blake "professes drawing from life always to have been hateful to him; and speaks of it as looking more like death, or smelling of mortality. Yet still he drew a good deal from life, both at the academy and at home. In this manner he has managed his talents ... " (xxii). In this passage, Malkin's use of the word "professes" and his subsequent assertion that Blake did in fact draw "a good deal from life" contradict Blake's famous anti-natural outbursts, suggesting something of Blake's habitual polemical nature, which may have caused him occasionally to make claims in bad faith. In the paragraph immediately following the one quoted above, Malkin goes on to declare that Blake, who was considered mad by many of his peers, is "highly esteemed" among those particular colleagues "who can distinguish excellence *under the disguise of singularity*" (xxiii; emphasis added). Like Frederick Tatham, who understood that "many of [Blake's] Eccentric speeches, were thrown forth more as a piece of sarcasm, upon the Enquirer, than from his real opinion" (quoted in B 529), Malkin believed that people who took Blake at his word when he spoke, among other things, of despising nature were the ones most likely to misunderstand his genius.

Blake's important patron Henry Crabb Robinson noted similar contradictions in Blake's philosophy. In reporting one of his conversations with the poet, for example, Crabb Robinson wrote that Blake claimed not to "believe in the *omnipotence* of God – The language of the Bible on that subject is only poetical or allegorical. Yet soon after [making this claim] he denied that the natural world is anything" (quoted in B 316). Concerning Crabb Robinson's remark, Mark Schorer asks: "Did [Blake] want it both ways?" (1959, 22). That is, did Blake wish to deny *both* a transcendent *and* an immanent God? This is an important question; for generally, in Blake's era, a theological denunciation of material nature implied an affirmation of transcendent deity, and vice versa, and Blake, if Crabb Robinson can be trusted, refused to take a firm stand on either side of the dualistic divide. Thus, before citing Blake's conversations and fragmentary jottings to dismiss nature as anathematic to his thought, we would do well to question the poet's own dismissals of nature and analyse the tensions that arise between Blake's obviously contradictory positions on the subject. For if Blake often rejects nature (in his annotations, conversation, and epistolary correspondence), he tends often to affirm nature in his early poems and in his late epics, works that, significantly, "are not the productions of a moment's mood of dismay but of a studied effort to state his view as, most soberly, he held it" (ibid., 124–5).

Blake's unsettled attitude towards nature is also reflected in his discourse on Deism, which, contrary to the assertions of many of his readers, is often conflicted and contradictory. As Steve Clark and David Worrall have recently suggested, the "assumption of a purely oppositional relation [on Blake's part] to a monolithic and oppressive Enlightenment has precluded a fuller understanding of Blake's diverse, unpredictable, and by no means unproductive responses to the culture of his time" (1994, 18). An examination of Blake's rather unstable relationship to the Enlightenment discourse on Deism is important to an environmentally engaged study of Blake's *œuvre*, for the concept of "nature's economy" is largely the product of eighteenth-century physico-theology. There can be no doubt that Blake explicitly opposed his own philosophy to that of the Deists, but his denunciations of the latter are by no means as comprehensive as they might at first glance seem. Most significantly, Blake shared with the Deists the belief that the institutions of priesthood and monarchy destroyed intellectual and spiritual liberty (Damon 1988, 101). It is perhaps because twentieth-century criticism has tended too quickly to celebrate rather than to question Blake's self-proclaimed prophetic authority that it has also tended to take the poet entirely at his word when he denounces, and so distances himself from, the philosophical tenets of Enlightenment Deism.

Perhaps the aspect of Deist doctrine most important to a study of Blake's attitude towards nature is its rejection of the orthodox notion that nature, being fallen, is evil. Undeniably, there are moments when Blake, following orthodoxy, seems to impute such radical evil to nature. Consider, for example, one of his annotations to Watson: "The Bible tells me that the plan of Providence was Subverted at the Fall of Adam & that it was not restored till ... Christ" (E615). If Blake is in fact affirming here the doctrine of a fall that leaves no remedial recourse to the natural world (and this is by no means clear, given Blake's common habit of questioning what the "Bible tells me"), the doctrine is one that Blake does not dwell on or consistently emphasize in his work. Schorer remarks that, among Blake's repertoire of attitudes towards nature, this view of nature as radically evil is "least characteristic" (1959, 114). Indeed, given Blake's critique of dualism in *The Marriage of Heaven and Hell*, where he imputes the concept of evil in part to the error-causing "Bibles or sacred codes" (E34) and ascetic doctrines of a self-interested "Priesthood" (E38), one might point out that Blake is at least in partial agreement with Deism's proposition that evil is a state of mind arising in human society as a result of institutional corruption, which imposes upon the individual mind the erroneous notion that evil is *in fact* real (Schorer 1959, 115).

The notion that evil is not an essential or natural category is typically "primitivist," part of a doctrine that Blake's era tended to associate with the Deistical writings of Jean-Jacques Rousseau. Given Blake's overt hostility towards Rousseau, it is perhaps surprising to find traces of the primitivist doctrine in Blake's own writing. Consider, for example, Blake's repeated defence of pagan beliefs in his annotations to Lavater, where he asserts that "True superstition is ignorant honesty & this is beloved of god and man" (E591), and that superstition is "honest feeling & God who loves all honest men. will lead ... the poor enthusiast in the paths of holiness" (E598). Can we simply dismiss as momentary eccentricity Blake's assertion that "the Innocent civilized Heathen & the Uncivilized Savage who having not the Law do by Nature the things contain in the Law" (VLJ; E559)? One cannot deny that Blake vehemently opposes Deistical doctrine in his early tractates on Natural Religion (E2–3) and in his address "To the Deists" in *Jerusalem* (52; E200ff), but this opposition must be considered in light of contrary assertions like "Truth is Nature" (E609) and "Natural Religion is the voice of God" (E614), assertions that express, using the vocabulary of physico-theology itself, something like "true deistical equanimity" (Schorer 1959, 114).

I do not mean simply to reverse the common critical reading of Blakean nature by denying the importance of Blake's critique of Deism. On the contrary, as I will demonstrate in chapter 2, the poet's arguments against certain aspects of eighteenth-century physico-theology can help to clarify crucial theoretical problems inhabiting Enlightenment models of holism. Crucial to understanding the holistic dynamics of "nature's economy," for example, is the physico-theological "argument from design," which claimed that God's ways could be known through careful observation of the complex interrelationships existing among natural phenomena. As Linnaeus's disciple Isaac Biberg argued in the mid-eighteenth century, the "oeconomy of nature" (a phrase of Biberg's own coinage) refers to "the all-wise disposition of the creator in relation to natural things, by which they are fitted to produce general ends, and reciprocal uses" (1759, 31). "Things on this our terraqueous globe," Biberg continues, "are so connected, so chained together, that they all aim at the same end" – to "make manifest the divine glory" – "and to this end a vast number of intermediate ends are subservient" (32). Biberg's remarks on "nature's economy," which, in their focus on the innumerable interconnections existing among natural phenomena, prefigure the holistic claims made by many of today's ecological philosophers, would have been offensive to Blake (though, as we shall see, by no means entirely so) for a number of reasons. Notably, the "all-wise disposition of the creator" was optimistically understood by physico-theologians as manifesting itself in the universal "perfection" of nature's design. But, as Arthur O. Lovejoy has pointed out, this kind of "perfection in no way implied either the happiness or the excellence of the finite parts of the system. On the contrary, the fundamental and characteristic premise of the usual proof of [Enlightenment] optimism was the proposition that the perfection of the whole depends upon, indeed consists in, the existence of every possible degree of imperfection in the parts" (1953, 211). Hence the "intermediate ends" proper to the parts of Biberg's natural economy remain "subservient" (Biberg 1759, 32), in the greater cosmic picture, to the larger ends of an inscrutable Providence.

Blake would certainly have been troubled by this proposition: his persistent concern for the "minute particulars" of existence – the manifold parts that together comprise the universal "whole" or organic body of Christ-Albion – is well known. Since the Deistical model of "nature's economy" tended, like the doctrine of utilitarianism, to privilege the general happiness over that of the particular, it is necessary, in Blake's view, to consider the plight of the particular with careful critical attention. This exigency becomes especially apparent given the instrumental underpinnings of Deistical theology; for when the argument from design is inevitably transposed into the social realm, it becomes clear that the only necessary rational knowledge is that which helps humans "to conform properly to the design of things" (Charles Taylor 1989, 272). Rousseau seems to advocate such a stance in *Émile* when he cries "O Man! confine thine existence within thyself, and thou wilt no longer be miserable. Remain in the place which Nature has assigned to thee in the chain of beings, and nothing can compel thee to depart from it" (quoted in Lovejoy 1953, 201). Such a view of humanity's role in the natural order may promote humility, but in its static conception of human identity it also encourages quietism and complacence, thus implicitly favouring and perpetuating the prevailing *status quo*. Indeed, on a political level, the notion that individuals must conform to a pre-given natural design endangers individual liberty, privileging as it does the larger order over its elemental constituents, the "whole" over its parts. Such holism can be manipulated to justify social totalitarianism by "naturalizing" the authority of the political totality, that is, by equating totalitarian government with the very nature of things. Finally and perhaps most crucially, the Deistical separation of general and particular ends presupposes the separation of divinity (the general) and humanity (the particular), thus not only perpetuating the dualisms (spirit/body, good/evil, heaven/hell) that Blake's work tends largely to decry but also necessitating the perpetuation of theological and scientific "Priesthoods," which, by claiming authoritatively to know the cosmic "whole" wherein God's will is made manifest, set themselves up to interpret and prescribe *the* proper role and function of its constitutive particulars, whether human or otherwise.

ENVIRONMENT AND INDUSTRIALISM IN BLAKE'S ENGLAND

Blake was a metropolitan artist who preferred to live in London rather than in the country, and this simple aspect of his biography – which distinguishes him sharply from such contemporaries as Wordsworth and Coleridge – has itself helped to establish and perpetuate Blake's reputation as nature's Romantic adversary. Despite his metropolitanism, however, Blake was far from hostile to country life. Indeed, he spent much of his residence in London living on or near the edge of the open countryside, where he was well situated to witness the city's gradual urban encroachment upon the natural landscape. During his childhood, when Blake lived with his family in Broad Street, the areas north of Tyburn Road and Oxford Street consisted primarily of pleasant meadowlands (Erdman 1969, 473), but these pastoral landscapes were interspersed with brick kilns, foul ditches, and unsightly piles of industrial refuse. The young Blake, a vigorous child who spent whole days wandering among these scenes (Ackroyd 1995, 31–5), could not help but have been struck by the ecotonal contrasts[3] of these liminal spaces in which urban and rural environmental realities met and interacted. Perhaps it was on these walks that Blake first developed his distaste, seldom noted by his major interpreters, for the "cities turrets & towers & domes / Whose smoke destroyd the pleasant gardens & whose running Kennels / Chokd the bright rivers" (FZ 9:167–9; E390).

Even in his adult life, Blake was never far from the countryside. Contemporary Lambeth, where William and Catherine resided from 1790 until 1800, was sparsely populated, containing large tracts of meadow and undeveloped swampland. To quote James King, Lambeth retained at the time "a pastoral air, as if Blake had chosen to dwell where the urban and suburban could be, in a sort of compromise, blended" (1991, 68). When Blake writes in *Milton* of "Lambeth ruin'd" (25:48; E122), however, he is pointing at one level to the destruction of this kind of compromise, where the major symptoms of human corruption are social *and* natural environmental degradation. Blake could not have been unaffected by Lambeth's transformation into "a peculiarly repellent urban slum" (Ackroyd 1995, 128), for he claimed, in his final epic, that the very "Foundations" of Jerusalem began in "*lovely* Lambeth" (J 84:4; E243; emphasis added). With this foundational site "ruin'd," the hope of building Jerusalem in "Englands green & pleasant Land" (M 1:16; E96) becomes remote, entailing the need for reclamation and transformation even before the project of building can commence.

David V. Erdman points out that even when the Blakes moved in 1803 to South Molton Street, the scene where the author of *Jerusalem* depicts himself as writing "In regions of Humanity, in Londons opening streets" (J 34:43; E180), they were "just keeping up with the receding 'meadows green.'" In South Molton Street, if Erdman is correct, Blake would have witnessed "the arts of peace overshadowing the gallows of war," regarding the suburban expansion that occurred in London during these years as a positive effect of the long-awaited but ultimately unsuccessful Peace of Amiens (1969, 473–4). Referring to Blake's lyric "The fields from Islington to Marybone," Erdman remarks that Blake "welcomed the 'golden builders' who were expanding London's suburbs" (1961, 18):

> What are those golden Builders doing
> Near mournful ever-weeping Paddington
> Standing above that mighty Ruin
> Where Satan the first victory won. (J 27:25–28; E172)

Despite Erdman's optimism, it is hard not to see some significant ambivalence in this stanza: Blake does not exactly welcome or celebrate the presence of his golden builders; rather, he emphatically *questions* it. Although these builders are "golden – and although they stand "above" the "Ruin" commemorating Satan's first victory (a position suggesting their spiritual superiority to Satanic ruination) – Blake situates them near "*ever*-weeping Paddington," whose characterization as such suggests the possible futility of the builders' constructive enterprise. At any rate, given Blake's experience of the ruination of Lambeth Marsh, it is difficult to believe that he would have been without at least some reservations concerning London's rapid expansion at the turn of the nineteenth century.

Blake's only extended residence in the country proper was in Felpham, Sussex, where he and his wife, Catherine Blake, lived under the patronage of the well-known poet and author William Hayley from 1800 until 1803. During the early days of their Felpham sojourn, Blake praised country life in the highest of terms. In a letter to John Flaxman (21 September 1800), Blake claimed that Felpham was a "more Spiritual" place than London, a place where the "voices of Celestial inhabitants are more distinctly heard & their forms more distinctly seen" (E710). Writing a day or two later to Thomas Butts, Blake goes so far as to link this visionary aspect of Felpham directly to its natural landscape, expressing this connection in language that is reminiscent more of Wordsworth's writing than his own. As he told Butts, "the sweet air & the voices of winds trees & birds & the odours of the happy ground" make Felpham "a dwelling for immortals" (E711). Finally, in a letter he wrote to William Hayley in the spring of 1804, Blake suggests a direct correlation between the open country landscapes and the positive expansion of human intellect: "the country," he declares, "is not only more beautiful on account of its expanded meadows, but also on account of its benevolent minds" (E751). Coming from an habitual city dweller obsessed with mind-expanding visionary experience, such comments amount to high praise for the rural life.

Each of these letters was, of course, written in the context of the vicissitudes surrounding Blake's turbulent relationship with Hayley. It is likely that Blake idealizes Sussex in his early Felpham correspondence at least partially in order to justify his decision to move there in the first place, while the letter written to Hayley after the Felpham years is probably coloured by Blake's gratitude for the role his patron played in helping him through the infamous Scofield sedition trials. At any rate, three years in Felpham was certainly a long enough country sojourn for the Blakes, both of whom were more than content to return to Albion's centre of arts and commerce in London. But Blake's return to London need not be seen as marking any kind of ultimate rejection of the natural world. The notion of the "Romantic retreat" to nature is, in extreme forms, a species of philosophical separatism that is ultimately untenable: In the modern world, one can never obtain more than a temporary escape from the looming political, social, and environmental realities of industrial society. Blake, wishing to play a key role in the transformation of his society's thoughts and practices, could not remain immured at a physical and intellectual distance from that society; rather, he had to work for change at the very centre of national activity, where the need for "Mental Fight" (M E95) is most pressing and urgent. Indeed, in his pastoral preface to *Milton*, Blake presents the highly social activity of "Mental Fight" as a necessary prerequisite to the building of Jerusalem in "Englands green & pleasant Land" (1:16; E96). As I shall argue in chapters 3 and 4, Blake sets key passages of *Milton* and *Jerusalem* in places like Felpham in order to affirm the role that nature's green and pleasant landscapes might play in human imaginative expansion.

Ultimately, Blake may have preferred the city to the country, but his love for the former was by no means uncritical: his concern for the adverse social implications of England's urban industrialization is well known. Thematically, both *Milton* and *Jerusalem* are all but obsessed with human industry and technology. Los's role in these epics as master of the forge and Enitharmon's supervision of the looms are indicative of their status as artisan labourers, as is evident, for example, in the design to plate 100 of *Jerusalem* (see Figure 4). Here, Los's hammer and tongs and Enitharmon's distaff or spindle – not to mention the easy, unconstrained, and open postures of the workers holding these tools – are affirmative symbols of local non-industrialized labour and "simple workmanship" (65:17; E216). Yet there are other contexts in which Los and Enitharmon can be called Blake's "great industrial figures," figures functioning in the late epics as veritable symbols of the industrial revolution (Bronowski 1947, 83). Although the industrialization of London did not begin in earnest until after Blake's death (English industry having been based primarily in the North), Blake was familiar with industrial monuments like the Albion flour mill; and his "dark Satanic mills" are at one level images of the oppression that haunts such wonders of English industry. Moreover, as a working-class artisan and son of a hosier, it is not unlikely that Blake would have sympathized, like Lord Byron, with the plight of such workers as the Nottingham Luddites, who destroyed industrial machinery in early-nineteenth-century protests against the labour policies of capitalist factory owners. As Thomas Frosch has pointed out, Blake's poetic representations of technological manufacture, which constitute in his late epics "an almost continuous narrative matrix," are often associated with

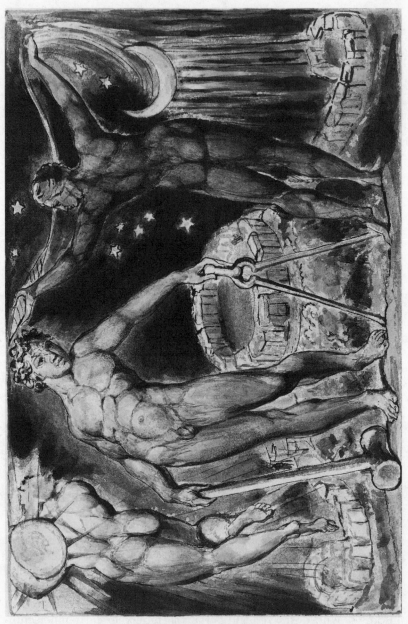

4   *Jerusalem*, plate 100
Yale Centre for British Art, Paul Mellon Collection

torture, imprisonment, and warfare, reflecting as such the "deep fail-
ure" of "Blakean man" (1974, 38–9). And although many of Blake's
technological and industrial images comprise important aspects of
the sublimity of the Blakean text (which itself is the product of an
explicitly technological process), it is difficult to imagine Blake con-
curring with Thomas Carlyle's Victorian notion that the English
industrial landscape was "sublime as a Niagara" (quoted in Houghton
1957, 198).

A non-industrialized worker himself, Blake was an engraver and
printmaker who had a keen awareness of the material basis of his
poetic art. He would likely have appreciated Milton's argument in *The
Christian Doctrine* that the verb "to create," in its Hebrew, Greek, and
Latin forms, implies "to make *of something*" (quoted in Danielson 1982,
39; emphasis added); for, as an engraver, Blake worked with concrete
materials such as polished copper plates, upon which he carved chan-
nels (by graver, or using aqua fortis) to guide the distribution of his
ink in the printing process. The fact that these channels were techni-
cally called "furrows" enriches our speculations concerning Blake's
employment of the plough metaphor. Since he was, metaphorically
speaking, a ploughman himself, Blake's poetic references to the
plough likely contain a self-reflexive element, suggesting, perhaps,
that he aligned his own localized, non-industrial labour practices with
the ploughman's environmental imperative to "labour well the teem-
ing Earth" (J 55:53; E205).[4] Because of its "simplicity," at any rate,
Blake's artistic workmanship is "like the [simple] workmanship of the
plowman" (J 65:17–18; E216), which, as we have seen, Blake explicitly
opposes to the complex workmanship characterizing the technology
of the socially oppressive and ecologically harmful industrial mill.

Ultimately, as we shall see in chapter 3, Blake uses the image of
the mill to critique not only the social and environmental implica-
tions of English technology and industrialization but the philosoph-
ical underpinnings of these phenomena in the physical science of his
era. For in *Milton*, Blake presents the workers of the dark Satanic
Mills as slaves to a contemporary pan-mechanistic cosmology whose
Prime Mover epitomizes and consolidates the tyranny of immutable
law and rigid hierarchy. In Blake's mythology, this cosmic order, a
conceptual universe of self-contained physical object-systems subject
to the endless repetition of rigidly governed cyclical processes,
enslaves the workers of the mill by foreclosing the possibility of
creativity, novelty, and intersubjective communion between entities.
To combat such a vision, Blake offers in his poetry an alternative
model of the universe, one that may be usefully considered in light
of his radical and idiosyncratic theology of creation.

CREATION THEOLOGY: BLAKE, MILTON, AND THE ANTINOMIAN TRADITION

William Blake's avowed and sustained Christianity – which differentiates him sharply from many of his English Romantic contemporaries – can tempt one to place his thought squarely in the context of a tradition whose environmental politics have become dangerously suspect in recent years. According to Lynn White, Jr, for example, orthodox modes of Christianity violate the rights of non-human nature by authorizing its total subjugation under human instrumental control (the "dominion" of Genesis 1:26–8). Worse, as White argues, Christianity tends ultimately to negate the natural world by constructing and advocating a paradigm of transcendental salvation in which humans must ultimately reject natural creation in favour of an abstract realm of spirit (1996, passim). Since it was first published in 1967, White's critique of the Judaeo-Christian approach to nature has garnered much critical response, especially from writers working within the emerging interdisciplinary field of ecotheology. While most of these writers are willing to admit that Western Christian tradition has tended, during the past three hundred years or so, to neglect crucial scriptural teachings advocating human respect for, and care of, the natural world, others suggest that polemical arguments like White's are misguided and distorting at best. Thus, for example, Richard J. Clifford (1994, 5–6) and Michael S. Northcott (1996, 179–87) offer alternative readings of Genesis 1, in which the concept of dominion is understood in terms of a responsible and caring human stewardship over a natural world beloved of God. One should also take note of the logical Christian claim that Christ's earthly incarnation entailed a redemptive valuation not only of fallen humanity but also of the embodied natural world in which his incarnation was manifested (Northcott 1996, 133). Although White's ground-breaking environmental critique of Christian tradition is important, we must remember that Christianity is by no means a monolithic structure reducible to a singular mode of praxis.[5] In Blake's era, indeed, Christianity – especially in its schismatic subcultural forms – comprised a highly heterogeneous and diverse system of related customs and beliefs. Blake's own Christianity, moreover, is highly personal, unorthodox, and idiosyncratic: during his lifetime he held no final allegiance to any established church. In the following pages, I shall examine Blake's particular Christian theory of natural creation in light of its philosophical relationship, particularly, to antinomian and Miltonic cosmogonies; for these models provide contexts and analogues that can helpfully illuminate the complex environmental implications of Blake's own theological beliefs.

In a general sense, antinomianism refers to the doctrine (embraced by such schismatic subcultural groups as the Muggletonians and the Ranters) that the coming of Jesus had rendered the moral law superfluous, so that the believer may obtain salvation through personal faith alone.[6] Because it undermines the established Church's prerogative to codify and administer social morality, antinomianism is potentially subversive. From an environmentalist standpoint, however, antinomian doctrine is far less revolutionary, for it tends to crystallize and perpetuate destructive dualisms. In the Muggletonian tradition of antinomianism, for example, matter itself is radically evil: the self-proclaimed prophets and fathers of the Muggletonian sect, John Reeve and Lodowick Muggleton, argue that "without Controversy Earth and Water were uncreated Substances, eternally distinct from the God of Glory" (1760, 8). Obviously, if matter is entirely distinct from a God seen as the source of all goodness, material nature must be radically evil and, therefore, ultimately irredeemable. Such a view of creation (which has important parallels in Gnosticism and Manichaeism) helps to explain Muggleton's doctrine that the post-apocalyptic Earth will be the ultimate site of Hell itself. As the Muggletonian Thomas Tomkinson argued early in the eighteenth century, "the Devil and his Angels are to be punished with eternal Torment ... upon this Earth, for this Earth is the lowest Place in which the Devils can be cast down into" (1724, 9).

Blake may have been influenced, directly or indirectly, by Muggletonian doctrine, but he would by no means have countenanced its dualistic view of creation. On the contrary, Blakean nature, being part of the indivisible body and spirit of Christ-Albion, must of necessity be redeemable if human salvation is to be at all possible. Blake concludes the lyrical preface to Part Four of *Jerusalem*, for example, by asserting that Albion's inhabitants must awaken to the imminent apocalypse, "Reciev[ing] the Lamb of God to dwell" not only within the "ancient walls" of its cities but "In Englands green & pleasant bowers" as well (J 77; E233). This passage recalls *Milton's* opening tribute to "Englands green & pleasant Land" (M 1:16; E96), but with a crucial difference: the explicitly natural reference in the later poem to "bowers" rather than to "land" suggests that England's redemption as a human nation must not exclude the redemption of its natural landscapes.

In much antinomian thought, the primal dualism of spirit and matter involves much more than an indictment of earthly nature; it also serves to explain and justify the very possibility of humanity's fall from grace. According to Reeve and Muggleton, Adam's substantial body of clay is precisely responsible for his original act of disobedience: "though the Soul of *Adam* through the divine Purity of its Nature was immortal, and uncapable of the least Motion of any Kind of Rebellion against the glorious Spirit of its Creator, yet, because his Body was natural, and had its Beginning of Dust, and so was subject ... to be changed from its present Condition, his immortal Soul having its Being in a Piece of Clay, was become subject through Temptation to be transmuted from its present created Glory also" (1760, 161). Although Reeve and Muggleton argue elsewhere that the human body and spirit are indivisible, their contradictory primordial dualism allows them to place the blame for the fall on the corrupting influence of the body's physical substance. Blake, as we shall see, represents this kind of argument as a specious construction of "Priesthood," part of the project of "abstraction" that he criticizes in *The Marriage of Heaven and Hell* (11; E38).

In more mainstream seventeenth- and eighteenth-century English theology, the notion that material nature had "fallen" as a result of humanity's free and wilful disobedience towards a benevolent God is much more common than the antinomian notion that the Earth's impure constitutive matter, being primordially separate from God, is itself the cause of humanity's fall. Milton's theology is a case in point. In Book Five of *Paradise Lost*, for example, Raphael tells Adam that "All things proceed ... [from] one first matter" (1992, 5.470–2). This is the doctrine of Creation *ex Deo*, for the "one first matter" to which Raphael refers is an efflux or emanation from Deity. Milton's monism is ultimately heretical, for it posits a substantial God (a God who literally "fill[s] / Infinitude" [7.168–9]); however, such a monistic cosmogony is crucial to Milton's theodical project of "justify[ing] the ways of God to men" (1.26), since it guarantees both God's omnipotence *and* the goodness of his created works (Danielson 1982, 38; Hill 1977, 326). If "there is but one God, the Father, of whom are all things" (1 Corinthians 8:6); if God is omnipotent and good; and if "all things" are "of him, and through him, and to him" (Romans 11:36),[7] then humanity logically cannot trace the etiology of its fallen condition to any shortcoming in God's design or any defect in the material dust of his creation.

But the original goodness of creation in Milton's theology by no means guarantees the ultimate redemption of all created beings. As Raphael warns Adam, "All things proceed [from God], and up to him return, / *If not depraved from good*" (Milton 1992, 5.470–1; emphasis added). J.H. Adamson interprets this proposition in light of Milton's belief that, once matter itself had emanated from God, it became, like humanity, "mutable and therefore subject to taint" (1971, 87). But it is also important to note that, despite matter's essential goodness, the *original* products of creation do not share the same degree of perfection for Milton: from the outset, his representation of prelapsarian paradise seems to involve two kinds of nature, only one of which ultimately finds favour in his eyes. In *Paradise Lost*, for example, Milton opposes the "goodl[y]," "gay," "lovely" "landscape" of the human-tended Edenic garden (1992, 4.146–53) to the "grotesque and wild" tracts of land surrounding and enclosing this paradisiacal setting (4.135–6). Whereas the Edenic environment is a well-ordered one containing "circling row[s]" of productive fruit trees (4.146), the tangled "wilderness," with its untended growth, "perplexe[s] / All path of man or beast" (4.176–7). The Miltonic world of primordial nature is only truly redeemed, it seems, when it is occupied and tended by Man, who, as the poet tells us, has "the regard of heaven on all his ways." And this heaven, Milton plainly states, "takes no account" of the doings of "other animals" (4.620–2).

Blake occasionally follows Milton and the writers of Scripture by using the metaphor of "wilderness" to describe that which perplexes and retards human spiritual progress.[8] But his own cosmology – despite its thoroughly anthropocentric character – is one that questions the exclusive right of humans to God's regard and salvation. In Blake's highly interrelational universe, for example, "A Robin Red breast in a Cage / Puts all Heaven in a Rage" (AI 5–6; E490). Or, as Blake characterizes this inclusive dynamic in *Jerusalem*, "not one sparrow can suffer, & the whole Universe not suffer also, / In all its Regions, & its Father & Saviour not pity and weep" (25:8–9; E170). This notion that wild animals do indeed have the regard of heaven has biblical sanction in Matthew 10:29, Blake's allusive emphasizing of which may well be part of his thoroughgoing critique of "Miltons Religion" (M 22:39; E117). To be fair, however, we must acknowledge the fluidity or inconsistency of Milton's natural philosophy, recognizing that his dualism of humanity and nature is less than absolute. Consider, for example, the "songs" in *Paradise Lost*, which, as Adam declares, "Divide the night, and lift our thoughts to heaven" (4.688). It is interesting to note that these songs, which encourage human heavenly aspiration, issue from "the steep / Of echoing hill or thicket" (1992, 4.680–1). If we recall Milton's earlier reference to the "steep savage hill" surrounding Eden with its impenetrable thickets (4.172–7), we must concede the possibility that the songs to which Adam refers issue from the untended wilderness rather than from the domesticated Edenic garden. Later in the poem, indeed, after portraying an Edenic world of breathing flowers, Milton declares that "all things that breathe, / ... send up silent praise" (9.193–5).[9] These passages render problematic the earlier claim that only humans have "the regard of heaven" (4.620–2); for in Milton's theology, a creature's ability to acknowledge the Creator (something Satan cannot do) provides substantial proof of its goodness.[10] Still, Milton hesitates to attribute an *inherent* goodness to the natural world (whether wild or Edenic), using articulate language as the criterion for a continued ethical separation of humanity and nature. Nature may sing and even praise God, but the full potential of these acts is realized only when Adam and Eve join their own "vocal worship to the choir / Of creatures wanting voice" (9.198–99). In these lines, Milton attributes language to non-human entities (by calling nature a "choir"), only to take it away again (by declaring that nature's choir "want[s] voice"). For Milton, quite simply, nature's unaccompanied song lacks the substantive significance of the redemptive Logos.

In the ensuing chapters, I shall examine the environmental implications of Blakean parallels to this kind of linguistic predicament. In *The Book of Thel*, for example, Blake attributes voice to such non-human entities as a Lilly, a Cloud, and a Clod of Clay, all of whom speak, in various ways, of their relationship to a God who "smiles on all" creatures (1:19; E4), whether they occupy lofty or "lowly" places (5:1; E5) in the cosmic hierarchy. When we understand, however, that Thel is actually projecting her own human voice onto these animals, colouring their utterances with the ideological discourses that constitute her own subjective makeup, Blake's distrust for human notions concerning the capacity of the non-human world to signify becomes sharply apparent. But this distrust need not imply a devaluation of nature as such, for it is based on a problem of *human* interpretive practice. As I will demonstrate in my discussion of Blake's epic poem *Milton*, Blake is willing to attribute even the highest linguistic capacity – the inspired faculty of prophecy itself – to non-human entities, asserting that "Trees on mountains" can speak "instructive words to the sons / Of men" (M 26:7–10; E123). The major linguistic problem for Blake is that humans, in their present fallen condition, are simply unequipped to understand these visionary and prophetic utterances. And so, whereas John Milton's *Paradise Lost* tends to deny nature an articulate voice (ensuring a firm conceptual separation of humanity and nature), William Blake's *Milton*, by contrast, denies humanity an understanding of *nature's* articulate voice. In both cases, the result is similar: there is a radical disjunction between, and problematic separation of, human and non-human entities. But, whereas in *Paradise Lost* nature's redemption depends on human presence, in the above-quoted passage from *Milton* the salvation of *humanity* is partially contingent upon the human ability to apprehend the meaning of nature's own "instructive words." By considering Blake's representations of nature and natural signification in *The Book of Thel* and in *Milton*, chapters 2 and 3 will explore the environmental implications of Blake's own linguistic human/ nature divide.

The question whether Milton's primordial nature is good or evil is, as we have seen, a complex and difficult one to answer. One thing of which we may be certain, however, is that the "fall of Man" in Milton's work also entails the fall of nature, as it does in Blake's mythology. Such a doctrine has crucial ecological ramifications, because, historically, "the idea of nature as darkened by the effect of the Fall of Man drew a heavy curtain between the supernatural and the natural and veiled the spiritual significance of the order of nature and the Divine Origin of this order from many eyes" (Nasr 58), thus serving to demonize nature by separating it from the goodness of God. In the postlapsarian setting of *Paradise Regained* (1671), Milton's Satan, having successfully tempted humankind in Eden, has gone on to "posses[s]" "This Universe" (1992, 1.49), effectively claiming the Earth as his own "fair empire" (1.63). Satan is so entirely confident of his earthly and natural dominion that he believes he can conquer Christ merely by removing him from human society and "exercis[ing] him in the wilderness" (1.156). Part of this exercise would involve the ingestion of natural food: the banquet Satan offers the Saviour by way of temptation is one, or so he claims, that "Nature" "hath purveyed / From all the elements" (2.333–4). The perilous nature of this elemental banquet is evident, however, in Satan's address to his subordinate "Demonian spirits," for these demons are themselves the elemental "Powers of fire, air, water, and earth beneath" (2.122–4).

In Blake's mythology, Albion's fall is also related to Satanic temptation, carrying consequences for the material world similar to those stemming from the human fall in *Paradise Lost*. In *Jerusalem*, for example, the Satanic "Reactor" "hath compelld Albion to become a Punisher" and, as a result, "hath possessd / Himself of Albions Forests & Wilds!" (43:16–17; E191). And in *Milton*, Satan's possession of nature is every bit as complete as it is in *Paradise Regained*: we are told that "all the Living Creatures of the Four Elements ... in the aggregate are named Satan / And Rahab" (31:17–19; E130). Indeed, from the perspective of an environmentally engaged critical practice, it is possible to argue that Blake's association of Satan with elemental nature is even more insidious than Milton's, for Blake's Satan is not simply the colonizer or usurper of an earthly "Empire"; he is, rather, nature "in the aggregate," in other words, the whole of nature itself. But we must not proceed too quickly with this line of argumentation, for the reference in this passage to the performative act of naming (a ubiquitous theme in Blake) highlights the crucial difference in Blake's writing between the proposition that nature is indeed fallen and the notion that institutionalized discourse plays a central role in *constructing* a fallen nature. Although Blake often suggests in his poetry that nature is in fact fallen, he is simultaneously uncomfortable with the idea, for he sees it as potentially complicitous with the perpetuation of the institution of "Priesthood," which sets itself up as the ultimate remedy to postlapsarian creation by inventing and authorizing its own system of *transcendental* salvation. Obsessed as he is with questions of law and moral virtue, Blake's Satanic "Reactor" is himself the highest priest in the land; thus, he has a great deal to gain from the invention of such a system of ostensible redemption.

Paradise Regained solves the dilemma of life in our fallen world by advocating its ultimate transcendence. Indeed, Christ's exemplary behaviour in this brief epic, if not his verbal justifications for it, emphatically underlines the need for a transcendental resolution to the problem of the fall. For example, when Christ righteously refuses Satan's offer of elemental nourishment from the Satanic "spirits of air, and woods, and springs" – spirits who ostensibly come to "acknowledge" him as Lord and pay him "homage" (1992, 2.374–6) – he does so with the following justification: "Shall I receive by gift what of my own, / When and where likes me best, I can command?" (2.381–2). This simple rhetorical question makes it plain that Satan has *usurped* control of nature from Christ's own rightful command, suggesting that fallen nature, like fallen humanity, is indeed redeemable. Unlike humanity, however, nature's potential redemption is not played out in the ensuing drama of the poem. After his triumphant defeat of the Satanic tempter, for instance, Christ chooses to command in the wilderness not the bounty of nature but a *super*natural banquet, "A table of celestial food, divine, / Ambrosial, fruits fetched from the tree of life, / And from the fount of life ambrosial drink" (4.588–90). Moreover, at the end of *Paradise Regained*, choirs of angels tell Christ that "A fairer Paradise is founded now / For Adam and his chosen sons, whom thou / A saviour art come down to reinstall" (4.613–15). Although Christ comes "down" to earth to "*re*install" lost paradise, the paradise regained by his act is of questionable ontology: paradise may be "founded now," in the temporal present, but it is spatially manifest not on earth but in Milton's utterly distant and abstract realm of heaven. In other words, the new paradise is a celestial image derived from material nature; but because it has no ultimate material point of reference, it functions as a rhetorical and discursive device *to negate* that nature. For Blake, this unearthly abstract spirituality was the most offensive aspect of "Miltons Religion." Hence he counters it with a radical reinstatement not only of the human body (Frosch 1974, 160) but of the body's material contexts as well.

Blake's reinstatement of the body is part of his famous critique of dualism and related ascetic practices, a critique that is not without important environmental implications. In practice, asceticism involves a profound psychic conversion, a righteous disavowal of all "base" or material attachments in order to gain a properly spiritualized apprehension of God. Under the influence of negative theology, the penitent understands that the world is not God, and that God, being *wholly other*, can only be approached through a "turn" away from the things of this world – and then by turning away from the desire implicitly motivating the conversional turn itself.[11] From this ascetic standpoint, the penitential subject's conversion is understood to involve a profound exercise of free will. A radical critique of dualistic practice, however, conceptualizes this notion of subjective free will as illusory, considering ascetic doctrine rather in terms of what Judith Butler has called "a foreclosure that structures the forms that any attachment may assume." In short, institutionally sanctioned dualism entails the instantiation of "a regulatory ideal ... according to which certain forms of love become possible and others, impossible" (1997, 24, 25). From an environmentalist standpoint, the orthodox construction and privileging of the soul as spirit without matter entails a *founding* psychic prohibition of love not only for the human body but for the material world that is its dwelling place, or *oikos*.

Blake, a staunch opponent of the moral Law and its accompanying prohibitions (especially those prohibitions that take the subtle and insidious form of internalized "mind-forg'd manacles" [sie; E27]), sees the dualism underpinning ascetic practice as an insidious error. For Blake, dualism involves nothing less than the institutionalization of "a system" that "enslav[es] the vulgar by attempting to realize or abstract ... mental dieties [sic] from their objects" (MHH 11; E38). He combats this oppressive separation of "mental dieties" (souls) and "objects" (material bodies) by arguing that "Man has no Body distinct from his Soul for that calld Body is a portion of Soul discernd by the five Senses" (MHH 4; E34). Elsewhere, in defence of his self-proclaimed "mode of representing spirits with real bodies," Blake argues similarly that "A Spirit and a Vision are not, as the modern philosophy supposes, a cloudy vapour or a nothing" (E541). In each of these cases, Blake's thinking is in line with the antinomian theology of John Reeve, who declares, first, that the soul and body "are both of one nature, and so both but one Creature," and second, that "the spirit is nothing at all without a body, and a body is nothing at all without a spirit; neither of them can live or have a being without the other" (1652, 42, 44). On the surface, it appears that the philosophies of both Blake and Reeve could provide foundations upon which to construct an ethics of respect for the body and its physicality, perhaps even for the corporeality of non-human nature. But, as we have seen, the Muggletonian affirmation of the body is necessarily foreclosed by a foundational cosmogonic dualism of spirit and matter. Hence Reeve's "body" is in fact *form*, what he refers to as "a spirituall body" rather than a body of clay (14). A similar problem is evident in Blake's philosophy. For if a "Spirit and a Vision" are not "a nothing," neither are they substantial: "they are organized and minutely articulated *beyond* all that the mortal and perishing nature can produce" (E541; emphasis added). To deny that Blake's "beyond" points towards some realm of the supernatural would entail, at the very least, a distortion of his poetic vision.

Yet we should not too quickly dismiss Henry Crabb Robinson's remark that Blake's "greatest enjoyment consists in giving bodily form to spiritual beings" (B 450); for although Blake's writing tends often to spiritualize the material realm, it also demonstrates, as it were, a propensity to materialize things abstract or spiritual[12] in the interest of human redemption. At the very least, Blake's critique of dualistic abstraction prioritizes the role of corporeal experience to the apprehension of the transcendental. Consider, for example, the oft-cited opening quatrain to "Auguries of Innocence":

> To see a World in a Grain of Sand
> And a Heaven in a Wild Flower
> Hold Infinity in the palm of your hand
> And Eternity in an hour[.] (E490)

With these lines Blake harnesses highly abstract metaphysical concepts ("World" and "Heaven," "Infinity" and "Eternity") to mundane experiences of material nature. He represents spatial "Infinity" as something that must be grasped in the human hand, thus advocating a necessary connection between the metaphysical realm and the body's experience in the natural world. Similarly, "Eternity" is to be sought *within* the human experience of time – and not within the relative abstraction of a lifetime but in the more easily apprehensible (because much more mundane) experience of "an hour." In Blake's view, the seeker after truth, rather than turning away from nature and the body, must seek salvation (i.e., "Heaven") in the simplest *natural* objects, in such minute particulars as individual wild flowers and single grains of sand;[13] for such particulars provide "the ultimate material starting points of [Blake's] visions" (Erdman 1961, 22).

Blake's affirmation of bodily experience in nature also informs his conception of the proper way for humans to approach or know God. Since Blake's understanding of the relationship between humanity and spirit contains interesting parallels to the antinomian theology of Reeve and Muggleton, it will be helpful first to consider the views of the latter, who argue on epistemological grounds against the idea of God as a formless Spirit. "If the Creator should be an infinite formless spirit, as some Men vainly imagine ... it were impossible for any Spirit of Man or Angel to be made capable of fixing his Understanding upon any such spiritual Creator" (1760, 4). On an allegorical level, Blake says much the same thing as Reeve and Muggleton when, in his annotations to Swedenborg, he declares: "Think of a white cloud. as being holy you cannot love it but think of a holy man within the cloud love springs up in your thought. for to think of holiness distinct from man is impossible to the affections. Thought alone can make monsters, but the affections cannot" (E603). These Muggletonian and Blakean assertions may seem quite similar, but they contain some subtle and important differences. While the Muggletonian God is not "a formless spirit," its human corporeal "form or likenesse" (Reeve 1652, 14) is by no means substantial but ultimately abstract, a distinctly "spirituall body." Blake retains in his philosophy the similar notion of a spiritual body, but his allegorizing of Spirit as a mundane natural phenomenon – an earthly cloud – is by no means insignificant. For Blake, in short, the logic of a Reeve or a Muggleton must itself be brought, as it were, down to earth, as if the antinomian "Creator" or "Spirit," whether formless or otherwise, is already too abstract an entity to be grasped by the human understanding. In Blake's allegory, there is a subtle, if often embattled, sense that human understanding requires a grounding in proximate nature even to *begin* to apprehend Spirit and related concepts like holiness. As Blake so concisely and honestly declares in his Annotations to Lavater, "it is impossible to think without images of somewhat on earth" (E600).

For similar reasons Blake's vision of the New Jerusalem is also of an apprehensible material character. In contrast to St Paul, who in his Epistle to the Galatians (4:25–6) opposes the earthly fallen Jerusalem to an ideal "Jerusalem which is above," Blake chooses to represent the heavenly city not only as earthly but as situated on England's own green and pleasant terrain. Such heterodoxy was bound to raise objections. For example, in poet laureate Robert Southey's authoritative opinion, according to Crabb Robinson, *Jerusalem* failed as a work of art partly *because* of Blake's "perfectly mad" notion that "Oxford Street is in Jerusalem" (B 229). But, for reasons both social and environmental, there is sound method in Blake's ostensible madness. If Blake, in the spirit of Miltonic epic, is writing for the benefit of his nation, he must concretize what would otherwise remain absolutely distant and abstract. In other words, just as humans cannot love a God understood as a spirituous vapour but must clothe this ideal in a human corporeal form, they must also attribute a familiar corporeality to the New Jerusalem, or this ideal holy city will be unimaginable, hence unattainable. Blake solves this largely epistemological problem quite simply by indigenizing the heavenly city.

Admittedly, this process of indigenization runs the risk of effacing the historical Jerusalem's cultural specificity by denying its geographical reality. Thus, to a certain extent, Blake's apocalyptic vision must face the charge of poetical imperialism. History has shown, however, that the Eurocentric fetishization of the historical Jerusalem inevitably gives rise to the "holy Crusade" and its attendant military and cultural violence; and Blake shares with antinomian divines like Reeve and Muggleton a principled repugnance for all physical violence and bloodshed. For each of these writers, the use of the "Sword of Steel" (as distinguished from the intellectual or "spiritual sword" [J 9:18; E152]) cannot be justified under any circumstance, since to kill any human whatsoever is to slay "the Image of God" (Reeve and Muggleton 1760, 9–10), or what Blake similarly calls "The Divine Image" (E12).

On a philosophical level, Jerusalem's English locus in Blake's mythology grounds its ideality as the heavenly city in the materiality of a specific, local geography, a geography that Blake's contemporary readers would have known most intimately. By bringing Jerusalem home to his own nation, Blake's text articulates a kind of bioregionalism, an environmentalist philosophy advocating the need for human society "to be more conscious of its locale, or regions, or lifeplace" (Plant 1997, 132). Suddenly, for the sympathetic reader of *Jerusalem*, contemporary Oxford Street, a muddy thoroughfare whose intersecting lanes and alleys were "no more than repositories of ordure and offal" (Ackroyd 1995, 31), is the *ultimate* reality. And if Oxford Street is a dirty, noisy, and unpleasant place, then it is up to its inhabitants to change it for the better. If English people are to attain the *heavenly* city, in other words, they must not utter empty prayers for transcendental displacement out of this realm of urban chaos and into an abstract realm of harmonious ideality. Rather, in

Blake's view, they must focus their attention and energies on trans-forming their *immediate* situation, since active concentration on local reality is the only way the English people can "buil[d] Jerusalem, / In Englands green & pleasant Land" (M 1:16; E96).

HYLOZOISM, GAIA, AND THE PROBLEM OF LIFE

Jerusalem may be Blake's holy city, but the attribute of "holiness" extends far beyond its borders in Blake's imaginative vision of the cosmos. Indeed, as Blake declares in *The Marriage of Heaven and Hell*, "every thing that lives is Holy" (25; E45). But what, exactly, does "Holy" mean in Blake's vocabulary? Perhaps, before attempting to define this adjective, we would do well to ask what Blake means by the substantive phrase "every thing that lives?" How, in short, does Blake define *life*? Despite the centrality of this term and its cognates (alive, live, living, etc.) in the Blakean canon,[14] Blake's critics have rarely ventured to offer a definition of Blakean life. Underlying this critical omission, perhaps, is the assumption that life is an unchang-ing given – that it was the same in Blake's time as it has always been in every era, and that we all of course *know* what it is. So seemingly self-evident is Blake's definition of "life," for example, that S. Foster Damon's monumental *Blake Dictionary* does not even list it as a term. But *is* life – and especially Blakean life – really such a transparent concept or phenomenon?

Hardly. Life, as Lyall Watson has remarked, "is impossible to define. Many have tried drawing up lists of essential characteristics like growth, metabolism, movement and reproduction – only to stumble over exceptions" (1990, 22). And the exceptions are, as it were, substantial. The problems attending a definitive understanding of life have implications not only for the idealistic and conceptual pursuits of speculative philosophy but also for the empirically grounded research of the cutting-edge "hard sciences." In recent years, for example, one of the major problems confronting NASA's massively expensive search for extra-terrestrial life has been the very question "What is life, and how should it be recognized?" (Lovelock 1987, 2). Closer to home, in Blake studies, we may attempt to define life by proceeding deductively. One thing we can know with relative certainty is that Blake's understanding of life involves a polemical response to institutionalized Christianity, whose rhetoric of dualism attacks the "pagan" notion of an animate universe by locating vitality in an abstract, hyper-hygienic realm of spirit. We may also read Blakean life as a response to institutionalized science, whose rhetoric of objectivity attacks animism and Christian anthropomorphism by postulating a cosmos composed of pure lifeless matter.

The eighteenth-century animistic and panvitalistic philosophies with which Blake was familiar were largely rooted in the Greek philosophical tradition. The Stoics and Platonists, as Bishop Berkeley put it, saw life as "infused throughout all things." And this infusion was "an inward principle, animal spirit, or natural life, producing and forming within as art doth without, regulating, moderating, and reconciling the various notions, qualities, and parts of the mundane system" (quoted in Worster 1995, 81). Although Blake explicitly voices his distaste for the philosophy of the ancient Greeks,[15] he does not, as his patron Crabb Robinson insightfully noted (B 310), entirely reject their cosmology. In his own mythology, he adopts and adapts the organic viewpoints of panvitalism and hylozoism,[16] for they provide him with a model of universal existence stressing the interrelationship of all entities as integral parts of a divine unified organism. As Blake writes in *The Book of Thel*, "every thing that lives, / Lives not alone, nor for itself" (3:26–7; E5). If this quotation, the implications of which we shall examine closely in chapter 2, does not define Blakean life as such, it certainly delineates Blake's understanding of its principal dynamic: the interconnection and interdependence of all entities. In many ways, Blake's cosmological vision accords with Hans Jonas's view that "life is essentially relationship; and relation as such implies 'transcendence,' a going-beyond-itself on the part of that which entertains the relation" (1968, 4).

But Jonas's notion of "transcendence" must not be confused with Christian notions of the same; for in the latter tradition, transcendence is usually seen as a "going beyond" the material world, the world embodying the very interrelational dynamic of which Jonas speaks. In short, by privileging soul over body, Christianity gradually adopted the Orphic formula "*Soma – sema*, the body – a tomb" (ibid., 13), thus relegating life out of this world and into the abstract realm of spirit. Such a view of material existence is not at odds with the antinomian doctrine of the Muggletonians, which posits matter as "eternall death ... void of all spirit or life" (Reeve 1652, 12) – at least until the Creator takes it upon himself to "compose dead Matter into compleat living Forms" (Reeve and Muggleton 1760, 34). According to theological systems privileging Spirit as the fundamental locus of life, the soul becomes an "alien injection into what is otherwise unrelated to life" and the physical universe itself is "formed after the mystery of the corpse" (Jonas 1968, 14, 15). In his epic mythology, Blake opposes this ontology of death by positing Albion, the human form divine, as the living, organic structure of the cosmos itself. In

Jerusalem, indeed, the myth of Albion's fall into "Eternal Death" – in which process he is virtually transformed into a corpse – and the ultimate resurrection and renovation of his body enables Blake to articulate a profound visionary critique of a dualistic mode of Christianity that negates life under the insidious guise of celebrating it.

But Blake is fighting his philosophical battle on two epistemic fronts, and his hylozoism is also a response to what he perceived as the deathly tendencies of mainstream Enlightenment science. While pre-modern panvitalism viewed life as the universal norm and death as its anomalous exception, Enlightenment science reversed this formula, positing a vast and lifeless universe in which death became the norm and life the anomaly. By privileging a model of pure, utterly lifeless matter as the very stuff of material creation, the physical sciences developed a highly authoritative, universal ontology of death (ibid., 9). Moreover, by examining material phenomena strictly in terms of extension and motion, the new sciences denied significance to the so-called "secondary characteristics," those aspects of the human experience of natural phenomena that were not mathematically quantifiable and manipulable. This scientific "suppression of the secondary – or the suppression of the subjective *as* the secondary" (Black 1990, 136) – is part of the Enlightenment's thoroughgoing epistemological attack on anthropomorphic paradigms of knowledge, which constructed a universe based on a projection of human self-experience (or what Rousseau calls the "perception of our action upon other bodies" [1993, 262]). But, as Jonas points out in his discussion of Hume's philosophy, this attack, taken to its logical and self-consistent conclusion, had to deny even "the explanatory concept of force as anthropomorphic, and as unverifiable by a mere measuring account of extensity" (1968, 36). According to Hume, in other words, even the efficient causation of Newtonian physical science was derived from or based on human bodily intuitions of cause and effect.

While the Enlightenment's relentless attack on anthropomorphic modes of epistemology has enabled us in many ways to pursue a more adequate understanding of nature's otherness, it has also had less positive implications for our conceptualization of nature and human-nature relations. As Jonas argues, "*without* the body and its elementary self-experience, without this 'whence' of our most general, all-encompassing extrapolation into the whole of reality, there could be no idea whatever of force and action in the world and thus of a dynamic connection of all things: no idea, in short, of any 'nature' at all" (ibid., 24). To rephrase Jonas's insight, one might say that the "human body and its elementary self-experience" provide the very ground for ecological formulations of the dynamic interconnectedness of all things. Blake's mythology embodies a profound awareness of this concern: it combats the Enlightenment's seeming negation of human subjective and bodily experience by imagining a universe that is, on one level, human experience itself – the complex psychological and physiological life-experience of the giant Albion.

Blake's human-centred cosmology is analogous to, perhaps even inspired by, Emanuel Swedenborg's notion that the constitutive parts of the cosmos compose, in the aggregate, a "Grand Man." Swedenborg's anthropomorphic vision is based on the ancient philosophical notion that there exists in the universe a profound interrelationship between microcosm and macrocosm. By positing a complex system of correspondences between finite particulars and larger wholes, Swedenborg constructed an organic holism that offered visionary thinkers like Blake an attractive metaphysical alternative to the seemingly reductive atomistic cosmology belonging to mainstream physical science.[17] But despite his lifelong fascination with Swedenborg, Blake was not ultimately an orthodox Swedenborgian; and the important implications of his own cosmic anthropomorphism can be further clarified by considering its relationship to other contemporary philosophical analogues. In the seventeenth century, for example, Henry More contended that there was "a Soul of the World, or Spirit of Nature," an active force that he called the *anima mundi* (quoted in Worster 1995, 42). Although many of Blake's English contemporaries used More's organicism to combat the ontological claims of mechanistic science, the concept of the *anima mundi* would have been distasteful to Blake for reasons I have already discussed: the idea of a "Soul of the World, or Spirit of Nature" was far too abstract to be useful to him, if only because the categories of "World" and "Nature" are themselves too vast to be apprehensible. Whether Blake was aware of it or not, his notion of Albion as both the "human form divine" *and* the vast form of nature resembles more closely the scientific hylozoism of James Hutton than the panvitalism of More. In a 1785 lecture to the Royal Society in Edinburgh, Hutton, the father of modern geology, suggested that the proper analogue for geological study was animal physiology, arguing that a significant parallel existed between the biospheric cycling of the elements and the physiological circulation of the blood (Lovelock 1987, viii). The major difference between Blake's vision and Hutton's is that Blake concretizes, in his mythology, the analogical terms supporting Hutton's remarkable argument. In other words, Blake sees natural objects and processes as veritable *parts* of Albion's physiology; and it is this cosmic organicism that enables him to imagine "every thing that lives" as profoundly interconnected and interdependent. In such an interrelational universe, indeed (as American environmentalist Aldo Leopold was aware), even the traditional distinction between the animate and the inanimate becomes hollow (Nash 1989, 65), so that rocks, stones, and grains of sand may be understood as no less alive than organic, biological entities.

In recent years, the notion that the world is alive has been resurrected in the scientific community through the research of J.E. Lovelock, who proposes, in his controversial "Gaia hypothesis," that "the entire range of living matter on Earth" can be "regarded as constituting a single living entity, capable of manipulating the Earth's atmosphere to suit its overall needs and endowed with faculties and powers far beyond those of its constitutive parts" (1987, 9). From a Blakean perspective, Lovelock's hylozoistic Gaia hypothesis is interesting precisely because of its "holism";[18] by explaining the functioning of all earthly organisms in terms of the role they play in the larger workings of the biosphere as a whole, the Gaia hypothesis articulates a significant conceptual alternative to the atomism characterizing the traditional methodology of the physical sciences. Moreover, by attributing a kind of intentionality to the biosphere (Lovelock, xii, calls it "a self-regulating entity"), the Gaia hypothesis implicitly affirms a model of final causation over the external efficient causation of much Enlightenment mechanistic theory. But Lovelock's hypothesis would ultimately have been unsatisfactory to Blake, because it locates life only within earthly nature, failing in "terracentric" fashion to extend the principle of organic vitalism beyond the confines of our planet's biosphere. In Blakean terms, this problem is largely an imaginative one, a problem involving what Blake refers to as the limit-setting "ratio" of cognitive reasoning. But, as Errol E. Harris has argued, Lovelock's privileging of the biosphere as the finite locus of life is insupportable on scientific grounds as well, for the earth's biosphere is itself subject to extra-terrestrial relational influences: "The earth cannot be treated in isolation from the solar system, if only because its own motion and physical state depend almost totally on the sun's gravity and energy outflow. Nor can the solar system be separated from the galaxy, or the galaxy from the rest of the universe. If, as the physicists assure us, the universe is one system ... then we must presume that there is ultimately only one universal morphic field" (1991, 98). In Blake's mythology, the ultimate morphic field, of which the Earth is a crucial part (but by no means a final whole), is Christ-Albion, the divine humanity.

It is perhaps in this cosmological sense that we should try to understand Blake's doctrine of final causation. Properly speaking, such a doctrine does not imply the causative influence of future events so

much as "causation empowered by the ordering principle of an orga-
nized whole" (ibid., 27). Accordingly, as Harris puts it, "a teleological
explanation is one which explains the part in terms of the whole, and
not vice versa. It is one for which the whole takes precedence, so that
the explanatory principle is that which organizes the system" (ibid.).
In such a scenario, in other words, the mutual relations of a structure's
parts "are governed by a principle of order or organization that per-
vades the entire structure" (18). In Blake's mythology – despite its
relentless emphasis on the necessary integrity of "minute particulars"
– Albion provides such an explanatory structural principle: his vast
corporeality organizes and orchestrates the workings of the entire
Blakean cosmos. Indeed, one might say that Albion exemplifies the
process that E.O. Wilson has termed "mutualistic symbiosis," the sce-
nario in which distinct biological entities, existing together, coopera-
tively comprise a single living organism (1992, 178) (as in the
inglorious case of intestinal bacteria, which help to support digestive
processes in, and therefore the very lives of, larger animals). Since, in
the Blakean universe, minute particulars co-exist to form a single
giant complex organism, one might argue that Blake's Albion takes
this concept of mutualistic symbiosis to its most radical and expansive
extreme. In Blake's *cosmic* organizational scenario, in other words,
virtually all things, as vital parts of Albion's vast form, are mutually
interrelated, working together in infinitely various ways to comprise
the complexity of Albion's multiplicitous but nonetheless individual
being. Blake's reiterated notion that "every thing that lives is Holy"
(MHH E45; VDA 8:10, E51) might be conceived, from Albion's cosmic
standpoint, as an affirmation of a vast (w)holism which sees all
entities as vitally interconnected and interdependent.

For a number of reasons, however, Blake's human teleological
holism is problematic. First and most obviously, it tends imperialis-
tically to conceive the cosmos in decidedly anthropocentric terms;
and second, it is, like all teleological explanations of natural phenom-
ena, unverifiable and therefore fraught with mystery – a problem of
no small importance for readers of a poet who claimed overtly to
oppose the metaphysics of mystery. Since Blake's time, and in accor-
dance with its own systematic critique of anthropomorphism and
mystery, mainstream biological science has gradually developed a
wholly empirical conceptual model to explain the appearance of
goal-directed activity in nature, invoking the evolutionary model of
natural selection to account for developmental processes in the bio-
logical world (Mayr 1992, *passim*). For his own part, Blake might be
excused for courting teleological mystery, since he was the product
of a pre-evolutionary and largely theistical era. But it is nevertheless

possible to appreciate his likely motives for resisting the increasing priority given to empirical over teleological concepts. Although biology was gaining importance and legitimacy as a scientific discipline during Blake's lifetime, physics understandably remained the scientific discipline *par excellence* because it so successfully lent itself to empirical modes of investigation. As Blake must have noticed, strict non-deistical physical empiricism was more than willing to explain the what and how of natural processes; but in order to avoid raising the anthropomorphic and metaphysical spectres of teleology, this same contemporary science largely refused to address the all-important question of *why* things happen as they do (ibid., 122). It is likely, then, that Blake would have regarded the avoidance of such a fundamental question as a failure of imagination, if not a symptom of moral cowardice. Thus, throughout his career, he stubbornly adhered to an increasingly outmoded discourse to account for the workings of the cosmos. Perhaps it was in recognition of the inherent mysteriousness of much contemporary teleological thinking that Blake championed the giant Albion as a wholly human model of holistic cosmic activity. By thoroughly humanizing teleology, in other words, Blake conceptualized a humanly familiar, relatively non-abstract universe within which his readers might feel a sense of unalienated community with all things.

ANTHROPOMORPHISM, ENVIRONMENTAL ETHICS, AND ANIMAL RIGHTS

As we have seen, Blake's cosmology is unabashedly anthropomorphic. From the perspective of an ecological ethics, his foundational anthropomorphism (implicit in the theological notion that Albion's body constitutes the organic structure of the universe in its entirety) is questionable, for, like the concept of "environment" itself, anthropomorphism centres humanity while relegating non-human life forms to the periphery of things, thus foreclosing the possibility of valuing non-human entities on their "own" terms. Much of chapter 2 will be devoted to an examination of this problem as it is articulated in *The Book of Thel*. For the moment, however, it will suffice to point out that anthropomorphic practice can take many forms, having diverse environmental and ethical implications. On the one hand, as David L. Clark has argued in a related discussion, "sentimentalizing anthropomorphisms make genuinely ethical thought ... impossible, for, under the guise of a certain pathos, they peremptorily annihilate differences in the name of the (human) same" (1997, 169). In his pastoral poetry, Blake often employs the pathetic fallacy in ways that sentimentalize nature and so colonize its difference (as, for example, in poems like the pastoral "Night," where Blake depicts the "lions ruddy eyes" as "flow[ing] with tears of gold," lines 34–5; E14). In his epic writing, however, Blake's pathetic fallacy, far from affirming a sentimental identification with nature, often highlights a sense of human-nature alienation. Consider, for instance, Blake's "Trees of Malice: Revenge: / And black Anxiety" (J 13:42–3; E157) and his "fierce Vegetation" where "the Oak frowns terrible" (J 16:3–5; E159). By attributing malevolent human motivations and emotions to non-human beings, descriptions like these remain thoroughly anthropomorphic: like their sentimental counterparts, they take humanity as the very measure of nature, thus annihilating the sheer profundity of nature's difference. Yet Blake's fearful anthropomorphisms suggest at least something of nature's otherness by figuring non-human entities as agents of potential menace to humanity. (This is significant in an age where all living things were being subjected to the most painstaking taxonomy as part of science's Baconian effort to bring all of nature under the "dominion of the human race"; Bacon 4:114). At the very least, by alternating between a sympathetic *identification with* the natural world and a fearful *alienation from* it (in his sentimentalizing and menacing anthropomorphisms, respectively), Blake's poetical practice helps to unsettle the complacency of our expectations regarding human-nature relations.

Blake's anthropomorphic cosmology – his radical privileging of human experience in Albion's giant form – has played a crucial role in establishing and upholding the prevailing critical viewpoint that Blake's philosophy is antagonistic to nature. But, as Alexander Wilson has pointed out, anthropomorphism "can be a radical strategy in a culture like our own, where the frontier between the human and the non-human is well policed" (1992, 128). As I argued earlier, such philosophical policing of the human/non-human distinction can be seen in works like *Paradise Lost*, which sharply distinguishes human from non-human beings on the basis of articulate language. Blake's organicism challenges mainstream Christian representations and valuations of nature not only by blurring the human-nature divide but by attacking the very conceptions of God and cosmic hierarchy invoked to authorize such division. The contemporary Christian establishment would have been offended by Blake's cosmological privileging of the "human form divine," for such a structural anthropomorphism eradicates the traditional distinction between humanity and divinity, thus doing away with the need for an institutionalized, priestly mediation between these terms. Blake's foundational anthropomorphism also challenges the theological underpinnings of deistic mechanism; for rather than assuming the existence of God as an autonomous designer and Prime Mover existing *outside* the great cosmic machine, it presupposes, like all organicist cosmologies, a God who cannot exist "apart from the nexus of relations that determine its reality" (Oelschlaeger 1991, 343). In either case, Blake's decentralization of cosmic authority implies a radical critique of traditional forms of hierarchy, a critique that has important philosophical implications not only for human society and government but for human-nature relations as well.

Consider, for example, the following passage from *Jerusalem*:

> Cities
> Are Men, fathers of multitudes, and Rivers & Mountins [*sic*]
> Are also Men; every thing is Human, mighty! sublime!
> In every bosom a Universe expands ... (34:46–9; E180)

The argument that "every thing is Human," ubiquitous in Blake's canon, has important ethical consequences; for Judaeo-Christian morality, as epitomized in the Old Testament's Decalogue, concerns itself exclusively with relationships between and among humans, or between humans and the God who created them in his own image (Nash 1989, 113). Arguably, Blake's radical expansion of the category of humanity involves an emphatic questioning of this traditional exclusivity. Despite its anthropomorphism – or rather, because of it – Blake's cosmology provides a firm conceptual foundation for a spiritually pragmatic environmental ethic; for if all nature is considered human, the commandment "Thou shalt not kill" must necessarily be generalized far beyond a narrow conception of humanity, to include literally "every thing that lives." We witness something of this ethical dynamic at play, for example, in Blake's watercolour entitled "The Wood of Self-Murderers: The Harpies and the Suicides" (see Figure 5). In this painting, Blake illustrates a passage from *The Inferno* (13.2–108), in which Dante tears a branch from a tree embodying Pier delle Vigne, a politician who committed suicide after falling out with his emperor, Frederick II (see Butlin 1981, 563). There can be no doubt that the painting gestures towards a harmful violation of distinct categories of identity: its humanized trees, and the bird-human hybrids that perch in their upper branches, are clearly monstrous, functioning as iconographic indictments of the act of suicide and its violent negation of the divine human form. And yet if we consider "The Wood of the Self-Murderers" in light of Blake's human cosmology, we can understand that Dante's assault on the tree is at one level an inexcusable response to his encounter with delle Vigne. One of the most striking things about "The Wood of the Self-Murderers" is that the tree

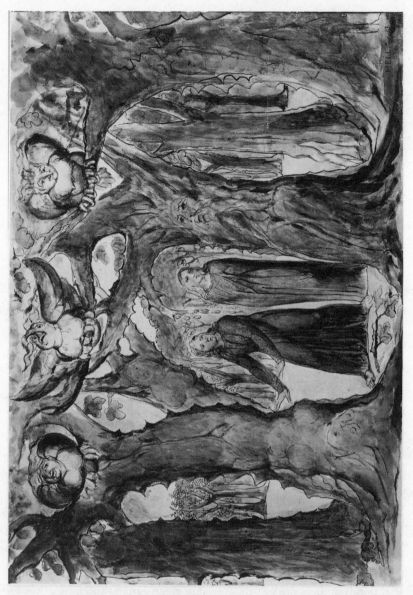

5 "The Wood of the Self-Murderers: The Harpies and the Suicides"
© Tate, London 2001

embodying delle Vigne bleeds profusely as a result of Dante's act. In the original watercolour, which hangs in the Tate Gallery, the blood that issues from the broken branch is offset against the forest background in dramatic red, continually drawing the viewer's attention to the centre of the painting and to Dante's act of violence. Interpreted in the context of Blake's human organicism, which sees *all* things as particulars of the divine humanity, Dante's mutilation of this vegetated form is more than a tyrannical "punish[ing of] the already punishd" (J 45:34; E194): it is an act of *self*-mutilation. Indeed, if the aggressive Dante is seen as attempting to murder the humanized tree, he must also be seen as committing precisely what the painting's title designates – an act of "self-murder," or "suicide."

Blake did not formulate this kind of ethico-poetical "argument" in a philosophical vacuum. The late eighteenth and early nineteenth centuries witnessed numerous debates concerning what environmentalists now refer to as the "rights of nature." Eugene C. Hargrove attributes the rise of present-day environmental ethics to the taxonomical activities of eighteenth-century biological naturalists, whose understanding of species difference promoted an awareness of, and desire to protect, the diversity of life; and he traces the history of today's animal liberation movements to the same era's popular concern to protect the welfare of domesticated animals (1992a, xix). Although contemporary Neoplatonists like Thomas Taylor had contempt for the idea that ethical consideration should be given to non-human creatures per se (Taylor famously used the notion of the "Rights of Brutes" to parody Mary Wollstonecraft's ground-breaking argument for the "Rights of Women"), writers like Jeremy Bentham and John Lawrence spoke very much in support of animal rights. In a footnote to his 1789 *Principles of Morals and Legislation*, Bentham argued that "the day *may* come, when the rest of the animal creation may acquire those rights which never could have been withholden from them but by the hand of tyranny" (Bentham 1948, 310–11n.1).[19] Writing seven years later, Lawrence spoke with a far greater sense of urgency, arguing not for the gradual evolution and distant realization of animal rights but for animals' inherent possession of what he emphatically termed "certain natural and unalienable rights" (1976, 84). Lawrence proposed, indeed, that "the Rights of Beasts be formally acknowledged by the state, and that a law be framed ... to guard and protect [animals] from acts of flagrant and wanton cruelty, whether committed by their owners or others" (123).

The pioneering arguments of Bentham and Lawrence, despite their importance to the history of animal rights ethics, are, from a postmodern eco-critical perspective, flawed for at least two crucial reasons.

Bentham's ethics were grounded upon the utilitarian principle of "the greatest happiness for the greatest number." In an age that subscribed to the Cartesian notion that animals were automata, machine-like entities incapable of experiencing pleasure or pain, Bentham's argument for animal rights would have been difficult to support, for the notion of animal "happiness" would have been widely incomprehensible or at least subject to serious dispute. This is perhaps why Lawrence is careful to refute the Cartesian view of animality (82), going so far as to argue that "every living creature, is vivified and informed by a *soul*, or portion of intellectual element super-added" (78). But Lawrence's anti-Cartesian ethic is in turn compromised by his notion that "man" must treat animals with humane kindness "in return for the benefit he derives from their services" (120). Such an argument is utilitarian and therefore anthropocentric, since it focuses on the instrumental role animals play in relation to human society. And since human interests are subject to change, the notion of use-value cannot provide a substantial basis for an enduring ethic of care. Indeed, most environmental ethicists agree that utilitarianism's anthropocentric instrumentalization of the non-human world is a primary *cause* of the environmental crisis (Hargrove 1992a, xi). It is interesting to note, then, that Blake, in denouncing cruelty to animals in such poems as *Auguries of Innocence*, avoids invoking the utilitarian concepts of pleasure, pain, or instrumental value. Rather, he advocates humane treatment of animals on the basis of the holistic interdependence of all entities in his organic universe. In the interrelational cosmos Blake envisions, the abuse of *any* living creature is necessarily symptomatic not only of pathology on the part of the abuser (who cannot be entirely isolated as such) but also of a structural pathology in the larger systemic whole.

Such a notion is clearly at odds with prevailing views of the implications of animal abuse in the late seventeenth and eighteenth centuries. In *Some Thoughts Concerning Education* (1693), for example, John Locke declared that people "who delight in the Suffering and Destruction of Inferiour Creatures, will not ... be very compassionate, or benign to those of their own kind" (quoted in Nash 1989, 19). According to Locke's line of argumentation, children should be educated to respect animals not because animals are themselves deemed worthy of human respect but because cruelty against animals is ultimately harmful to humans and human society. In a similar vein, Blake's acquaintance Thomas Taylor suggested that the wanton mistreatment and destruction of animals would damage the very fabric of civil society; for such acts were means by which "the brutal energies of our nature grow strong, and savage desires encrease" (1792, 29). At the end of the eighteenth century, secular arguments for the humane

treatment of animals tended to be articulated on much the same log-
ical basis. More common, however, was the religious argument
against animal abuse, which emphasized not the biblical importance
attributed to animals as creatures sharing "the divine-inspired char-
acter" of created life (Northcott 1996, 184) but explicitly anthropocen-
tric concerns. In general, the English movement supporting what John
Lawrence called "the Rights of Beasts" understood cruelty against
non-human creatures as a moral evil that harmed the *human* soul,
especially the soul of the human animal abuser (Nash 1989, 19, 24–5).

Considered in this context, Blake's declaration, in *Auguries of Inno-
cence*, that "A dog starvd at his Masters Gate / Predicts the ruin of
the State" (9–10; E490) can best be understood to partake in the more
secular contemporary critique of animal mistreatment. According to
the logic of this aphorism, the dog's abused condition signifies not
the master's individual culpability – the "ruin" of his own individ-
ual, immortal soul – but the culpability of the governmental or state
structures that condone such cruelty by supporting an anthropocen-
tric system of legislated rights. This logic is especially interesting
given the hesitancy of contemporary English lawmakers to prohibit
animal owners from mistreating what was regarded as their own
animal "property." To quote eco-historian Roderick Nash, property,
in the early nineteenth century, "remained too sacrosanct, too much
a natural right in itself, to be challenged by [an assertion of] the
natural rights of nonhuman beings" (1989, 25). In Blake's aphorism,
however, the fact that a human "Master" owns the "starvd" dog in
no way excuses the cruelty underpinning its abused condition. On
the contrary, the dog takes on a strange agency, at odds with the
notion of its subordinate status as an object of ownership, as the very
consequence of its mistreatment: it actively and prophetically "Pre-
dicts the ruin of the State" whose capitalist system of ownership
allows such abuses to occur with impunity.

Indeed, Blake's aphorism is radical even by standards commonly
embraced by writers of the late-twentieth-century environmental
ethics movement. According to J. Baird Callicott's early writings, for
example, the present-day animal liberation movement falls short of
articulating a genuine environmental ethic precisely because it
locates moral value in individual organisms. For Callicott, in short,
a genuine environmental ethic is not "atomistic or distributive" but
"*holistic* or collective," since it values as its highest priority the good
of the whole community (1992b, 59), that is, the good of the ecosys-
tem in which individual creatures have their being. Similarly,
although Blake speaks of a singular "dog starvd at his Masters Gate,"
his concern is not atomistically limited to the welfare of the individual

dog. By shifting the aphorism's focus from the individual dog and Master in the first line to the fate of the whole "State" in the second, Blake articulates an emphatic concern for what the dog's condition signifies about the *relationship* between its abuse and the governmental structures that support such cruelty.

While the issue of animal rights is largely based on legality, Blake tends in antinomian fashion to oppose law, favouring the concept of "Liberty" over the juridical and moral concepts of "Right and Duty" (J 22:11; E167). Thus, in contrast to John Lawrence, who argues that "unless you make legal and formal recognition of the Rights of Beasts, you cannot punish cruelty and aggression" (1796, 125), Blake's "environmental ethic" avoids – perhaps too idealistically – making any pragmatic appeal to legislative force. But this aspect of Blake's philosophy does not stop him from speaking of animals in terms of legality. "One Law for the Lion & Ox is Oppression" (E44), he declares in *The Marriage of Heaven and Hell*, implying on one level that there is a kind of oppressive government that does in fact extend itself to the animal kingdom.[20] This oppression may even involve, for Blake, the fact that animals have been appropriated symbolically in poetic tradition to point towards explicitly anthropocentric concerns – like government itself (since traditionally the lion and ox have both been deployed as symbols of nobility[21]). Blake's disdain for homogeneous rule ("One Law") suggests that the law's main problem is its inability to acknowledge and respect the particular otherness of individual creatures and contexts, human or otherwise. The regaining of such respect would perhaps provide the basis for an environmental ethic emphasizing "liberty"; for, as we shall see in the next chapter, the best strategy for respecting the rights of non-human creatures might involve merely letting such creatures "be" – or at least attempting to imagine them as such from a respectful, relatively unintrusive distance.

This is not to downplay the importance in Blake's cosmology of the humanity of all things. As we have already seen, Blake's universe is thoroughly and unabashedly anthropomorphic, since the status of non-human entities in his poetic mythology is fundamentally and inextricably related to his understanding of *human* identity. Blake's discourse on nature would likely be distasteful to many thinkers in the fields of environmental ethics and deep ecology, who argue that non-human entities must be cherished for their "intrinsic value," their value, that is, apart from anthropocentric motivations and concerns.[22] From a Blakean standpoint, however, such a claim is ultimately problematic, perhaps even untenable. Since, for Blake, *all* notions of value have their source in human thought, ethical value must always be a distinctively human or anthropomorphic concern.

In attempting to delineate a Blakean position on animal rights and environmental ethics, then, we would do well at this point to reconsider Blake's discourse on the cloud, discussed above: "Think of a white cloud. as being holy you cannot love it but think of a holy man within the cloud love springs up in your thought" (E603). For Blake, as I have argued, a certain kind of anthropomorphism *enables* our ability to conceive of the "holiness" of non-human entities, and thus to treat such entities with love and respect. By considering Blake's discourse on the cloud in light of his famous claim that *all* things are human, we can begin to imagine a radical extension of the idea of "holiness" to all entities, human or otherwise. The potential respect for nature implicit in such a stance might offer a new perspective from which to consider the popular claims that Blake is an opponent of "tyranny in *all* its guises" (L. Clark 1991, 10; emphasis added), and that he is "deeply concerned with the disruption and transformation of hegemonic discourses" (Mee 1992, 10). Whereas Milton, Blake's most influential poetic precursor, vows to work towards "the liberation of all human life from slavery" (1992, 323), Blake's radical humanism goes much further. An almost limitless expansion of the concept of liberty is apparent, for example, in the concluding lines to Blake's "Song of Liberty," wherein the poet asserts that "every thing that lives is Holy" (E45). If we consider this quotation in relation to Blake's assertion that "every thing that lives, / Lives not alone, nor for itself" (BT 3:26–7; E5), we can understand that holiness and relationality – the defining attributes of all Blakean "life" – provide the conceptual bases for an environmental ethic that "would respect otherness as part of a whole in which one participates" (Vogt 1982, 416). But when we recall that "holiness" refers, etymologically, to that which is itself healthy and intact, we can recognize that Blake's concern for the relationality of an entity does not imply a negation of its particularity. Without a consistent focus on *particular* identity, as I shall argue in the next chapter, the concept of holistic relationality can itself become insidious, for it can be deployed to justify and "naturalize" the institutionalized modes of government that Blake so abhorred.

2 Anthropocentrism, Nature's Economy, and *The Book of Thel*

> ... animate and inanimate Nature, the Seasons, the Forest and the Field, the Bee and the Ant, the Larva, Chrysalis and Moth, have lent their real or supposed Analogies with the Origin, Pursuits, and End of the Human Race, so often to emblematic Purposes, that Instruction is become stale, and Attention callous.
>
> (Henry Fuseli)[1]

ANTHROPOMORPHISM AND CRITICAL PRACTICE

For most critics of William Blake's *The Book of Thel* (1789), the Eagle and Mole of "Thel's Motto" have represented virtually anything and everything but eagles and moles. Among other things, these creatures of the Blakean sky and pit have been seen as poetic figures for objective versus subjective modes of knowing (Levinson 1980, 291); sight versus touch (Johnson 1970, 263); human poetic, prophetic, and inspirational insight versus the animal blindness of natural religion (Pearce 1978, 34); imaginative experience versus physical experience (Beer 1968, 200); divine or higher innocence versus regenerative experience (Tarr 1971, 193) – and the list goes on. As far as I am aware, only Gerda S. Norvig has discussed these complex symbols in terms that invite a consideration of the non-human entities for which they are named: *Thel*'s Eagle and Mole, Norvig remarks, refer to "animals appropriated by common parlance as epistemological emblems" (1995, 267). Norvig's insight encourages me to examine the *discursive* uses such linguistic "appropriation" of non-human entities serves in *The Book of Thel* and its criticism; for as I hope to demonstrate in this chapter, Blake's poem is acutely concerned with the ways our understandings of such creatures are inevitably constructed in and produced by institutionalized discourse. For Blake, I shall argue, concepts associated with vegetation and animality have important implications not only for human identity but also for the lives of the myriad creatures who enter discourse under the homogenizing signs of the "plant" and the "animal."

In my introduction, I attempted to delineate some of the ways Blake shows us that our thinking about "natural" objects is always discursive, involving at the most basic level what Michel Foucault refers to as a "violence that we do to things," or "a practice we impose" upon them (1972, 229). To this extent, it is virtually impossible, when we consider the existence of non-human creatures, to catch even a fleeting glimpse of something "other" than ourselves. And yet the fact that many people today take for granted the notion that animals have certain inalienable rights – a state of affairs that would likely have exceeded the most optimistic hopes of an eighteenth-century animal rights advocate like John Lawrence[2] – proves that the practices we impose upon non-human creatures are not so rigid that they cannot be dramatically transformed. By attempting at least to imagine the needs of the non-human world, we can open ourselves to very real change, change that can mitigate or at least temper the ecological violence that accompanies so many of our discursive practices.

In many ways, however, the institution of literary criticism – and of Blake criticism in particular – has remained closed to such change. Indeed, in most present-day readings of *The Book of Thel*'s symbolism, critical practice tends to involve a subtle but violent effacement of the plants and animals from which so many of the poem's linguistic figures derive their names. Consider, for instance, the following reading of the pasqueflower in *Thel*'s frontispiece design (see Figure 6). A.G. den Otter perceptively characterizes the bud of this flower as "slither[ing]" up to Thel's knee, thus symbolizing "the serpent in Paradise, tempting the Eve-like Thel" (1991, 646). Without denying the interpretive efficacy of this reading, one might point out that the pasqueflower's botanical referent is revealingly absent in it. For den Otter, Blake's pasqueflower represents not its biological species but a serpent – which in turn symbolizes, for most Blake scholars at least, all that is harmful to human existence. As an embodiment of evil, the pasqueflower would be well served if Thel, following God's dictate in Genesis 3:15, were to treat it as Satan's offspring, exacting vengeance for its act of temptation by crushing it beneath her righteous heel.[3]

The anti-natural violence implicit in this traditional and rather narrow reading of the pasqueflower's referentiality is subtly pervasive in *Thel* criticism. A remarkable instance of such violence occurs, for example, in Marjorie Levinson's insightful commentary on the Motto's opening lines, wherein Blake asks: "Does the Eagle know what is in the pit? / Or wilt thou go ask the Mole" (E3). In response to these questions, Levinson advocates a convergence of what she

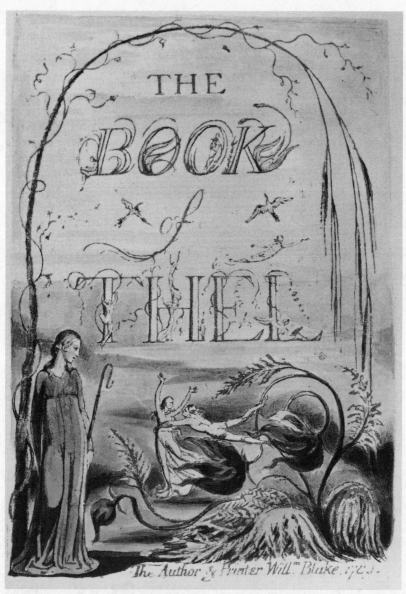

The Author & Printer Will. Blake. 1789.

6   *The Book of Thel*, frontispiece
By permission of the Houghton Library, Harvard University

reads as the objective and subjective viewpoints symbolized by the Eagle and the Mole – and she does so in a particularly telling way: "The marriage between Eagle and Mole vision would occur when the Mole brought his sense of the Eagle into the Pit. The Pit, unable to contain this unstable potential, would *explode* and produce a finite third term: double-vision, seeing the divine in the human and the human in the divine" (1980, 292; emphasis added). If one chooses to read Blake's symbols in a manner that centres or privileges their animal referents, Levinson's interpretation of Thel's Motto becomes rather ominous. At the very least, the hypothetical and figurative "explosion" of the Mole's underground pit suggests something of the violence inhabiting anthropocentric notions of divinity ("the divine in the human and the human in the divine"); for in the natural world, such a circumstance would do away with troublesome moles once and for all quite simply by killing them. One might ask at this point whether biological moles wish to alter or abandon their subterranean homes, or whether they envy the experience of eagles – but the question would be all too human, entailing its own anthropomorphic violence. Perhaps the only thing that can be said of biological moles is that they remain, from the human standpoint, unknown and unknowable. To respect these animals in their otherness, then, would entail learning simply and unintrusively to let them "be" – itself perhaps an impossible task.

Admittedly, my commentary on Levinson's reading is hardly fair, literalizing as it does the figurative terms of her ground-breaking argument. Nevertheless, I would like to propose that Blake deploys the Motto's Eagle/Mole dyad in part to query the "speciesism" that underpins our devaluation of "lesser" animals, indeed of animals in general, in our symbolic practices.[4] Traditionally, Europeans have appropriated the eagle as a figure of transcendence – valuing it not for its "eagleness" but for the cultural or conventional roles it can be made to assume. And these roles, far from being innocent, tend to be regulatory in character. A brief discussion of Foucault's critique of "governmentality" will help to clarify this point. According to traditional Judaeo-Christian belief, the soul is that which ultimately guarantees human freedom from corporeal strife. Seen as an historical effect or as a figure of understanding, however, it is an aspect of human identity in which various ascetic denunciations of corporeality are traditionally carried out. To this extent, the soul functions politically as an instrument of corporeal subjection. Indeed, by inhabiting the human subject and bringing it to existence, the "soul" is "a factor in the mastery that power exercises over the body. The soul is the effect and instrument of a political anatomy; the soul is the prison of the body" (Foucault 1995, 30).

These claims may sound hyperbolical, but they are part of a thoroughgoing political critique in which traditional notions of human sovereignty are seen unwittingly to play into the hands of power. Crucially, the imprisonment of which Foucault speaks involves not external coercion so much as conditioned acts of individual conscience; for as the ostensible voice of the soul, the conscience makes possible a mode of *internalized* surveillance linking "total obedience, knowledge of oneself, and confession to someone else" in a panoptic structure Foucault refers to as "pastoral technology" (1988, 70, 63). And this technology of power is not without important environmental implications. Allied with the hyper-hygienic realm of spirit in a binary equation subordinating the Earth as the source and locus of corporeality and its attendant corruption, the soul in orthodox thinking imprisons not only the individual body but material nature in general, subordinating nature to a humanity understood as the earthly locus of transcendent spirit. This subordination of the natural or physical realm brings us back to the question of *Thel*'s Eagle. As an embodiment of spirit or spiritual desire, this symbol points at one level towards a process of linguistic imposition in which its earthly animal referent has been utterly negated in the name of the human "Same."

According to Kathleen Raine, such imposition is ubiquitous in Blake's poetry: Blake derives *all* of his natural symbols "from some already established symbolic tradition," seeing "nature through symbol, not symbol through nature" (1985, 71). To the extent that all humans apprehend the things of nature *through* language, Raine's insight is certainly correct and relevant. But what if Blake, a rigorously self-reflexive poet and iconoclastic champion of "Mental Fight" (M 1:13; E95), appropriates such creatures as eagles and moles in his poetic practice in part to *question* the implications of animal symbolism? Often, following Robert Gleckner (1959, 162), Blake's readers have privileged eagle symbolism over mole symbolism by appealing to Blake's hellish proverb that "When thou seest an Eagle, thou seest a portion of Genius" (MHH; E37). What tends to be forgotten in this standard appeal is that the espied eagle is not Genius itself but "a *portion* of Genius," a *part*, in other words, of a greater morphology of spirit; and there is no evidence in Blake's proverb that this larger whole excludes the pit, the mole, or any other earthly or heavenly particular. As for *Thel*'s Mole, it is nothing new to suggest that this blind and seemingly immanental creature has a kind of experiential *insight* to which the transcendental Eagle can never have access, for although the Eagle can "see" where the Pit opens onto the landscape, it cannot "know" what is "*in* the pit" (except perhaps that its occupant, once vulnerably exposed to the light of the sun, is a potential morsel of nourishment). Arguably, both the Eagle and the Mole of Thel's Motto have "experience" that is peculiarly and distinctively their own. And whatever this experience may comprise, the Motto, by providing us with questions rather than doctrinal assertions, does not explicitly favour any single experiential perspective (Rajan 1990, 240) and hence does not privilege or even necessarily "pit" either one of its represented animals over or against the other. But this insight provides only a tentative starting point for a socio-ecological reading of *The Book of Thel*. For the question remains: how can we as humans *respect* the irreducible alterity of non-human creatures like moles and eagles in our symbolic practices? Can we even begin to "ask the Mole" or the Eagle what they "know" about earthly life without destroying their nests, without "exploding" their natural habitats, without the violence of anthropomorphic colonization?

When Blake asks in Thel's Motto whether "Wisdom" can "be put in a silver rod? / Or Love in a golden bowl" (E3), he explicitly raises the question of anthropomorphic projection: as we decide how to answer these questions, we must consider the ways human characteristics or valuations are indeed "put in" or projected upon external (in this case human-made) objects. But these questioning lines, following as they do the Motto's references to the Eagle and the Mole, also underscore by their ultimate positioning in the quatrain the human tendency to consider *non*-human creatures in terms of institutional or governmental categories; for at a certain referential level, they structurally connect the "natural" realm of wild eagles and moles to the discursive realm signified by the silver rod and the golden bowl (respectively, "the state rod of office" and "the golden chalice of orthodox Christian ritual"; Mellor 1974, 37). More important, however, these lines – these questions – *question* the relationship between institutional discourse (as a nexus of power and knowledge) and the animal inhabitants of non-human nature. Among other things, they ask us: Can "Wisdom" or "Love" be expressed in a symbolic order or economy that subjugates natural entities? Is anthropocentrism a Wise or Loving stance? Does such a stance express infinite Love or an all-encompassing self-interest? (This is certainly a question we must ask of a poet who asserted, only a year prior to the etching of *Thel*, that "He who sees the Infinite in all things sees God. He who sees the Ratio only sees himself only" [NNR; E3]). Among the numerous questions that the Motto's perplexing questions raise, Blake seems to be asking whether it is possible to consider objects in "Infinite" terms rather than in narrowly anthropocentric ones.

But such a question raises the larger problem of the overtly anthropocentric epistemology involved in Blake's philosophical privileging

of the divine human form. Those critics who emphasize Blake's sus-
picion of nature at the expense of his desire to see "the Infinite in all
things" tend to be convinced that Blake dismisses the natural world
as a possible source of redemptive knowledge or wisdom. From such
a standpoint, Blake is an anthropomorphic Swedenborgian, endorsing,
as Désirée Hirst would have it (1964, 206–7), Swedenborg's dictum
that "God is very Man. In all the Heavens there is no other Idea of
God, than that of a Man." But is Blake's 1788 annotation to this pas-
sage really an endorsement *per se*? Blake responds: "Man can have no
idea of any thing greater than Man as a cup cannot contain more than
its capaciousness But God is a man not because he is so perceivd by
man but because he is the creator of man" (E603). Blake does not say
here that "there is *no* other Idea of God, than that of a Man," but that
"*Man* can have no [other] idea" of God. This assertion is much more
equivocal than Swedenborg's. Indeed, Blake's response to Sweden-
borg invites a further qualifying question: If "God is a man ... because
he is the creator of man," might it not logically follow that God is, for
example, a lily, because he is the creator of the lily? Blake's notorious
anthropocentrism comes undone at moments such as this one, reveal-
ing, I would argue, an understanding of creation that is not absolutely
human centred but open to radical perspectival shifting.

Such multi perspectivism certainly informs Blake's conception of
human-nature relations in "The Fly," one of the *Songs of Experience*
written approximately three years after the etching of *Thel*:

Little Fly
Thy summers play,
My thoughtless hand
Has brush'd away.

Am not I
A fly like thee?
Or art not thou
A man like me?

For I dance
And drink & sing:
Till some blind hand
Shall brush my wing.

If thought is life
And strength & breath:
And the want
Of thought is death;

Then am I
A happy fly,
If I live,
Or if I die. (E23–24)

These seemingly simple lines, inspired by the speaker's "thought-less" act of violence, embody a profound meditation on the difference between human and non-human identity. While the speaker con-structs the fly in anthropomorphic terms (conceiving its activity as "play"), he goes on to entertain the possibility that human identity may be zoomorphically constructed in turn, asking "Am not I / A fly like thee?" Although this perspectival reversal does not escape the economy of anthropomorphism (since it presupposes that the fly can engage in something like thoughtful dialogue with the human speaker), it is nevertheless unsettling, involving a concerted effort "to imagine a complete interchangeability between animal and human" (Buell 1995, 185). While this imaginative shifting of perspective may seem like idle intellectual play, it carries important ethical implica-tions and consequences. When he asserts in the fourth stanza that "the want / Of thought *is* death," the speaker logically pronounces a subtle but severe judgment on the action perpetrated earlier in the poem by his "thoughtless hand": according to the poem's internal logic, thoughtless acts are not only potentially deadly; they are them-selves forms of death. Thus, the speaker learns an important lesson from his encounter with the fly, a lesson that will likely encourage him thoughtfully to alter his future behaviour. Indeed, by calling himself a "happy fly" at the end of the poem, the humbled human speaker pays fitting tribute to the tiny creature whose inadvertent death has inspired his ethical anthropomorphic musings.

It remains to be seen whether this kind of multiperspectivism is applicable to a reading of *The Book of Thel*. Following the example of the Motto, one might rephrase this problem as a question: Can Thel, like the speaker in "The Fly," learn anything worthwhile from the natural entities she encounters in the Vales of Har? One critic has recently argued that when Thel begins in the poem to realize that the Lilly, Cloud, and Clod of Clay know relatively little about "being a human being," she correctly doubts the relevance, applicability, and truth of the knowledge that they offer her (den Otter 1991, 644). Certainly, as I shall presently argue, the knowledge that these natural entities articulate is not "their own" so much as Thel's ventriloquistic and discursively influenced projection. But this does not mean that Thel cannot gain important insights from her interaction with the non-human inhabitants of Har. On the contrary, Thel's encounters with the Lilly, Cloud, and Clod of Clay offer her opportunities to

examine carefully her complex implication in the discourses that con-
stitute her subjective view of the world and her understanding of its
non-human inhabitants.

PASTORALISM, INSTRUMENTALISM, HIERARCHY

Although Blake does not explicitly delineate Thel's social back-
ground, we know from the poem's outset that she is a shepherd – so
we may surmise that she is the product of a distinctively pastoral
mode of social organization. It is significant, then, that Thel's first act
in the poem is one of social rebellion: "The daughters of Mne Sera-
phim led round their sunny flocks. / All but the youngest; she in
paleness sought the secret air" (1:1–2). Thel's abandonment of the
social totality represented by the "All" that designates her sisters is
obviously a rejection of the duties that belong to her assigned station
in the pastoral order. Mary Lynn Johnson has interpreted Thel's
rebellion as an undutiful abandonment of responsible activity, an act
justifying the rebuke that Thel is "locked in selfhood, in a hell of her
own making" (1970, 265). More recently, however, critics have
become somewhat less severe in their judgment of the youthful shep-
herd's behaviour. Brian Wilkie sees Thel's rebellion as a part of her
effort to break free from the confines of a "limited world" (1990, 52);
and den Otter sees Thel's rejection of her duties as symptomatic of
a failure on the part of the authority figures responsible for her edu-
cation (1991, 637). According to these latter critical arguments, there
is something unsatisfactory or lacking not so much in Thel herself
but in the pastoral world she inhabits.

If we entertain for a moment the possibility that Thel is rebelling
in the opening lines of her "Book" against the same dull "round"
(1:1) of a stultifying human pastoralism, her "paleness" of complex-
ion need not necessarily be symptomatic of a "diseased life" (Johnson
1970, 264–5). Rather, it might be read as signifying Thel's awareness
of the profundity of her transgression against a questionable but
nonetheless authoritative pastoral regime. Thel's rebellion is socially
suspect only if we adhere to the traditional view that pastoral society
was the product of an ideal "golden age," a benevolent age of peace
and plenty. We must remember, however, that Blake was no passive
inheritor of literary conventions; indeed, there is much evidence in
his early work to suggest that Blake suspected the pastoral ideal,
regarding it as a political fiction subserving and perpetuating an
oppressive hegemonic order. To clarify the political and historical
underpinnings of the pastoral, it will be helpful to quote a relevant

passage from Raymond Williams' critique of eighteenth-century pas-
toral literature. As Williams points out, the feudal economy charac-
terizing England's so-called "golden age" – a social order numerous
historians have invoked as a positive model against which to criticize
postmodern capitalism – "was an order of exploitation of a most
thoroughgoing kind: a property in men as well as in land; a reduction
of most men to working animals, tied by forced tribute, forced labour,
or 'bought and sold like beasts'; 'protected' by law and custom only
as animals and streams are protected, to yield more labour, more
food, more blood; an economy directed, in all its working relations,
to a physical and economic domination of a significantly total kind"
(1973, 37–8). Is there evidence that *The Book of Thel*'s eponymous
heroine senses something of this pervasive violence, a violence affect-
ing inhabitants of both the human *and* non-human worlds? Certainly
Thel's propensity to refer to herself in the third person (see 1:8, 2:11,
3:3) suggests an implicit sense of alienation[5] that is at odds with the
peaceful and organically unified existence traditionally associated
with the pastoral ideal. By focusing on Thel's alienated condition, we
can understand that the "air" she seeks – as if her customary life has
been suffocating her – is "secret" (1:1–2) because a genuine sense of
communal interaction with the human and non-human beings inhab-
iting her world has never been available to her. Indeed, it is possible
that the youthful Thel at some level blames Har's pastoral society for
her sense of alienation in the midst of a world of seeming plenitude.
What I am proposing, in short, is that Thel's behaviour signifies her
intuitive dissatisfaction with the socially oppressive and narrowly
anthropocentric world view that Har's pastoral regime has bequeathed
her. Such a situation, at any rate, would help to explain her rebellious
actions: she longs perhaps "To fade away" from a "mortal day" (1:3)
defined not so much in terms of a contrast between immortal life and
earthly mortality (the standard interpretation) but in terms of
humanity itself; for in a secondary adjectival sense, "mortal" can
mean quite simply "relating to humanity" (Oxford English Dictio-
nary, 1st ed). We must remember, moreover, that Thel is fleeing "*her*
mortal day" – not the day of some abstract universal humanity but,
as the genitive construction specifies, the quotidian day of the pas-
toral economy that defines the ratio or "round" of her own pastoral
mode of life.

Thel's repeated articulation of her rebellious desire in terms of
"gentleness" is telling in this regard: "Ah! gentle may I lay me down,
and gentle rest my head. / And gentle sleep the sleep of death. and
gentle hear the voice / Of him that walketh in the garden in the
evening time" (1:12–14). In this brief passage, Thel's insistent repetition

of the word "gentle" suggests an awareness that her life has involved a customary or habitual violence; it implies, moreover, an emphatic desire to escape this context, which, among other effects, disrupts or prohibits her ability to gain access to the Word – "the voice / Of him that walketh in the garden" (1:13–14). But an ominous note has already been sounded: Thel's characterization of her life in terms of transient phenomena – rainbow, cloud, reflection, shadows, dreams (1:8–10) – suggests that the violence affecting her is strangely insubstantial and thus difficult to understand or even to pinpoint with any kind of precision.

Perhaps this is why Thel has such difficulty in the poem escaping her troubling predicament. Levinson astutely observes that most of *The Book of Thel* consists of its protagonist's "ventriloquism," inasmuch as the entities that Thel encounters "do no more than repeat Thel's own knowledge" (1980, 290, 288). This ventriloquism, or linguistic projection, stems, I would argue, not from a narcissistic compulsion on Thel's part but from the *discursive* conditioning constituting Thel's view of the world (I shall examine the nature of this conditioning presently). Indeed, Thel's anxious concern about what the inhabitants of Har think of her – implicit in her troubled belief that "*all* shall say, without a use this shining woman liv'd" (3:22; emphasis added) – demonstrates that she has internalized the surveillance of power, that she is subject to a regulative mode of *self*-surveillance that would contain her rebellion even prior to its outbreak. Thus, if the authoritative gaze of Mne Seraphim – the senior shepherd or watcher in Thel's world – can no longer fall upon Thel when she escapes to the "river of Adona," Mne Seraphim can at least rest assured that Thel, the transgressive daughter, has already been taught most circumspectly to watch *herself*. Because her subjectivity is the very product of her social milieu, moreover, Thel's experience of the natural entities she will encounter in the Vales of Har will be largely pre-determined, even though she has physically removed herself from the watchful presence of her seraphic parent and obedient sisters.

That Thel's subjective experience of Har is constituted discursively can be clarified by examining the question of utility as it is articulated in her poem, for Thel tends to consider non-human entities almost entirely in terms of their use-value in Har's human-centred pastoral economy. The poem's concern for this utilitarian ethic begins on plate 1, where the Lilly characterizes herself in passing as a "weed" (1:16), a derogatory term tending to connote non-useful plants. Thel, perhaps disagreeing with this implicit self-disparagement, attempts to defend the Lilly's value; but she does so in a highly questionable

manner, characterizing the plant solely in terms of the various func-
tions it performs in a distinctly human-oriented pastoral economy.
According to Thel, the Lilly is praiseworthy because it nourishes the
lamb and cleanses its mouth of "all contagious taints," "purif[ies]
the golden honey," and "Revives the milked cow, & tames the fire-
breathing steed" (2:5–10). These are certainly valuable services (Mellor
1974, 24), but they are aimed precisely at humans, the ultimate con-
sumers of the products of a domesticated nature. For Thel, in short,
the Lilly belongs to a natural order that "is simply and decisively on
its way to table" (Williams 1973, 30). With this overt instrumentalism
in mind, one might read the Lilly's rather abrupt departure from the
narrative as a poetic response to the anti-natural insult implicit in
such a narrow anthropocentric valuation. Because Thel cannot think
of the Lilly as having any value exceeding that of its practical useful-
ness to humans, in other words, the Lilly *itself* disappears from the
scene. Not so the question of use-value, however, which Thel brings
to bear on her subsequent encounter with the Cloud. For immediately
after she describes the many *useful* functions of the Lilly, Thel
declares, "But Thel is like a faint cloud" (2:11). Here, the conjunction
"But" sets up a grammatical antithesis, implying that a cloud is an
apt symbol for the uselessness that Thel herself feels. The poem's
personified Cloud, so inscribed, echoes back this ideology in its sub-
sequent encounter with Thel (speaking of her "great … use" as "the
food of worms" [3:25–6; E5]), demonstrating that the discourse con-
stituting the human protagonist's subjectivity extends to itself as well.

But Thel is clearly at odds with this instrumentalism, which she
cannot help but speak. If she indeed advocated such a doctrine, she
would not have rejected, at the poem's outset, her duties as a shepherd
– duties that should, presumably, define the scope of her own useful-
ness in life. Thel's act of rejection, I have suggested, stems from her
intuitive awareness that her role in the social structure of Har is
haunted by an intangible violence. Her inadvertent or residual sub-
scription to a doctrine of utility in her encounter with the Lilly and the
Cloud signifies not a personal failure, then, but the overarching power
of Mne Seraphim's pastoral – but nevertheless discursive – regime.

The Book of Thel brings established notions of utility into question in
at least two ways. First, it questions anthropocentric biases by gestur-
ing towards a radically expansive conception of use. For example, the
poem's representation of the human body's usefulness as "the food of
worms" (3:23–6) suggests that Blake is willing to shock us into con-
sidering use in the widest possible terms, as a principle of life in gen-
eral, not just the life of human beings. Second, in the Cloud's advice
to Thel, Blake introduces a principle that exceeds the instrumentalism

of an ethics based on use-value. The Cloud certainly tells Thel that "if thou art the food of worms ... / How great thy use"; but he qualifies this assertion with the crucial clause "how great thy blessing" (3:25–6). This latter clause might be read as a paying of lip service to the realm of the sacred, or as implying that "blessing" is *derived* from utility. But there is something excessive about the Cloud's philosophical gesture. The Cloud goes on to tell Thel that "every thing that lives, / Lives not alone, nor for itself" (3:26–7). If Thel's use-value arises because each and every creature lives "not ... *for* itself" but in the purposeful and practical service of others, her "blessing" might be said to stem from the fact that each living thing "Lives not alone" but as part of a cosmic community in which no entity need be alienated. If Thel could free herself from the anthropocentric ratio that circumscribes her existence – if she could open herself to the vitality of a relational infinity that includes but also surpasses human-centred utility – she would begin to understand the interrelational holiness of *all* life, the intrinsic value or "bless[edness]" of literally "every thing that lives." The wisdom implicit in such an understanding would dispel the particular utilitarian anxiety that is part and parcel of the sense of alienation that Thel feels in Har; it would enable her to reformulate her view of the world so that she might at least begin to "find [her] place" (2:12) in it. According to her present viewpoint, Thel occupies the centre of a cosmic web of connections designed to serve her *own* needs. Perhaps her simultaneous desire for, and fear of, "fad[ing] away" is part of a larger but frightening desire to free herself from this economy of self-centredness by positioning herself upon a *strand* in the cosmic web rather than at its focal point.

In light of Thel's subtle but significant preoccupation with the notion of hierarchy, however, such a reading becomes problematic. For when Thel articulates her desire to find her "place" in the order of things, the Lilly answers her by addressing her as "Queen of the vales" (2:13; cf. also 3:29 and 5:16), seemingly shoring up Thel's anthropocentric notion that she occupies, as the poem's human representative, a "pearly throne" (2:12) near or at the pinnacle of the *Scala Naturae* or Great Chain of Being. Later in the poem, Thel's response to the Cloud's story of his courtship with the Dew further demonstrates her subscription to some such notion of hierarchy. As she puts it, "I walk through the vales of Har. and smell the sweetest flowers; / But I feed not the little flowers: I hear the warbling birds, / But I feed not the warbling birds." This discourse culminates in Thel's declaration of her own uselessness, her fear that she lives "*only* ... to be at death the food of worms" (3:18–20, 23; emphasis added). Thel wishes, in short, to be of use to the fragrant flowers and the pleasantly "warbling birds," but she is disgusted by the thought of serving lowly worms. In other words, she seems willing to condescend – with as little psychological inconvenience to herself as possible – to be of "use" only to what she has learned to conceive of as "higher" beings, pleasing entities situated in relatively close proximity to her own "pearly throne."

Although the hierarchical concept of the Great Chain of Being has been characterized as anti-utilitarian (Lovejoy 1953, 186) and even as "a description of ecological relatedness" (Worster 1995, 46), it also derives from and reinforces the biblical sanction of human "dominion" over nature (Genesis 1:26–8) and can thus be manipulated discursively to justify numerous forms of human-centred violence against "lower" beings.[6] Blake's poem certainly incorporates the language of hierarchy, but it does so in ways that question the legitimacy of such vertical structure, thus problematizing the notion of Thel's ascendency. Over forty years ago, for example, Robert F. Gleckner pointed to the Lilly's "silver shrine," the cloud's "airy throne" and the Clay's "crown," to support the idea that each speaker is a kind of regal entity, "an important personage, if not the ruler, in his own special realm" (1959, 173). I would take the implications of Har's ubiquitous regality much further and argue that these poetic characterizations dismantle the hierarchical thinking that upholds and sustains the very concept of royalty as it is traditionally understood. Such dismantling is certainly evident in Blake's portrait of the Clod of Clay, who presents herself as "the meanest thing" (4:11), but who is nonetheless convinced that "he that loves the lowly" has given her "a crown that none can take away" (5:1,4). It is important to note that, as a figure for eternal sovereignty, the Clay's crown defies any ideology of transcendence that would devalue the realm of material existence in favour of a "heavenly" afterlife. The Clay's royal status thus functions to problematize the very hierarchy that constructs it as "mean" and "lowly" in the first place.

In *The Book of Thel*, literally "*every* thing that lives is Holy" (MHH; E45), holistic, valuable, because "every thing that lives, / Lives not alone, nor for itself." In such a relational universe, the very identity of *each* living thing is infinitely deferred in context, allowing no space or moment in which the entity may crystallize as a stable "being" on a hierarchical chain. This is the profound "ecological" insight at the heart of *The Book of Thel*. Yet the poem also embodies a profound awareness that such a philosophical holism is not without its attendant dangers; for holism can be invoked and manipulated to serve the self-interested ends of governmental discourse. It is to a consideration of this problem that we now turn.

SEXUAL POLITICS: ERASMUS DARWIN AND NATURE'S ECONOMY

We can begin to analyze the governmental implications of a holistic naturalism in Blake's thought by situating *The Book of Thel vis-à-vis* the eighteenth-century concept of "nature's economy," a perspective on nature that, as I have previously noted, conceptualized all earthly entities as integral but interdependent parts of a complexly unified, interactive whole. To a certain extent, Blake supports such a model of existence in *Thel* by problematizing the notion of identity as hierarchically stratified and self-sufficient. But Blake's poem also points to a profound ambivalence in the holistic concept of "nature's economy." On the one hand, as I shall demonstrate, Har's natural economy epitomizes a highly ethical mode of mutual coexistence, an approach to life that the alienated, instrumentally obsessed Thel would do well to emulate. On the other hand, Thel must approach Har's natural economy with a degree of scepticism or self-critical caution; for this economy, far from being "innocent," is ultimately "known" to Thel through internalized orthodoxies that efface the alterity of Har's natural entities by naturalizing various modes of social hierarchy.

It is highly probable that Blake was indeed aware of contemporary thinking on nature's economy when he composed and engraved *The Book of Thel*. Certainly this thinking was "in the air" in late-eighteenth-century England: it belongs largely to the contemporary discourse of botany, which, during Blake's lifetime, was the most popular branch of natural history. Indeed, according to the *Critical Review* of 1763, botany had, "by a kind of national establishment, become the favourite study of the times" (quoted in Jones 1937, 347). Now if this "national establishment" – a telling phrase from the perspective of Blakean iconoclasm – evaded or excluded Blake's working-class experience, Blake could have learned about nature's economy from a number of concrete sources. During his three-year residence in Felpham, for example, Blake would have had the opportunity to read about or discuss botany with his patron and daily companion, William Hayley, whose library contained, by my count, no fewer than forty English-language volumes related to the subject (Munby 1971, *passim*). In contrast to younger contemporary poets like Samuel Taylor Coleridge, however, Blake was not an enthusiastic reader of such texts. And the Felpham period, it must be noted, postdates the publication of *The Book of Thel*. What we know for certain is that Blake had read the first edition of Erasmus Darwin's *The Loves of the Plants* (1789) before completing *Thel*, and that shortly thereafter he had become familiar with Darwin's *Economy of Vegetation* (1791),[7] for which he engraved at least one illustration.

Admittedly, there is no shortage of critical speculation concerning Darwin's influence on *Thel* and on Blake's subsequent works. But such discussions can be misleading if they fail to acknowledge at the outset the vast differences between Blake's and Darwin's poetic philosophies. One can only imagine, for example, the fury of Blake's response to Darwin's advertisement prefacing *The Loves of the Plants*, wherein the naturalist-cum-poet forthrightly states that "the general design of the following sheets is to inlist Imagination under the banner of Science, and to lead her votaries from the looser analogies, which dress out the imagery of poetry, to the stricter ones, which form the ratiocination of philosophy." In contrast to scientific enthusiasts like Darwin, Blake is famous for his much-touted polemical conviction that the "ratio" of philosophical rationalism *destroys* the Imagination. As a persistent champion of imaginative endeavour, then, Blake would have had a great deal of cause to react unfavourably to Darwin's stated agenda. Critics have disagreed, however, on the precise extent or nature of this reaction. For some readers, Blake's cosmogony is largely influenced by Darwin (Leonard 1978, *passim*), as is his sexual politics (Erdman 1974, 34; Worrall 1975, 400); while for others Darwin's thought becomes a subtle "spectral presence" haunting Blake's *œuvre* (Hilton 1981, 37). Although these writers approach Darwin's influence on Blake in diverse and sometimes mutually contradictory ways, they share a common omission: none of them has considered the Darwin-Blake connection in light of the contemporary discourse of nature's economy and the role it plays in the history of ecological thought.

How, exactly, did Darwin conceptualize the economy of nature? Among other things, he learned from Linnaeus that all earthly things participate in a vast web of interrelated cyclical processes (McKusick 1996, 378). This understanding of natural process did not cause Darwin to abandon a methodological atomism; on the contrary, he tended, quite productively, to reduce complex ideas and systems into their component parts for the purposes of scientific study (Hassler 1973, 14–15). Nevertheless, in his poetic representations of terrestrial life, Darwin often focused on the complex interactions of discrete entities and natural processes. In *The Loves of the Plants*, for example, he argues that primeval vegetation produces the soil in which later botanical species will grow (1973a, 1.295n.); he discusses ocean and subterranean currents as natural phenomena that have implications for plant life that are nothing less than hemispheric in scope (3.345n.); and he considers the crucial role played by "Vegetable Respiration" in the production of air and the purification of water (4.161n.). Although he did not begin comprehensively to articulate something like a systematic philosophy of organic creation until *The Economy of Vegetation*, Darwin speaks implicitly, in *The Loves of the Plants*, of terrestrial life as comprised of an interrelated community of diverse species and processes; and he uses the phrases "economy of vegetation" or "vegetable economy" on numerous occasions in his footnotes to the poetry (see, for example, 1.211, 3.184, 3.188). One might say that the seeds that would produce *The Economy*'s ideal of a holistic cosmos in which "Orbs wheel in orbs, round centres centres roll, / And form self-balanced, one revolving Whole" (1.111–12), had already been sewn in *The Loves of the Plants*.[8]

Does Blake entertain this notion of natural creation as a balanced system of interconnected processes? Certainly he represents a cyclical and synergistic nature at various points in *The Book of Thel*. On the third plate of the poem, for example, Blake's Cloud discusses his own meteorological activities in terms of a perpetual cycle of evaporation and precipitation – where his "steeds drink of the golden springs" (BT 3:7; E4) in order subsequently to shower "food" upon all the "tender flowers" of the Vales of Har (3:16). Whether Blake was aware of it or not, the Cloud's poetic commentary accords with the scientific observations that Linnaeus's disciple, Isaac Biberg, recorded in his influential essay "The Oeconomy of Nature," first published in 1751. After tracing the flow of rainwater from its highland sources, along the courses of rivers, and then to the sea, Biberg declares: "Thus the water returns in a circle, whence it first drew its origin, that it may act over the same scene again" (1759, 36). In "The Oeconomy of Nature," the hydrological cycle sustains all forms of earthly life (McKusick 1996, 378); just as, in *The Book of Thel*, it brings nourishment to flowers, which themselves participate in the complex cycle of earthly sustenance. Blake's cloud summarizes his holistic philosophy by affirming the interconnectedness of all biological entities in nature; for in response to Thel's complaint that she exists "without a use" (BT 3:22; E5), he gestures towards a cyclical food chain that implicates all living creatures (3:25–7).

It is necessary at this point to emphasize that *Thel*'s natural cycles need not necessarily be understood as representations of the simple "cyclical recurrence" that Northrop Frye, in *Fearful Symmetry*, disapprovingly contrasts with the temporality of "infinite extension" (1970, 368); for *Thel*'s cycles tend at one level to function according to principles of mutuality and self-annihilation in the benevolent service of others. The common critical consensus that Blake saw *all* natural processes in terms of "the same dull round" of a rigidly repetitive natural cyclicity must be reconsidered, if only on the grounds that such a vision would imply Blake's agreement with the mechanistic paradigm of nature he ubiquitously indicts. In Blake's later mythology, at any rate, only processes associated with Satan's Newtonian Mill conform to the pattern of a perpetual, unchanging circularity. I shall consider Blake's view of nature's cyclicity in detail in chapter 3. Suffice it to say here that, as early as *The Book of Thel*, Blake begins to problematize such a static view of natural cyclicity; for in this pastoral poem he represents cyclical systems as open, intertwined, and therefore complex. Thus, the Cloud's hydrological cycle functions *in concert*, as we have seen, with the natural cycle of birth and death, feeding flowers that die to nourish lambs, whose lives and activities provide sustenance for human shepherds, whose own bodies, at death, play an alimentary role in the life-cycles of helpless worms. In the process of this interactivity, Luvah's horses are "*renew*[ed]" by "golden springs" belonging to a water cycle inter- acting with the light and heat of a cyclically regenerative "risen sun" (BT 3:7–8, 3:14, E4–5). This "*risen* sun" is not a mere symbol of mun- dane recurrence; rather, it is connected homonymically to the theme of *spiritual* renewal through resurrection in the "risen *Son*." In the natural world, to be sure, processes repeat themselves, but the con- texts in which these repetitions occur continually alter as minute particulars are rearranged in relation to one another. Hence, in the Vales of Har, an understanding of the life-cycle of a Lilly can illumi- nate and transform the material and spiritual existence of a "pensive" human "queen" (3:29), productively transforming Thel's view of her own pastoral "round" (1:1) and altering her understanding of her biological and ethical relation to worms and other "lowly" creatures. The Cloud hints at such expansive possibility by correlating an open- minded understanding of nature's complex round of birth and death with "bless[edness]" (3:26).

The male Cloud's holistic philosophy is shared in the poem by the Lilly and Clod of Clay, both of whom are female; but for these latter creatures, the implications of adhering to such a holism are double- edged. First, let us consider the Lilly in light of some of the positive consequences stemming from her understanding of the communal position she occupies in Har's natural economy. Unlike the despair- ing and alienated Thel, the Lilly is represented contextually as an integrated part of the natural community. She dwells peacefully "*in* the humble grass"; and although she declares individualistically that "*I* am visited from heaven and he that smiles on all. / … over *me* spreads his hand" (1:15, 19–20; emphasis added), she is not singled out or isolated by these providential gestures, for they are accompanied by an imperative directed at the Lilly, the grass, and potentially at Thel as well: "rejoice thou humble grass, thou new-born lilly flower, / Thou gentle maid of silent valleys" (1:21–22). As a whole, the Lilly's narrative expresses her easy awareness that she "Lives not alone" (as the Cloud will later put it) but as part of a community of interrelated beings. Blake's choice of words in this passage suggests, moreover, that this dynamic community potentially embraces Thel herself; for logically, when Thel finds the gentleness she so desperately seeks (1:12–13), she will take her place as the "*gentle* maid of silent valleys" and so will discover that she too can "rejoice."

And yet, despite this hopeful possibility, all is not well in the Vales of Har. We can begin to approach what is perhaps *Thel*'s central philosophical problem by considering Blake's explicit response in the poem to the eighteenth-century understanding of nature's economy as a *sexual* economy. Crucially, eighteenth-century botanical writing "was so imbued with socio-sexual implications that no botanical description was entirely removed from these concerns" (Bewell 1989, 134). Blake's representations of plant life are certainly no exception to this general rule. In particular, *Thel*'s graphic designs demonstrate Blake's acute awareness that the botanical naturalism of his era tended to read human sexual politics into plants in ways that functioned to naturalize and thus reaffirm hegemonic models of *human* gender relations (ibid.). In *Thel*'s frontispiece design, for example (see Figure 6), Blake graphically literalizes the anthropomorphic projection of human sexuality onto the Realm of Flora: he depicts two human figures, a male and a female, emerging from the blooms of a pasqueflower plant, while Thel stands by idly observing the beginnings of their sexual embrace. A number of critics have interpreted this design in light of Erasmus Darwin's botanical writings to support the thesis of Thel's developmental failure in the poem: her failure, in a sexually fecund world, to embrace her own "naturally" blooming sexuality.

David Erdman points out, for example, that the stamens of the pasqueflower, or *Anemone pulsatilla*, were said to remain enfolded within the flower's petals until the latter were touched by the wind, at which time the petals would open, enabling the sexual process of pollination to occur. Referring to a passage from *The Botanic Garden*, Erdman goes on to suggest that we "might take Thel herself for Darwin's 'sad Anemone' pining for the wind's 'cherub-lips,' since the two small figures beside her are performing Darwin's script" (1974, 34). For David Worrall, the sexual self-doubt that Thel expresses in the poem is, significantly, "not reflected in the plant world of the two figures emerging from the flower" (1975, 400). Both Erdman and Worrall,

along with a host of other critics, imply that the "Virgin" Thel's ulti-
mate refusal in the poem to embrace her developing sexuality is
*un*natural and so deserving of the reader's disapproval. From this
perspective, the clearly aggressive posture of the male figure in *Thel*'s
frontispiece design would suggest that Blake advocates the *natural-
ization* of masculinist sexual aggression in the human social world.

A re-examination of the figure of the Lilly, however, will help to
bring such a reading into question. On the one hand, this "modest"
creature (BT 2:17; E4) exhibits a profound sense of self-contentedness;
for in sharp contrast to the perplexed Thel, the Lilly expresses "love"
for her condition (1:17) and great hope for the future (1:23–5). And
yet there is something unsettling about this simple portrait of love
and faith; for the Lilly achieves her serenity, as well as her holistic
sense of communal belonging in Har's natural economy, in part by
way of a questionable self-effacement. The Lilly has likely been per-
suaded by patriarchal discourse to conceive of herself as a mere
"weed" (1:16), as Helen Bruder has pointed out. Indeed, as the ulti-
mate consequence of minding "her numerous charge among the ver-
dant grass" (2:18), the Lilly forfeits her very life (Bruder 1994, 151);
for she will be eaten by the supposedly "innocent" but significantly
male lamb who "crops [her] flowers" (BT 2:5–6; E4). Among other
things, the Lilly's literal self-sacrifice is an insidious consequence of
her religious convictions. To quote Friedrich Nietzsche, the great
nineteenth-century opponent of transcendentalism and priestcraft,
"Life ... come[s] to an end where the 'kingdom of God' begins" (1982,
490). In short, the Lilly has succumbed to an all-too-earthly ideology
that naturalizes its power as knowledge by way of the discourse of
a transcendentalist theology offering vague rewards in "eternal
vales" in exchange for obedience and an earthly self-abnegation.
(More accurately, I must emphasize, Thel has *projected* this discourse
upon the humanized Lilly, which, in the design to plate 4 [E plate 2;
see Figure 7], significantly resembles Thel in posture, form, and
dress.) Hence it is possible to read the Lilly's representation of her
harmonious existence as signifying her unwitting internalization of
the gender-based hierarchy serving the institutionalized self-interest
of patriarchal religion.

Let me clarify this point by examining the doctrine articulated by
the male Cloud. Whereas the Lilly achieves the serenity of her osten-
sibly harmonious existence by way of a philosophy of passivity and
self-abnegation, the Cloud "speaks" of his own harmonious existence
in terms of self-centred activity and agency. As Bruder points out, the
Cloud – the sole adult male Thel encounters in the Vales of Har – is
markedly different from the other creatures whom Thel meets (152).

Why should the mistress of the vales of Har, utter a sigh.

She ceasd & smild in tears, then sat down in her silver shrine.

Thel answerd. O thou little virgin of the peaceful valley.
Giving to those that cannot crave, the voiceless, the o'ertired
Thy breath doth nourish the innocent lamb, he smells thy milky garments,
He crops thy flowers, while thou sittest smiling in his face,
Wiping his mild and meekin mouth from all contagious taints.
Thy wine doth purify the golden honey, thy perfume,
Which thou dost scatter on every little blade of grass that springs
Revives the milked cow, & tames the fire-breathing steed.
But Thel is like a faint cloud kindled at the rising sun:
I vanish from my pearly throne, and who shall find my place.

Queen of the vales, the Lilly answerd, ask the tender cloud,
And it shall tell thee why it glitters in the morning sky,
And why it scatters its bright beauty thro' the humid air.
Descend O little cloud & hover before the eyes of Thel.

The Cloud descended, and the Lilly bowd her modest head:
And went to mind her numerous charge among the verdant grass.

7   *The Book of Thel*, plate 4 (E plate 2)
By permission of the Houghton Library, Harvard University

Unlike the self-effacing Lilly, that "weak" inhabitant of "lowly vales" (1:18, 17), and the "lowly" (5:1) Clay, both of whom Thel must look down upon to see, the Cloud actively shows "his golden head & his bright form ... / Hovering and glittering on the air before the face of Thel" (3:5–6). Moreover, when he passes away, "It is to tenfold life, to love, to peace, and raptures holy" involving a successful courtship with "the fair eyed dew ... / The weeping virgin, [who] trembling kneels before the risen sun, / Till we arise link'd in a golden band, and never part" (3:10–15). Bruder points to the "marked lack of enthusiasm" that the weeping and trembling Dew displays during the Cloud's courtship, suggesting that the Cloud *forces* himself upon an unwilling but acquiescent bride, the latter of whom offers an insidious model of feminine behaviour for Thel to emulate (152). In Har's natural economy, it is clear that the Cloud advocates a "self-interested" philosophy of environmental coexistence that is the perverse flip-side of that articulated by the abject Lilly and the all too "humble" Clay (4:9). In short, although all of these non-human entities agree that "every thing that lives, / Lives not alone, nor for itself," the self-effacing Lilly and Clay give themselves willingly to others, whereas the self-centred Cloud demands that others surrender their will to his own.

The gendered hierarchy supporting the privileged situation of *Thel's* Cloud is not unlike the model of hierarchy supporting the situation of "Man" in Erasmus Darwin's *The Economy of Vegetation*, various passages of which, read analogically, can shed light on the gender politics informing *The Book of Thel*. Darwin's poetical assertion that feminine "'Beauty fades upon its damask throne!' – / – Unconscious of the worm, that mined her own!" (1973a, 3.315–16) describes Thel's situation remarkably well; for Thel, despite the status signified by her "pearly throne," must "fade away like morning beauty" in her own inevitable encounter with the lowly worm (BT 2:12; 1:3; 3:23). Moreover, like Blake's male Cloud, Darwin's "Man" (represented at one point by Mr Brindley, the innovative "MECHANIC GENIUS" responsible for building numerous canals in eighteenth-century England) occupies a position that seems to transcend the feminized natural world in which he lives and conducts his work. As the fortunate recipient of "secret[s]" lovingly bestowed upon him by a personified feminine nature (Darwin 1973a, 3.323), the Mechanic Genius is immortalized by the fame attending his feats of engineering and their profound manipulation of the natural environment. Thus, in contrast to feminine "Beauty," the male Genius transcends death, attaining in the poem the pedestal of a statue erected in his honour, from which, in a state of eternal animation, he actively

"Counts the fleet waves, and balances the lands" (3.343–4). Brindley, Darwin seems to suggest, need not fear the worms that will inevitably devour feminine entities like "Beauty" (and, one might add, Thel); for by inscribing his human signature upon the natural landscape in the patently material lines of canals designed to encourage the advancement of "Plenty, Arts, and Commerce" (3.336), he ostensibly transcends the ecosystems in which Darwin represents animal and vegetable bodies as growing and dissolving in perpetual dynamic cycle (see 2.584n.).

Darwin's portrait of the "Mechanic Genius" as securely immortalized by his fame is certainly more a product of the poet's desire than of his certitude. One should note that Darwin's depiction of Brindley's statue is an imaginative one, not the contemporary depiction of an actual monument erected in Brindley's honour. Darwin's anxiety over the substantiality of Brindley's fame and the validity of his status as transcendent "GENIUS" is evident in a footnote to the poetry, wherein the poet asserts that Brindley "*ought* to have a monument in the cathedral church at Lichfield" (3.321n.; emphasis added). In contrast to Darwin's speaker, Thel arguably has come to understand that fame will *not* provide a cure for the mutability of her existence. Although she has fame in Har as a sort of queen on a "pearly throne" (BT 2:12–13; E4), she nonetheless seeks, in her "dialogue" with the Cloud, and especially in their discussion of the worm, to obtain something like an immanental (as opposed to transcendental) understanding of the nature of her mortal existence. Nevertheless, the fact that the male Cloud encourages such an understanding in Thel while insisting that he himself transcends natural systems (3:10–11) is troublesome. One gets the feeling that the Cloud may be attempting to take advantage of the earnest Thel by relegating her consensually to the corporeal realm that he himself has transcendentally devalued.

In both *The Book of Thel* and *The Economy of Vegetation* the gendering of nature's economy is fraught with violence. In the latter poem, as Darwin's speaker tells dame Nature, the "Mechanic Genius" had gained scientific knowledge when he had "Pierced all your springs, and open'd all your wells" (3.324). Such figurative language recalls that of Francis Bacon, who metaphorizes scientific pursuit in sexual terms as the penetration of nature's "womb" (1860, 4:100). Indeed, Darwin's poem goes so far as to depict the practical actualization of Bacon's metaphor as quasi-military "legions" of working men, who "tread the swampy heath, / *Pierce* with sharp spades the *tremulous* peat beneath" (Darwin 1973a, 3.463–4; emphasis added) – activities that "alarm" not only the plots of ground immediately subject to the attack but "a thousand hills" (3.333). In Darwin's view, Nature, alluringly fearful yet femininely submissive in the face of Man's sexualized technological advances, provides an ideal model for feminine behaviour in the human world:

> So should young SYMPATHY, in female form,
> Climb the tall rock, spectatress of the storm;
> Life's sinking wrecks with secret sighs deplore,
> And bleed for others' woes, Herself on shore[.] (3.441–4)

As in *Thel*'s Vales of Har, where the self-effacing Lilly and Clod exist in a state of feminine docility, thus helping to perpetuate the masculine Cloud's questionable pursuit of self-interest, Darwin's feminine Nature willingly supports the violent ideology and practice of the masculine Mechanic Genius. In other words, although "young SYMPATHY" deplores the "sinking wrecks" of a self-interested masculine mercantile economy gone wrong, her sympathetic compassion and figurative bleeding are here promoted as affirmative signs of a patriarchally prescribed feminine self-abnegation. Rather than vocally opposing violent and destructive masculinist pursuits, feminine Sympathy, as passive "spectatress," is capable of offering only an ineffectual critique consisting of inarticulate and impalpable "secret sighs."[9]

In contrast to *The Economy of Vegetation*, which envisions the gendered economy of human relations as properly continuous and correlative with a gendered "economy of nature," *The Book of Thel*, in its anthropomorphic allegory of human sexual politics, *questions* the ways androcentric ideology informs human views of nature. By making lilies, clouds, and clods of clay the gendered mouthpieces of an asymmetrical interlocking model of human gender relations, Blake demonstrates the ways our views of nature can "naturalize" the ideological interests of the *status quo*.

This point is implicit in Blake's poetic invention of the name "Vales of Har." In Erdman's edition of *Thel*, the word "Har" is followed on two occasions by a grammatically unnecessary period (3:18, 4:10), suggesting, perhaps, that Blake wanted his reader to pause over the term and – at least as one aspect of a polysemous interpretation[10] – mentally complete its seeming abbreviation, thoughtfully reading into "Har." a reference to "Harmony." Such a reading would certainly make sense in light of the fact that, during the eighteenth century, the pastoral mode – the genre in which most of *Thel* is self-reflexively written – was popularly associated with the notion of a harmonious "golden age." Indeed, if Blake wanted "the Vales of Har" to suggest the notion of pastoral Harmony, the possible pun on the word "vales" with "veils" raises the ironic possibility that Harmony functions in *Thel* as a *cover* for something insidious.

While an association between "Har" and "Harmony" in the poem is necessarily conjectural, it nevertheless raises some relevant and fascinating interpretive possibilities. One should note that the concept of harmony was an integral aspect of Enlightenment faith, so much so, indeed, that virtually all eighteenth-century philosophers used it "directly or indirectly, explicitly or implicitly" (Tillich 1967, 332–3). According to this concept, private vices were thought ultimately to produce public benefits, for the individual pursuit of self-interest was regarded as ultimately conducive to the proper functioning of the greater social whole. This kind of thinking was evident, for example, in Rousseau's concept of *volonté générale* and Adam Smith's "invisible hand,"[11] both of which quasi-natural models of social conduct tended to justify self-interested individualism in terms of balanced beneficial outcomes achieved at the larger social level (ibid., 334–7). Arguably, Erasmus Darwin's "self-balanced" cosmology involves an implicit gesture towards such a self-centred model of philosophical holism. But it is Alexander Pope's *Essay on Man* (1733) that offers the pre-eminent poetic representation of this kind of thinking. Asserting that "jarring Int'rests of themselves create / Th' according Music of a *well-mix'd State*" (3:293–4), Pope might well be summarizing the philosophical doctrine advocated by Blake's male Cloud; for the Cloud's approach to earthly mutuality implicitly partakes of this notion that his own pursuit of self-interest does not ultimately contravene a beneficial and "harmonious" holism.

Charles Taylor's recent commentary on John Locke's conception of the universe's "great interlocking order" can helpfully illuminate the philosophical underpinnings of this notion that the "partial Evil" of self-interest contributes to "the WORLD's *great Harmony*" (Pope 1733, 1:284, 3:295): "The principal thing that makes the entities in the world into an order is that their natures *mesh*. The purposes sought by each, of the causal functions which each one exercises, interlock with the others so as to cohere into a harmonious whole. Each in serving itself serves the entire order." On the one hand, Locke's view of nature is highly optimistic. Having the power to transform the pursuit of self-interest into its opposite, Lockean nature becomes a benevolent, even providential, principle of universal order. On the other hand, Locke's view of the interactions shared by nature's elementary constituents reveals an underlying pessimism that is hard to ignore; for at the individual level, "things *feed* each other" in an "efficient-causal" manner. As this latter scenario suggests, the established hypothesis of a harmonious interlocking order involved a highly questionable leap of faith: such a world was *too* good – not to mention too complacently satisfied with the reigning order of things – to be generally believable (Charles Taylor 1989, 275–6, 322). For his own part, Blake was incred- ulous. In his 1798 annotations to *The Works of Sir Joshua Reynolds*, for example, Blake places Harmony (along with "Demonstration" and "Similitude") among the accursed "Objects of Reasoning" (E659), declaring derisively that "One Species of General Hue over all is the Cursed Thing calld Harmony it is like the Smile of a Fool" (E662).[12] One gets the impression that *The Book of Thel*'s female Lilly, who "sittest smiling" (BT 2:6; E4) into the face of the male lamb that will devour her, might unwittingly be displaying such a fool's smile.

Arguably, Thel's act of rebellion in the opening lines of her "Book" stems from an awareness of the ideological artificiality of her "har- monious" existence in Har, which place Donald Pearce has ironically dubbed "Happy Valley" (1978, 28). The sole adjective in the opening line of the poem certainly suggests something like caricature. Mne Seraphim's flocks, depicted entirely in terms of sunlight, are perhaps too "sunny" to be believable, as if somehow, in the process of their discursive domestication, these animals have been reduced to mere reflective aesthetic surfaces. Thel leaves these domesticated sheep, her habitual animal companions – whose docile condition parallels her own in the Vales of Har – to seek the company of creatures that have not been subjugated to such an obvious degree by Har's pas- toral economy. Her discomfort with Har's superficial "morning beauty" (BT 1:3; E3) – the "harmonious" aesthetic surface of a human- centred view of the non-human environment – manifests itself as a rejection of the harmony of the pastoral myth.

What Blake is advocating, in his ironic portrayal of natural "har- mony" in *The Book of Thel*, is not a devaluation of nature itself, but the need for incessant vigilance regarding the ways nature is con- structed in and produced by social discourse. For Blake, self-interest generates not harmony but a complex web of social oppression. Indeed, the philosophical valorization of self-interest *naturalizes* this oppression, even rendering it good. In the Vales of Har, the self- interested Cloud speaks the magnanimous language of goodness when he declares that he and his docile bride "walk united, bearing food to all our tender flowers" (3:16). Instead of accepting these words at face value, however, we would do well to pose the follow- ing questions. First, to what extent is the Cloud's notion of matrimo- nial unity at least subtly coercive, the production of a discursive (rather than "natural") economy forcibly linking the Dew to the Cloud by way of the "golden band" (3:15–16), or bond of conven- tional legality? Second, might the "tender flowers" that the Cloud charitably feeds be facing an earthly fate similar to that of the sacrificial Lilly? The possibility that gendered behaviour is discursively produced and regulated in *The Book of Thel* brings the common critical notion that Har is a land of primal Innocence – an "exquisite and harmless" world of "equalitarian *harmony*" (Frye 1970, 241; Erdman 1969, 132; emphasis added) – very much into question. Har exemplifies, rather, what Mary Wollstonecraft convincingly identifies as "the *arbitrary* economy of nature," an economy deriving its significance from a political system in which females are "kept in ignorance under the *specious name* of innocence" (1982, 82, 54; emphasis added). The philosophy that all is "harmony" cannot begin to solve the dilemma in which Thel finds herself, for such a model of earthly existence encourages her to stop worrying about her relationship to Har's social and natural environments, believing, quite simply, in Pope's highly conservative proposition that "whatever IS, is RIGHT" (1733, 1:286). From a Blakean perspective, the Enlightenment concept of "harmony" inevitably produces complacency and quietism, thus perpetuating the pastoral *status quo* that Thel rejects in the opening lines of her poem.

ANTHROPOCENTRISM, ANDROCENTRISM, AND NATURE'S ECONOMY

If nature, for Blake, is always in part the product of the social discourses that constitute our subjectivity, can Thel (or anyone for that matter) be open to nature's otherness without selfishly appropriating it? Thel's encounter with the Cloud emphasizes the difficulty of being so open. It is significant that Thel says she "is like" the Cloud even before his "bright form" emerges in the poem (BT 3:3, 5; E4); for this circumstance reveals her predisposition to assume similarity between human self and non-human other. Indeed, although Thel declares that she herself "is like" the Cloud, one suspects that she can say this only because she has already projected her own notion of selfhood onto this non-human entity. Unfortunately, her subsequent realization that she and the Cloud are *not* alike does not solve this problem but results, rather, in an unproductive sense of fear: by telling the Cloud "I fear that I am not like thee" (3:17), Thel makes it plain that she wishes it were possible to recapture her earlier sense of similarity between herself and this meteorological entity. Acknowledging the Cloud's specificity is indeed frightening for Thel, for it reinforces her earlier sense of her own alienation and purposelessness. Obviously, in her relationship with the Cloud, Thel has become trapped in a vicious cycle of discursive "saming" and "othering." Clearly, the overarching problem with each of these ways of relating involves Thel's use of self as the primary point of reference in the process of identification (*I* am like thee; *I* am not like thee). To see the Cloud on something like its "own" terms, Thel must learn to decentre her pastoral selfhood, to engage in a species of what Blake will call, in his later works, "Self-Annihilation."

Among other things, such a process of subjective decentring would help Thel come to terms with her instrumental or utilitarian anxiety, especially as it relates to the "place" she seeks for herself in the natural order (2:12). Once again, an examination of Thel's relationship to the Lilly and Cloud can help to clarify this point. Brian Wilkie points out (in contrast to my own argument) that the Lilly's notion that she is protected by heaven (1:19–25) implies a certain "self-sufficiency" on her part, and that the Cloud's discussion of the hydrological cycle demonstrates that he and his bride the Dew take more than adequate care of Har's "tender flowers" (3:16). But nature's self-sufficiency is not enough for Thel, who "nevertheless projects helplessness and need onto animals and flowers, and uselessness onto herself for failing to tend them, though it is abundantly clear that they already have all the attentive help they need" (Wilkie 1990, 59–60). Wilkie's point suggests that if Thel really wishes to serve the creatures of Har, she should not attempt needlessly to interfere in their lives and life processes but should reflect, instead, upon her own modes of understanding non-human existence, scrutinizing especially her ideology of use-value. What Thel might learn from her experience among the creatures of Har is, in short, the efficacy of a hands-off approach to the thinking and acting-out of human-nature relations.[13]

Perhaps the best way to attempt to apprehend such a relationship with the natural world is through a self-reflexive understanding of the environmental intrusiveness of language itself. Indeed, in her contact with the Worm, there is a suggestion that Thel begins tentatively to acquire such an understanding. First, if Thel is a ventriloquist who projects her own subjective discourses upon external others, then the fact that the Worm does not speak – is not "itself" represented as entering into language in the poem – indicates that Thel is beginning to acquire a sense of the ways the very language she speaks determines her experiences in the Vales of Har. In this regard, the series of questions that Thel poses to and of the Worm is particularly telling: "Art thou a Worm? image of weakness. art thou but a Worm? / ... Is this a Worm?" (BT 4:2, 5; E5). Most obviously, perhaps, the Worm's silence in the face of Thel's first question might be seen as underscoring the classic philosophical discourse of animality (derived largely from the writings of Aristotle), which distinguishes humanity from

animality by insisting that only humans have systematic and mean-
ingful language. From the human standpoint, language has long been
"the implacable standard against which the animal is measured and
always found wanting." Indeed, when it is understood as the only
vehicle of genuine articulation, human language becomes that which
"muffles, strangles, and finally silences the animal" (David Clark
1997, 191). On the one hand, then, the Worm's failure to respond to
Thel's linguistic questioning might be said to reinforce the anthropo-
centric bias of Western epistemology.

On the other hand, however, the Worm's silence is decidedly pecu-
liar, for it occurs in a poem where all other narratively central non-
human characters speak in a most articulate fashion. Thel attempts
to deal with the strangely silent Worm by infantilizing it: when it does
not speak, she immediately constructs it as an inarticulate and infan-
tile "image of weakness," "an infant" that *cannot* speak but can only
"weep" (BT 4:3–4; E5). Such anthropomorphism allows Thel to speak
for the Worm, to represent the silent creature in her own words. The
fact that Thel nevertheless feels driven repeatedly to question the
Worm's identity suggests that her anthropomorphic construction of
it remains haunted by an element of anxiety in the face of its stubborn
silence. Hence the Worm's silent response to Thel's first question
("Art thou a Worm?") might itself be interpreted as the sign of an
alterity that refuses, paradoxically, to be silenced by the symbolic econ-
omy of naming; for once comfortably identified as "Worm," this crea-
ture would be assimilated to a regulative system of inscription that
would definitively categorize it and thus attempt to contain its oth-
erness. Thel's second and modified question – "art thou *but* a Worm?"
– suggests that Thel is beginning to entertain the possibility that the
Worm may be *nothing* other than "itself" – no voicepiece for human
philosophical discourse (in marked contrast to the Lilly and Cloud),
no projection of desire, no anthropomorphic symbol, but precisely a
"Worm" – whatever that may be. Indeed, Thel's third question – "*Is
this* a Worm?" – suggests something like an awareness that the label
"Worm" itself is ultimately inadequate to the naming of this creature's
identity; that the very act of naming, which appropriates the "Worm"
into language, enacts a reduction, an effacement. This brief scenario
of anxious questioning on Thel's part probes some fundamental
issues concerning the relationship between language and the objects
it names, highlighting in the process the linguistic and discursive
basis of our worldly perceptions. It is no wonder that Thel is "aston-
ish'd" (4:1) by her encounter with the "naked" Worm (4:5).[14]

Although the Clod's subsequent verbal intercourse with Thel indi-
cates a resumption of the linguistic projection that Thel had practised

earlier in her meetings with the Lilly and Cloud, it nevertheless marks an important change concerning the status and capacity of language in the poem. For the central ontological insight articulated by the Clod – whom Gleckner has called "the great earth mother" (1959, 169) – emphasizes the inadequacy of language to the definition or signification of her own condition. Although the Clod insists that her "bosom *of itself* is cold. and *of itself* is dark" (BT 4:12; E5; emphasis added), she has already rendered questionable this notion of the "as such" in her proclamation that "we live not for ourselves" (4:10). The contextual nature of the Clod's identity – the extension of the finite "of itself" into an infinite realm of holistic interrelationship – causes this self-proclaimed "lowly" being to assume the elevated status of one who wears "a crown that none can take away" (5:4). The qualifying statement that immediately follows this assertion – "But how this is sweet maid, I know not, and I cannot know, / I ponder, and I cannot ponder; yet I live and love" (5:4–6) – brings into question the notion that it is possible to name the truth of such contextual identity. Such difficulty finds an analogue in one of the major challenges facing postmodern ecological study: ecosystems are often so complex that they defy precise objective analysis, especially "the efforts of instrumental rationalists to model them" (Dryzek 1995, 105). Perhaps this defiance of scientific analysis rests in part on the ways in which ecological interrelatedness exceeds linguistic definition. Because systems based on natural signs "provide no way to raise semiosis or consciousness above their systemic limitations" (Essick 1989, 126), the value of organic life cannot be posited logically; it can only be somehow intuited, as the Clod puts it, in "life" and in "love."

Whatever she learns from the Clod of Clay, the lesson is strong enough to persuade Thel to accept the Clod's invitation to "enter my house" (BT 5:16; E6). Subsequently, Thel finds herself in a "land unknown" (6:2), an environment whose characterization as such recalls the Clod's remark that she "know[s] not, and ... cannot know," the conditions of her existence. But this unfamiliar territory beyond the Vales of Har is only truly a "land unknown" to the extent that it can evade or disrupt Thel's ability to categorize and thus discursively contain and dominate it; it is unknown, that is, only insofar as it is able to unsettle the manifold anthropocentric presuppositions implicit in the doctrines of use-value, hierarchy, and harmony that have helped to constitute Thel's subjective experience of the Vales of Har. But let us be cautious. As David Farrell Krell points out in a discussion of Heideggerian ontology, "the charge of anthropomorphism and anthropocentrism is essentially duplicitous, for it always presupposes that a [mode of] thinking could, if only it were rigorous enough, erase the human backdrop and expunge the set of (human) existence" (1992, 130). Clearly, for humans, such erasure and expunction is impossible, as Thel discovers in the "land unknown." For here she finds not freedom from her anthropomorphic impulses but death, not (as it were) a new birth but her "own grave plot" (BT 6:9; E6). Thel's discovery suggests that something like a total escape from human-centredness can come only with death, indeed is tantamount *to* death. And Thel, understandably, does not want to die. Hence the "voice of sorrow [which] *breathed* from the hollow pit" (6:10; emphasis added) is a living, *aspiring* voice, reminiscent of the life-in-death characterizing "the couches of the dead," where Thel paradoxically espies the curiously living and organic "fibrous roots / Of every heart on earth infix[ing] deep its restless twists" (6:3–4). In a passage that has perplexed generations of Blake's readers, this voice from the grave significantly speaks not of living nature per se but of an explicitly *human* experience of material existence:

Why cannot the Ear be closed to its own destruction?
Or the glistning Eye to the poison of a smile!
Why are Eyelids stord with arrows ready drawn,
Where a thousand fighting men in ambush lie?
Or an Eye of gifts & graces, show'ring fruits & coined gold!
Why a Tongue impress'd with honey from every wind?
Why an Ear, a whirlpool fierce to draw creations in?
Why a Nostril wide inhaling terror trembling & affright.
Why a tender curb upon the youthful burning boy!
Why a little curtain of flesh on the bed of our desire? (6:11–20)

The violence pervading this passage – made abundantly explicit by its references to "destruction," "poison," "arrows," "fighting men in ambush," "terror trembling & affright" – is remarkable. But what, exactly, has this poetry to do with the kinds of anthropocentric violence I have been discussing in this chapter? Let us take a closer look.

"Why cannot the Ear be closed to its own destruction?" Perhaps the answer to this strange question can be found six lines later in the succeeding reference to the Ear, which emphasizes that this perceptual organ is itself destructive of external phenomena insofar as it is a centripetal or self-centred "whirlpool fierce to draw creations in." But the Ear is *itself* overtaken by the destruction that it perpetrates on external "creations" – it cannot be "closed to its *own* destruction" – because it cannot be "closed" to the influence of the human discourses that help to determine its social and physiological functioning.

In other words, insofar as discourses (like those associated with doctrines of utility, hierarchy, and "harmony") are constitutive of subjectivity, producing and determining the subject's apprehension of auditory phenomena, they cause all sounds to be heard *in certain ways*, thus "destroying" the "real" sounds that come to the ear, hence destroying the ear's *proper* (i.e., its "own") function of hearing. We witness an example of such destruction on plate 3, in Thel's inability to take "delight" in the songs of "the warbling birds." Thel's obsession in this passage with utility ("But I feed not the warbling birds") introduces into the "gentle and melodious" warble of the birdsong (Oxford English Dictionary, 1st ed.) an anthropomorphic mournfulness that is not necessarily present in the song itself, a sense of melancholy that turns Thel's thoughts away from living things and towards her own inevitable "death" (BT 3:19–23; E5).

Much the same thing can be said about the Eye's inability to "be closed" to the "poison of a smile." One might read this reference to the smile in terms of the various discourses of "Harmony" (productions, perhaps, of "a Tongue impress'd with honey") that Blake found so repugnant. For these discourses, as I have argued, offer questionable but smile-inciting versions of happy coexistence, a mere *appearance* of happiness, a deceptive *vision* of things (hence the problematic relationship between the "Eye" and the "smile"). Recall the Lilly's "smiling" openness to the devouring lamb, and Thel's assertion that the Lilly's ultimate physical destruction serves to purify the "contagious *taints*" poisoning the lamb's ostensibly "mild and meekin mouth" (2:7; emphasis added). In a sense, the Lilly's smile is *self-poisoning*, for she has been taught (by a male deity who significantly "smiles on all" [1:19]) happily to *embrace* a questionable self-abnegation. That the "land unknown" in Part Four of the poem represents an extreme corrective alternative to such veiled deception can be seen in its characterization as a land "where never smile was seen" (6:5).

The assertion that eyelids are "stord with arrows ready drawn, / Where a thousand fighting men in ambush lie" warns Thel of the need to approach her world with extreme caution. Here, the reference to "Eyelids" conjures up the theme of veils implicit in the pun on "vales of Har[mony]," suggesting a veiled "covering" of the human gaze. The subsequent reference to "fighting men" indicates, moreover, that Blake is thinking of an explicitly masculinist gaze. This gendering of the gaze suggests that anthropocentrism is not only related to but is, more precisely, *andro*centrism in Har's patriarchal economy. Hence Thel and all of the poem's female characters face the danger that the closed eyelids of an apparently peaceful male lover function to cover or disguise the violence implicit in a masculinist gaze, which, when it is finally cast, will objectify and "ambush" external "creations." This kind of objectification puts a "curb" (6:19) upon sexual expression by overdetermining and thus "denaturing" or "denaturalizing" *all* expression that occurs within the field of vision, transforming this field, one might say, into a deadly "field" of battle. We can therefore interpret the hymenal "curtain of flesh" (6:20) as another "veil," insofar as patriarchy projects upon the fetishized hymen a significance that transforms sex from a life-giving and life-affirming act of communal sharing ("everything that lives, / Lives not alone, nor for itself") into an act fraught with violence, thus generating the alienating emotions of "terror trembling & affright."[15]

In light of the lessons articulated by the "voice of sorrow" speaking from Thel's "own grave plot," how should we read the protagonist's sudden retreat "back ... into the vales of Har" (6:21–2)? The majority of Blake's readers agree with Robert Gleckner that Thel's retreat marks some sort of developmental "failure" (1960, 575).[16] Most logical and persuasive is Gleckner's argument (579–80) that it is necessary to read the Clay's invitation to Thel "to enter, / And to return" from the Clay's "house" (BT 5:16–17; E6) in light of Ezekiel 46:9 ("he that entereth in by way of the north gate to worship [cf. *Thel*'s "northern bar" (6:1)] shall go out by way of the south gate ... he shall not return by the way of the gate whereby he came in"). What Gleckner seems to have forgotten, however, is Blake's well-known opposition to Old Testament law, especially to negative commandments couched in the form of "Thou shalt not," which for Blake are the utterances of a Priesthood that desecrates the "Garden of Love" (SIE; E26). Thel's defiance of such a command gestures towards her desire to resist the moral legalism that so offended Blake's own seemingly antinomian sensibility. Thus, she need not be seen as an "Innocent" soul who fails ultimately to make the necessary transition through Experience en route to a higher "Organized Innocence" (as so many readers have argued). Indeed, if Thel has learned by the end of her "Book" that the natural "Innocence" of Har is *already* "Organized" by its discursivity – that she has never experienced the creatures of Har or their utterances except in terms of the social "ratio" that constitutes and so defines her own finite selfhood – then she must go back into Har *in order* to enter Experience: a critical experience that attempts self-reflexively to respect and appreciate natural entities in their alterity rather than solely in terms of their conventional discursive representations. In other words, if Thel has been constituted as an inquiring subject in Har, then her return to its vales might entail not regression or escapism but a self-reflexive genealogical consideration of her own historical "descent"[17] and the discursive systems that have constituted her view of the natural world and its inhabitants.

Clearly, for example, an instrumentalist anthropocentrism, by appropriating the things of nature to serve the ends of human life, tends to efface the life-needs of the appropriated natural organisms. Since Thel's very name means not only to desire (Perkins 1967, 65n.) but also "to flourish, abound, [and] bloom" (Norvig 1995, 262n.17) we might see her as subject to the psychological dynamic eminent biologist Edward O. Wilson has termed "biophilia" (1992, 349–51): the deep-seated human desire to understand, support, and be a part of nature's flourishing vitality.[18] Perhaps, when Thel returns to Har, she will attempt to dismantle the pastoral instrumentalism that has helped to consolidate her anthropocentric world-view, so that she may learn to respect natural beings for the "blessing," or holiness, that in Blake's view constitutes and guarantees their *intrinsic* value. Such activity would not, of course, remove Thel from the anthropomorphic economy, since it is inevitably human beings who discuss the concept of value. But even if it will always be impossible for Thel to encounter nature on its "own" terms, she can at least attempt upon returning to Har to clarify the *brute fact* of anthropocentrism, evaluate various anthropocentric stances, and choose the ones that may best sustain the diversity of the natural world in which she has her existence.

In this chapter I have argued that *The Book of Thel* uses animal symbolism in ways that interrogate the anthropocentric violence inherent in symbolic practice. The design at the bottom of *Thel*'s final plate, in which three children are depicted as riding a rather harmless-looking tethered serpent (see Figure 8), might be interpreted as an epilogue to this questioning, offering an iconographic corrective to the anti-natural violence inhabiting the symbolism of orthodox mythology. To a certain extent, Judaeo-Christian symbolism colonizes the natural world by associating such animals as the serpent with the curse of human moral transgression (see Genesis 3:14–15). Blake marks his distance from such moral discourse by carrying out, in *Thel*'s final illuminated design, an act of symbolical defamiliarization. Reunited with a renewed humanity (represented by the youthfulness of the children on its back), the transformed serpent and its riders glide over the words "The End," suggesting, in the spirit of Coleridge's Ancient Mariner, the end of a cynical and destructive anthropomorphic practice and auguring a transformation of the relationship between humans and the world of other blessed living beings.[19] At one level, Blake's design releases the serpent – perhaps the most "othered" member of the animal creation – from its discursive role as a symbol of all that is harmful to human existence.

But this is, I suspect, too "harmonious" a note on which to conclude the discussion, for it is possible to see *Thel*'s illuminated serpent in exactly the opposite light, as an insidious symbol of foreboding

IV.

The eternal gates terrific porter lifted the northern bar.
Thel enterd in & saw the secrets of the land unknown;
She saw the couches of the dead, & where the fibrous roots
Of every heart on earth infixes deep its restless twists:
A land of sorrows & of tears where never smile was seen.

She wanderd in the land of clouds thro' valleys dark, listning
Dolours & lamentations: waiting oft beside a dewy grave
She stood in silence. listning to the voices of the ground,
Till to her own grave plot she came. & there she sat down.
And heard this voice of sorrow breathed from the hollow pit.

Why cannot the Ear be closed to its own destruction?
Or the glistning Eye to the poison of a smile!
Why are Eyelids stord with arrows ready drawn,
Where a thousand fighting men in ambush lie?
Or an Eye of gifts & graces, showring fruits & coined
　　gold?
Why a Tongue impress'd with honey from every wind?
Why an Ear, a whirlpool fierce to draw creations in?
Why a Nostril wide inhaling terror trembling & affright.

The Virgin started from her seat, & with a shriek.
Fled back unhinderd till she came into the vales of
　　　　　　　　　　　　　　　　　　　　　　Har

The End

8　*The Book of Thel*, plate 8 (E plate 6)
By permission of the Houghton Library, Harvard University

evil. Read in the light of Joseph Wicksteed's iconographic principle that rightward movement in Blake's designs indicates spiritual progression, while leftward movement indicates a regressive corporeality (1971, 133),[20] one could argue that the leftward-moving serpent on *Thel*'s final plate is tempting its youthful riders away from the paths of righteousness, restaging in the process the original fall from Innocence. One must remember, however, that Blake had to etch his texts and designs using the engraver's technique of mirror-writing. Hence in order to arrive at the spatialized economy of value that Wicksteed advocates, it was necessary for Blake to *reverse* this economy on his copper template, since the left side of the plate becomes the right side of the finished design and vice versa. This aspect of Blake's technical practice necessitates, as it were, a conceptual marriage of heaven and hell, providing an instance in which material praxis would likely have affected iconographic theory. Arguably, Blake's major concepts and symbols are the loci of a similar double-take on value. Depending on the poetic context of a given utterance or the interpretive contexts readers bring to bear upon that utterance, such concepts as "holiness," "harmony," and even "nature" itself may be positively *or* negatively valued. In this sense, Blake's symmetry is indeed fearful, for it implies an equivocity that continually unsettles the interpretive will to establish a dogmatic reading of his texts and designs.

These remarks bring me back to the problem of *Thel*'s illuminated serpent. The fact that this creature can be interpreted as a symbol auguring *either* good or evil outcomes suggests that there is something much more complex at play in Blake's poem than a moralized reading (whether pointing towards good *or* evil outcomes) would suggest. To quote Brian John's succinct observation, "We misread Blake if we assume that certain images ... are intrinsically good or bad, for such intrinsicality denies change and organic growth" (1974, 29–30). It is possible, I propose, that Blake deliberately deploys a degree of symbolic ambivalence in his depiction of *Thel*'s serpent precisely in order to unsettle the kinds of interpretive closure that would deny the possibility of change and growth in our symbolic practices. For is not a conviction that Blake's serpent is somehow "good" as misguided and misleading as a conviction that it is patently "evil"? Or, more precisely, is not the desire to settle the problem of the serpent once and for all – even to consider the problem in moral terms – complicitous with a questionable will to power by way of a reductive symbolic taxonomy? Since, in Blake's later writing, the serpent becomes a figure for nothing less than "the vast form of Nature" (J 43:76, 80; E192–3), our desire to stabilize its symbolic status suggests, perhaps, a correlative desire to stabilize the meaning of this "vast form" itself. Here, it will be helpful to quote the ecological critic Kelly Parker: "If we have our being in the ongoing encounter with [the natural] environment, then to will that the environment become a fully settled, predictable thing ... is to will that we undergo no further growth in experience. The attempt to dominate nature completely is thus an attempt to annihilate the ultimate source of our growth ["to flourish, abound, bloom"], and hence to annihilate ourselves" (1996, 30). Parker, one should note, is not speaking here about Blakean "Self-Annihilation" but about pathological – and ecological – self-destruction.

In contrast to atomistic modes of natural taxonomy, "nature's economy" implies a holistic view of earthly life that is relatively unstable and indeterminate, based as it is on the changing relationships, at any given moment, between entities that live not alone, nor for themselves. This is why, as I have suggested, the Clod of Clay "cannot know" her condition. On the one hand, the epistemological instability implied by such a lack of knowledge[21] indicates the Clod's potential openness to new perspectives, an openness that Thel would do well to emulate. On the other hand, however, such openness can dangerously engender (and I use the term deliberately) a passivity – a lack, that is, of critical self-reflexivity – that would leave Thel open, like the Lilly and the Clay, to manipulation by such discourses as patriarchy, which, in the process of naturalizing its authority, would actively constitute her as a pathological, self-abnegating subject. These diametrically opposed possibilities exemplify *Thel*'s rather famous thematic ambiguity,[22] supporting Gerda Norvig's argument that Blake "forged the trope of liminality at every threshold, every barrier of signification in the text" (1995, 264).

At a certain level, *Thel*'s liminal vision is the product of a pastoral mode whose major enduring feature is its "double vision"; and if Blake's early poems are in a sense *anti*-pastoral, they are nonetheless, as Curran remarks, "meticulous in [their] representation of a double vision" (1986b, 88, 111). Blake's meticulousness in this respect can be seen in his ambivalent attitude towards the "contrary states" he represents in his pastoral *Songs of Innocence and of Experience* (both of which states have their particular problems and limitations). It can also be seen in his antithetical valuations of "nature's economy" in *The Book of Thel*. On the one hand, as I have suggested, a cosmic natural order in which "every thing that lives, / Lives not alone, nor for itself" (BT 3:26–7; E5) provides a conceptual basis for profound ethical mutuality in the social world. On the other hand, as *The Book of Thel* demonstrates in its depiction of Har's gender politics, such a model of relationality can be invoked instrumentally to support and sanction – indeed to disguise – oppressive and even deadly modes of social hierarchy and governmentality. Is it any wonder that Blake's *Thel* both celebrates *and* abhors such a model of nature?

The ambivalent or liminalist stance towards nature that we see in *The Book of Thel* extends, in various ways, to the entire Blakean canon. Blake's discourse on nature continually alternates between the highest praise – "Nature is Imagination itself" (E702); "Truth is Nature" (E609); "every thing on earth is the word of God & in its essence is God" (E599) – and the deepest scorn – "Where man is not nature is barren" (E38); "Nature Teaches nothing of Spiritual Life but only of Natural Life" (E634); "The Natural Body is an Obstruction to the Soul or Spiritual Body" (E664). Needless to say, these contrary sets of assertions are exceedingly difficult to reconcile: one cannot side with either version of Blakean nature at the expense of the other without distorting Blake's thought. In other words, because Blake's "spectrum of nature … ranges from barrenness to truthfulness" (Lussier 1996, 399), it would be as misguided to say that Blake is a forthright champion of nature as it has always been to argue that Blake despised and utterly rejected the material world. Or perhaps not quite. As an enemy of "single vision," Blake understood that liminality is by its very nature unsettling, disturbing. It resists the complacency and easy appropriative gestures that petrific doctrinal formulations of nature have tended to generate and cultivate. Undoubtedly, as a concept, nature can be dangerous indeed. History testifies to the multitude of ways this concept has enabled the *naturalization* of orthodoxies based on patriarchy, racism, classism, and even, somewhat paradoxically, the related discourses and technologies that devastate the planet's biosphere – often under the guise of respect and praise for the world of nature. A liminalist view of nature is, perhaps, one that can at least attempt to oppose such appropriations of nature and the "natural." From this perspective, the idealistic notion that the vegetative flourishes on the letters of the word "BOOK" on *Thel*'s title page (see Figure 6) suggest "a free interchange between word and world" (Eaves et al. 1993a, 82) can be balanced by the more sober and unsettling possibility that this iconography signifies the ways that human language and discursive systems inevitably impose themselves upon organic nature. The former view enables a celebration of the human-nature relationship; the latter necessitates the active and self-critical caution implicit in Blake's concept of "Mental Fight" (M 1; E95). In concert, these approaches to nature might productively inform an ecological critical practice that would have as its goal the emancipation of *both* nature and humanity.

3 "The Nature of Infinity": *Milton*'s Environmental Poetics

There are, it may be, so many kinds of voices in the world,
and none of them is without significance.

(1 Cor. 14:10)

You take a mule to climb and not a muse
Except in fable and figure: forests chant
Their anthems to themselves, and leave you dumb.

(Elizabeth Barrett Browning)[1]

NEWTON AND THE APOCALYPSE: BLAKE'S PROPHETIC FORESTS

In his reading of the Revelation of Saint John, Isaac Newton, best known to our age not as a Biblical exegete but as the father of physical science, takes great pains to safeguard the authenticity and authority of biblical prophecy against the foolish incursions of vulgar interpreters:

The folly of Interpreters has been, to foretel times and things by this Prophecy, as if God designed to make them Prophets. By this rashness they have not only exposed themselves, but brought the Prophecy also into contempt. The design of God was much otherwise. He gave this and the Prophecies of the Old Testament, not to gratify men's curiosities by enabling them to foreknow things, but that after they were fulfilled they might be interpreted by the event, and his own Providence, not the Interpreters, be then manifested thereby to the world. For the event of things predicted many ages before, will then be a convincing argument that the world is governed by Providence. (Newton 1733, 251–2)

With these words from his *Observations Upon the Prophecies of Daniel, and the Apocalypse of St John* (1733), Newton maintains a strict division between the word of God and the language of mere humans, placing authority – the legal governance provided "by Providence" – only in the former. Such an understanding of prophecy is consonant in

Blake's view with Newton's philosophy of nature. For if Newton believes that the providential governance of human history must be understood strictly by retrospective reference to the Book of Scripture and its laws, he also believes that the governance belonging to natural history must be understood only by reference to laws ostensibly written at the time of Creation onto the pages of the Book of Nature. And since, for Newton, the Book of Scripture and the Book of Nature are not only equally sacred but mutually affirming (Manuel 1974, 48), it is hardly surprising that the laws of Newton's physics themselves become something like prophetic instruments for the unprecedentedly accurate divination of future events in the physical universe.

I shall examine the legalism inherent in Newton's cosmology presently by considering its possible implications for William Blake's critique of legal authority. First, however, some contextualizing observations concerning Blake's approach to prophecy in *Milton* will be helpful. One of the most interesting aspects of *Milton* is its presentation of prophetic genius as inherent in all human beings: "Every one," Blake asserts, "is a fallen Son of the Spirit of Prophecy" (M 24:75; E121). Since the poem's first textual plate contains a quotation from Numbers – "Would to God that all the Lords people were Prophets" (E96) – one might argue that *Milton* is motivated in part by its author's desire to redeem fallen humanity by helping to restore the prophetic faculty to all members of the human community. Newton, on the contrary, opposes such an extension of prophecy,[2] rejecting, as we have seen, the notion that "God designed to make [readers of the Bible] prophets." If, for Blake, prophetic utterance entails the expansion of human communal relations through the intersubjective dynamic of "Mental Fight" (M E95),[3] then Newton, by opposing *universal* prophecy, might be seen as essentially opposed to such relationality. Such a stance, at any rate, would be consistent with the philosophical atomism commonly associated with Newton's scientific methodology. For his own part, Blake combats atomistic self-enclosure by attempting with his prophetic writings to actualize a holistic community of verbally engaged mutually interchanging visionary prophets.

But Blake, it must be noted, does not limit prophecy to the human community. Indeed, in his radical vision, he goes so far as to attribute prophetic genius to such *non*-human entities as "Trees on Mountains," which he depicts in *Milton* as "thunder[ing] thro' the darksom sky / Uttering prophecies & speaking instructive words to the sons / Of Men" (26:7, 9–10; E123). In Western cultural tradition there is nothing novel about attributing to trees and forests the ability to communicate. In the Old Testament, for example, "Mountains, and

all hills; fruitful trees, and all cedars" are included among the man-
ifold creatures who send praises up to God (Psalms 148:9). But what
are we to make of Blake's strange attribution of a distinctly *prophetic*
utterance to the realm of non-human nature? Once again, such
anthropomorphizing is not without biblical precedent. In Revelation,
for example, "the two olive trees and the two candlesticks" together
comprise St John's "two witnesses" which "shall prophesy a thou-
sand two hundred and threescore days, clothed in sackcloth" (Reve-
lation 11:3–4).[4] It is interesting to note that the antinomian divines
John Reeve and Lodowick Muggleton set *themselves* up as these "two
last Witnesses and true Prophets of the man Jesus" (Reeve 1652, 1),
arguing, in patently non-Blakean terms, that all other "Prophets ...
in this world" are "false" (3). But whereas Muggleton claims in his
commentary on Revelation that he will reveal prophetic truth to "the
sons of men,"[5] such truth in Blake's *Milton* will be revealed to "the
sons / Of Men" not by divine human agents but by divinely inspired
"Trees on Mountains" (M 26:9–10, 7; E123).

While Blake's prophesying trees may allude to the olive trees of
Revelation, their indefinite species, location, and number suggest
that they more likely symbolize that biblical bugbear, the archetypal
"wilderness." In a memorable passage from Book Four of *Paradise
Regained*, Satan attempts to manipulate Christ in such a setting by
conjuring a tempest in which "terrors, voices, [and] prodigies" will
function as "a sure fore-going sign" that Christ must act now, against
his earlier judgment, to take up his earthly throne (Milton 1992,
4.482–3). Since Blake's prophesying trees also speak in the ominous
context of a storm (M 26:8), we might interpret their "instructive
words" in the manner that Christ interprets the "voices" that afflict
him in the storm-ravaged wilderness of *Paradise Regained*. As Milton's
Christ tells Satan, nature's voices are "false portents, not sent from
God, but thee" (1992, 4.491). In *Milton*, however, Blake seems deliber-
ately to render such a reading inapplicable, since he carefully associ-
ates his prophesying trees not with traditional notions of Satanic evil
but with the divinity of Christ himself. For in direct reference to these
trees, Blake writes of seeing "the hem of their garments" (M 26:11),
alluding thus to Christ's garment, the mere touching of which was
thought to render humans "perfectly whole" (Matthew 14:36, and
also 9:20–2). Believing with St John that "the testimony of Jesus *is* the
spirit of prophecy" (Revelation 19:10; emphasis added), Blake
encourages his readers to exercise faith rather than scepticism when
considering the prophetic voices issuing from his mountain forests.

It is necessary, however, to consider Blake's use of this garment
metaphor in greater detail, since it occurs in the context of a statement

concerning the problems attending our capacity to understand the articulate language of non-human entities. In reference to his prophesying trees, Blake declares that we are able to "see only as it were the hem of their garments / When with our vegetable eyes we view these wond'rous Visions" (M 26:11–12). At first glance, one might be tempted to interpret this reference to our faulty "vegetable eyes" as an indictment of modes of vision available to humans within the limited order of "Vegetable Nature." The passage seems to suggest, in other words, that we must exchange our bodies of clay for "spiritual bodies" before we will be capable of "seeing" and understanding the trees Blake calls "Visions of Eternity" (26:10). But such a conclusion is also open to dispute, for Blake has already declared that these same trees – as it were the *real* vegetables in this passage – themselves view the world through the unobstructed lens of instructive prophecy. Arguably, then, Blake's faulty "vegetable eyes" can be interpreted as referring to a shortcoming that is not "natural" but distinctively human: our inability to "know" the things of nature in their irreducible otherness.

For Blake, in short, our encounters with non-human entities are always in some sense anthropomorphic encounters with ourselves, as the design at the bottom of plate 16 (E plate 17; see Figure 9) seems to suggest. In this remarkable illustration, a human figure confronts a tree and a rock, both of which Blake depicts as deformed humans (lacking head and torso, respectively). The startled pose of the human passer-by indicates his extreme discomfort in this encounter, suggesting something of the interpretive crisis he faces as a result, perhaps, of his inability to confront the things of nature without anthropomorphizing and thus disfiguring them. Yet the fact that the tree and rock are not entirely human in form but maintain a degree of their non-human alterity indicates something of their resistance to anthropomorphic inscription. At once human *and* inhuman, these strange hybrid entities disfigure human identity by both teasing and impeding our all-too-human interpretive impulses.

By repeatedly emphasizing the difficulties attending our interpretations of nature's visible signs, Blake is actually in limited agreement with Newton, who, like Galileo and Kepler, believed that the Book of Nature was written in a veiled language whose meaning was exceedingly difficult to penetrate. But Blake departs from his scientific predecessors in imagining the nature of this language; for while these luminaries argue that nature's language is in fact rational, mathematical, and therefore accessible to the learned initiate of science, Blake sees it as imaginative, prophetic, and therefore potentially accessible to the poet and the prophet. As many critics have noted,

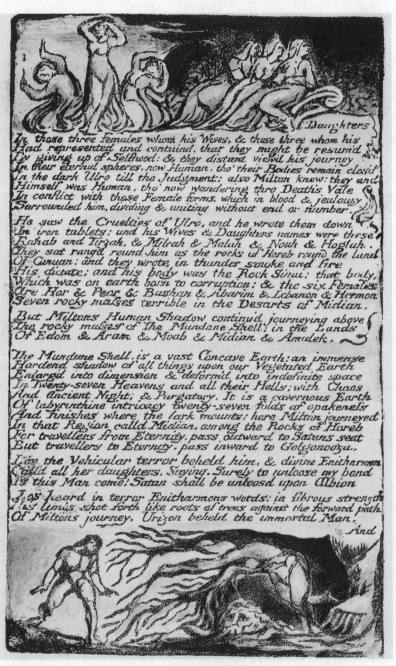

In those three Females whom his Wives, & those three whom his Daughters
Had represented and contain'd, that they might be resum'd
By giving up of Selfhood: & they distant view'd his journey
In their eternal spheres, now Human. tho' their Bodies remain clos'd
In the dark Ulro till the Judgment: also Milton knew: they and
Himself was Human, tho' now wandering thro Death's Vale
In conflict with those Female forms, which in blood & jealousy
Surrounded him, dividing & uniting without end or number.

He saw the Cruelties of Ulro, and he wrote them down
In iron tablets: and his Wives & Daughters names were these
Rahab and Tirzah, & Milcah & Malah & Noah & Hoglah.
They sat ranged round him as the rocks of Horeb round the land
Of Canaan: and they wrote in thunder smoke and fire
His dictate; and his body was the Rock Sinai: that body,
Which was on earth born to corruption: & the six Females
Are Hor & Peor & Bashan & Abarim & Lebanon & Hermon
Seven rocky masses terrible in the Desarts of Midian.

But Miltons Human Shadow continu'd journeying above
The rocky masses of The Mundane Shell; in the Lands
Of Edom & Aram & Moab & Midian & Amalek.

The Mundane Shell, is a vast Concave Earth: an immense
Hardend shadow of all things upon our Vegetated Earth
Enlarg'd into dimension & deform'd into indefinite space
In Twenty-seven Heavens and all their Hells; with Chaos
And Ancient Night; & Purgatory. It is a cavernous Earth
Of labyrinthine intricacy twenty-seven folds of opakeness
And finishes where the lark mounts; here Milton journeyed
In that Region calld Midian, among the Rocks of Horeb
For travellers from Eternity. pass outward to Satans seat
But travellers to Eternity. pass inward to Golgonooza.

Los the Vehicular terror beheld him, & divine Enitharmon
Call'd all her daughters, Saying. Surely to unloose my bond
Is this Man come! Satan shall be unloosd upon Albion

Los heard in terror Enitharmons words: in fibrous strength
His limbs shot forth like roots of trees against the forward path
Of Miltons journey. Urizen beheld the immortal Man,
And

9   *Milton*, plate 16
Rare Books Division, New York Public Library,
Astor, Lenox and Tilden Foundations

Blake's reading of the Book of Nature is similar to that of thinkers like Paracelsus and Emanuel Swedenborg, whose doctrines of "signatures" conceptualized nature as a text filled with obscure characters, ciphers, and words. According to this notion of signatures (also called "correspondences"), the universe functions as a complex system of mirrors in which all things, sharing a common identity, see themselves reflected in all other things. To quote Michel Foucault's discussion of pre-Enlightenment epistemology, such a universe was thought to be "filled with the murmur of words," since its myriad "mute reflections" or signatures were understood to "have corresponding words which indicate them" (1994, 27).

If the signs inhabiting Blakean nature recall this earlier episteme based on signatures or correspondences, they are also different in important ways. For according to the pre-Enlightenment paradigm, all things tended in fact to be *passive* signs, signs that had to be gleaned and read by the active human interpreter. As we have seen, however, the prophetic trees of *Milton* are far from passive: Blake depicts them actively "Uttering prophecies & speaking instructive words *to* the sons / Of men" (emphasis added). A few lines later, moreover, Blake depicts these trees, whom he lists among "the Sons of Los" (M 26:10, 23, 30), in the process of labouring to provide identities for formless human souls and "Sleepers." Indeed, speaking of these formless souls, Blake writes that "the Sons of Los clothe them & feed [them] & provide [them with] houses & fields" (26:30). Blake's trees are not passive resources waiting to be exploited by active humans; rather, they are agents of a sort, working and speaking in ways that benefit and indeed redeem a fortunate humanity.

In chapter 1 I examined Blake's notion that all things in the universe are human. Here, it is important to emphasize the fact that Blake identifies *Milton*'s prophesying trees as the "Sons of Los"; for, despite its flagrant anthropomorphism, such a nomination implies a radical rethinking of human identity. By conceptualizing trees as integral parts of the human community, in other words, Blake extends human identity far beyond its locus in an atomized human subjectivity or selfhood. And since such an extension of identity runs the risk of becoming an arrogant mode of anthropomorphic imperialism, Blake not only problematizes our ability to "see" these trees; he also refuses to concretize their prophetic effusions in the form of interpretable statements (for although he tells us that his trees speak, he does not represent the actual verbal content of their utterances). Blake's prophesying trees may be human, in short, but their inaccessibility to human apprehension allows them to maintain a significant degree of wildness, or non-human alterity. Most important, by calling his prophesying trees "the Sons of Los" Blake includes them in the category of the

"Lords people," *all* of whom he would transform into visionary prophets (E96). And since Blake privileges prophecy as one of the highest forms of human intercourse or communion, *Milton*'s imaginative representation of "Trees on Mountains" suggests that prophecy potentially provides for Blake a common ground upon which all beings, human and otherwise, might meet in visionary interchange.

BLAKE AND NEWTON: SPIRITUAL FRIENDS, CORPOREAL ENEMIES

In the work of most Blake critics (not excluding my own), Newtonian Reason tends inevitably to function as a negative counter against which to delineate and celebrate the figure of Blakean Imagination. In other words, "Newton" has generally come to represent in Blake studies all that Blake's philosophy is thought to abhor. While Blake's work no doubt encourages such a view of the father of physical science, we should beware of its reductiveness, for Blake's overall attitude towards Newton was ambivalent. To a great extent, indeed, Blake's anti-Newtonianism seems to involve a response more to Newton's contemporary reputation than to his actual writings. During the course of the eighteenth century, Newton had become, quite simply, a synecdoche for scientific genius itself. Thus, in one of his notable theological works, William Warburton poked fun at an over-zealous contemporary commentator whose celebratory rhetoric suggested "that as all *Midas* touched turned to Gold, so all Sir Isaac handled turned to Demonstration" (1742, 210). Or, as Voltaire noted more specifically, "There are people who think that if we are no longer content with the abhorrence of a vacuum, if we know that the air has weight, if we use a telescope, it is all due to Newton. Here he is the Hercules of the fable, to whom the ignorant attributed all the deeds of the other heroes" (quoted in Fauvel et al. 1988, 4). A glance at Newton's historical reception demonstrates the appropriateness of such remarks, for posthumously Newton's reputation achieved a status of truly mythical proportions: medals were struck bearing his countenance, statues were erected in his honour, and poets as famous as James Thomson and Alexander Pope invoked the muse to celebrate the man and his achievements in the most flattering of terms. Commenting on these developments, Geoffrey Cantor aptly observes that we "are all heirs to one of the most effective publicity stunts in the history of science – *the beatification, indeed the deification, of Newton*" (1988, 203). But the great scientist, despite his extraordinary intellect, was far from perfect, and those who deified him were content to ignore the many aspects of Newton's scientific, alchemical, and theological writings that were problematic and even mutually contradictory.

This is not to deny the profundity of Newton's contribution to the development of natural philosophy itself during the course of the eighteenth century and beyond; for Newton's writings helped to initiate an intellectual revolution of unprecedented magnitude. Under the influence of his thought, Enlightenment thinkers enthusiastically transposed the models and methodologies of physical science into fields as diverse as chemistry, botany, zoology, psychology, and theology, transforming in the process almost the entire terrain of European thought. We should be most careful, however, to distinguish Newton's actual writings from the discourse or legacy of "Newtonianism." Newton's highly influential celestial "mechanics" are a case in point. While many late-eighteenth- and early-nineteenth-century writers, including Blake, blamed Newton for disenchanting, dehumanizing, and devitalizing the universe by turning it into a vast machine, Newton's own writings often strenuously opposed the basic assumptions of strict philosophical mechanism. Before Newton, to cite an important example, René Descartes proposed that matter was entirely passive and inert, and that its apparent movements were the result of a chain reaction initiated by God at the time of Creation. Significantly, Newton opposed the principles of Descartes' scholastic physics by appealing in part to human bodily experience: "Do you learn by any experiment," he asks, "that the beating of heart gives no new motion to the blood ... or that a man by his will can give no new motion to his body?" (quoted in Henry 1988, 134). In order to explain what he saw as the spontaneous workings of nature in such phenomena as gravity and fermentation, Newton introduced in his 1687 treatise *Philosophiae Principia Mathematica* the notion of "active principles." Accordingly, matter was not passive and inert until acted upon by external forces. Rather, it was imbued with its own inherent active force or power. One should note at this juncture that Blake's opposition to mechanistic philosophy is based in part on objections similar to those that Newton aimed at Descartes; for as we saw in chapter 1, Blake imagines the cosmos as a human corporeal form endowed with the kind of spontaneous, unpredictable, and active will that Newton points to in his analogical refutation of Cartesian causality.

Blake's polemical alignment of Newton with mechanistic philosophy seems all the more unfair given the number of prominent eighteenth-century mechanists who strenuously objected to Newton's natural philosophy. The German philosopher and mathematician Gottfried Wilhelm Leibniz, for example, saw the theory of active principles as a betrayal of strict empirical rationality, and in a celebrated debate he charged Newton with occultism.[6] In his *Moses's Principia* of 1724, moreover, the English deistical philosopher John Hutchinson opposed Newton's physics on similar grounds but for a different reason. According to Hutchinson, the attribution of active principles to matter entailed a heretical denial of divine omnipotence, for it located power not solely in God but in the physical makeup of the cosmos itself. To combat what he saw as a latent pantheism in Newton's natural philosophy, Hutchinson reinforced a Cartesian cosmogony in which God's creative activity was entirely preserved in "the perfect perpetual motion machine" constituting an otherwise passive cosmos (Cantor 1988, 215). These brief examples render problematic Blake's famous equation of Newton and mechanistic philosophy, demonstrating the extent to which it involves a reductive misrepresentation of the complexities of eighteenth-century scientific debate.

If Newton was not exactly the arch-mechanist that Blake understood him to be, neither was he quite the progenitor of the deism that so troubled Blake's thought. Strictly speaking, the scientific inauguration of deism should be attributed not to Newton but to Galileo, who grandly proclaimed that the study of the universe's astronomical wonders contributed to the earthly glorification of God. Following Galileo's lead, numerous English writers (including such diverse thinkers as John Ray, Francis Willughby, Robert Hooke, Robert Boyle, and Henry More) began to extend this "argument from design" to the zoological, botanical, and chemical realms. Historically, the formal philosophical conjoining of Newton and deism was achieved in 1692, when Newton's disciple Richard Bentley attributed to Newton's system the ultimate philosophical verification of deistical ideology. While Newton had indeed granted Bentley permission to invoke his physics to celebrate God's glory, he nevertheless objected to numerous aspects of this deistical appropriation of his science, demonstrating no small degree of discomfort concerning the physico-theological uses to which his work was put during his own lifetime (Manuel 1974, 34–5).

From the foregoing discussion, it should be apparent that Newton and Blake shared at least some common ground: both of them were uncomfortable not only with strictly mechanical cosmologies but also with deistical adaptations of physical science (although Blake's opposition to these things is obviously much more emphatic than Newton's). Indeed, the similarities between Newton and Blake do not end here. Like Blake, Newton advocated a philosophy of final causation; he abhorred corruptions of Christianity for self-interested political ends; he opposed the glorification of theological mystery; and he had great disdain for the classical philosophies of Plato and Aristotle. In light of these similarities (which have been given insufficient attention in Blake criticism), one must concede that certain aspects of Blake's attack on Newton are misdirected.

Indeed, in the strictest sense, Blake's famous charge that Newtonian science is a product and progenitor of "Single vision" (E722) is somewhat unjust. As Jacob Bronowski has amply demonstrated, Newton's scientific method involved a "union of thought and fact, the rational and empirical streams [of natural philosophy] flowing together" in an unprecedented confluence of speculation and experimentation, philosophical theorizing and uncompromising material demonstration (1960, 40). Thus harnessing the speculative and empirical methods respectively associated with his precursors Descartes and Bacon, Newton's science marked a crucial synthetic shift in the Western approach to nature. Prior to the scientific revolution, nature had been an object of purely scholastic study. With Newton's marriage of speculative theory and empirical experimentation, however, history witnessed a move from purely abstract natural philosophizing towards a materially engaged praxis, as scientists attempted to test their theories from an objective standpoint in which nature itself was conceived as an actual object of study – an object that could and would change the way humans think. This epistemological shift was crucial to the historical development of ecology and environmental studies, if only for the obvious but nonetheless profound reason that it caused scientific thought to suppose, for the first time, "the existence of a *real* ... world" (Bronowski 1960, 113; emphasis added). One should point out, furthermore, that the ecological science that underpins environmentalist modes of activism, policy, and ethics is at bottom an empirical science whose "holistic" theorizing is based on the attempted analysis of causal connections existing in space and time between and among natural objects and systems.[7]

The point I wish to emphasize here is an important one. While it is fashionable (and to a certain extent justifiable) in ecological criticism to blame Newton for adversely objectifying, mechanizing, instrumentalizing, and otherwise disenchanting the cosmos, we must remember that this is a partial and therefore distorted view of his achievement and legacy. By subscribing to such a one-sided view of Newton, we ourselves succumb to a species of the "Single vision" Blake himself so emphatically decried. Hence as readers of Blake we would do well to approach the poet's own work in the critical spirit of "Mental Fight," acknowledging the limitations of his often scathing critique of Newtonian science. One might also point out that, in his more polemical moments, Blake all too often fails to differentiate Newton's historical legacy from Newton's actual work, unfairly blaming the scientist himself for the uses to which his work had been put by the mechanists, deists, and atomists who appropriated and modified its ideas.[8] And yet Blake's ultimate willingness to redeem Newton in the apocalypses of *Europe* (13:2–5; E65) and *Jerusalem* (98:9; E257) proves that his denunciations are by no means all-encompassing. Indeed, there is much evidence in his *œuvre* to suggest that Blake felt a grudging admiration for what S. Foster Damon has aptly called Newton's "extraordinary feat of imagination" (1988, 298).

These contextualizing observations bring me back to the point with which I began the present chapter: the question of the relationship between Blake's antinomian tendencies and his critique of Newton. For Blake's strongest objection to Newton involves not a simple and unequivocal rejection of his materialism, as so many critics have argued.[9] Rather, Blake's critique turns in part around the question of the relationship Newton's science establishes between material creation and law, whether the latter is formulated in natural or in social terms. Indeed, the history of Newtonian thought demonstrates that concepts of natural and governmental law cannot ultimately be separated; for during the course of the eighteenth century, Newton's laws of motion and gravitation were often invoked to support established ideologies and models of political authority. In his *Spirit of the Laws* (1748), for example, the Baron de Montesquieu described "an efficient monarchy ... in terms of gravitational forces attracting bodies to a system's centre" (Fauvel et al. 1988, 36). Later in the eighteenth century, T.N. Des Essarts invoked Newtonian cosmology to characterize the efficient functioning of a well-policed state, arguing in his 1787 *Dictionnaire Universel de Police* that France's magistrate-general "operates all the wheels that together produce order and harmony. The effects of his administration cannot be better compared than to the movement of the celestial bodies" (quoted in Foucault 1995, 213). Almost a century later, to cite one final example, the American critic E.P. Whipple gestured towards Newtonian theory to naturalize Adam Smith's celebrated theoretical offspring, the discourse of political economy: "The time will come," Whipple argued, "when it will be as intellectually discreditable for an educated person to engage in a crusade against the established laws of political economy as in a crusade against the established laws of the physical universe" (quoted in Ford 1965, 102–3).[10] From an iconoclastic and revolutionary standpoint such appropriations of Newton's physics are politically dangerous, serving as they do to "naturalize" socially constructed modes of governmental authority. What is less apparent is that these appropriations are, according to the logic informing

Blake's antinomian-influenced theology, perfectly consistent with the thrust of Newton's exegetical theory. If Newton detested theological mystery, and if his physics are part of an effort to demystify the workings of the cosmos, he nonetheless maintained, as we have seen, the absolute authority of an inscrutable Providence. As far as Newton was concerned, one worshipped God quite simply by obeying his commandments (Brooke 1988, 178). Since William Blake notoriously eschewed the authority of the Decalogue, positing an antinomian New Age based on faith rather than moral law, it is understandable that he would have found Newton's spiritual and physical doctrines distasteful and even insidious.

Blake's critique of Newton's theological and natural legalism is implicit in both the texts and designs of *Milton*. Consider, for example, the design comprising plate 15 (E plate 16; see Figure 10). Here, a naked and youthful Milton, who has taken off "the robe of the promise, & ungirded himself from the oath of God" (M 14:13; E108), encounters the fully clothed and aged Urizen, the false God whose hands grasp two gravestone-like tablets, icons of the moral law. In the poetic text, Milton strives to give the tyrannical Urizen "a Human form" (19:14; E112), so that he and his life-negating moral laws of "Deceit & False Forgiveness" (caption to plate 15) may be exposed and rejected as embodiments of human error. But Blake's iconography subtly suggests that such error extends beyond Urizen's theology to the realm of his physics. Significantly, at the top of the same design, on a curved green horizon[11] representing perhaps the curve of the earthly globe, numerous clothed figures circle Urizen like satellites compelled to orbit a parent star. Urizen's status as a symbol of physical law is reinforced iconographically by the east-to-west movement of the figures circling him[12] and by the fact that two of these individuals carry distinctively globe-shaped timbrels. By correlating religious and natural modes of law in this design, Blake suggests that Milton's annihilation of the former would be incomplete without a corresponding annihilation of the latter and its deterministic model of cyclical recurrence.

Blake makes a more subtle correlation between religious and scientific forms of legalism in his poetic depiction of Theotormon's Mills:

These are the starry voids of night & the depths & caverns of earth
These Mills are oceans, clouds & waters ungovernable in their fury
Here are the stars created & the seeds of all things planted
And here the Sun & Moon recieve their fixed destinations[.]
(M 27:51–4; E125)

10 *Milton*, plate 15
Rare Books Division, New York Public Library,
Astor, Lenox and Tilden Foundations

That this passage is a poetic depiction of Newtonian cosmology is evident in Blake's references to "starry voids,"[13] the creation of stars, and the "fixed destinations" of a "Sun & Moon" subject to the laws of gravitation. Theotormon's Mills, which at one level refer to the rotating "Starry Wheels" (3:43; E97) of Newtonian galaxies, are "ungovernable"; endowed with Newton's controversial "active principles," they are, as it were, *sources* of (gravitational) governance and therefore symbols of natural law itself. It is interesting to note that Blake uses the term "fixed destinations" to characterize both the physical motions of celestial bodies *and* the ostensible spiritual destinies of his "Three Classes of Mortal Men" (6:32; E100); for this terminological repetition suggests that Blake sees natural law and religious moralism as implying analogous forms of governmental constraint. Finally, it is significant that Theotormon's Newtonian "Mills are oceans, clouds & waters," since in Blake's mythology, the element of water often functions as a symbol for the legalism of the Old Testament.

This last point can be clarified by a brief discussion of the antinomian eschatology of the "Everlasting Gospel" (which Blake directly invokes in *Jerusalem* in his address "To the Jews" [J 27; E171]). According to this doctrine, there are three ages upon the Earth: the epochs of water, blood, and spirit. These epochs refer, respectively, to the past age of Mosaic legalism (or the Father of the Old Testament), the present age of Christian freedom from the Law (the Son of the New Testament), and the imminent age of Spirit (the Holy Ghost of the "Everlasting Gospel" [cf. Revelation 14:6]). In the apocalyptic age of spirit, the believer, it was thought, would internalize Christ as the Divine Image, becoming one with him so that "all existing forms of worship, ceremonies, churches, legal and moral codes … become superfluous" (Morton 1966, 37, 50).[14] With these three temporal categories of the Everlasting Gospel in mind, we can understand that Blake's association of physical science with water, the element of the first age, implies a pointed critique of Newtonian natural law. While Harold Bloom has argued in simple essentialist terms that the Newton-water association occurs "because water is a Blakean symbol for the delusion of materiality" (1963, 384), I propose that this association reflects, much more particularly, Blake's emphatic distaste for Newtonian *law*. In Blake's view, in short, Newton's privileging of static and immutable natural laws implies an insidious regression to a legalism analogous to that which ostensibly governed the Mosaic epoch of water. Blake's implicit thesis concerning Newton's utter immersion in legalism is most evident in the 1795 Tate Gallery print entitled "Newton" (see Figure 11). While this painting is notable for

11 "Newton"

its ambivalent portrayal of its eponymous subject,[15] it depicts him, significantly, sitting on a rock at the bottom of the ocean, completely submerged in the element of the first, legalistic epoch. Blake further concretizes the symbolic connection between Newton's physics and Old Testament law in this print (which he finished, significantly, in watercolour) by depicting the scientist wielding a pair of compasses, instruments used by the Son in the creation scene of *Paradise Lost* and by Urizen as he imposes order upon the universe in the frontispiece design to *Europe* (see Figure 12).[16] In "Newton," the rock upon which the eponymous subject sits as he performs his calculations suggests yet another correlation between Newton's naturalistic doctrines and the legalism of the Decalogue, for the latter was, of course, originally inscribed upon tablets of stone.

The connections I have been positing here between Newtonian physical law and the moral law of the Old Testament can helpfully inform a reading of Blake's *Milton*, for in this poem the protagonist's descent from heaven and his arrival on Earth arguably involve a comprehensive antinomian rejection of legalism in both its physical and moral manifestations. When Blake first introduces Milton in the poem, he presents a docile figure who has been fully subdued by the moral law: "Unhappy tho in heav'n, he obey'd, he murmur'd not" (M 2:18; E96). By the time Milton decides to leave this false heaven to "redeem" his "Sixfold Emanation" (2:19–20), his attitude towards the law has clearly changed: we are told that "He took off the robe of promise, & ungirded himself from the oath of God" (14:13; E108). This crucial passage, which Blake deems important enough to illustrate with a full-page design on plate 13 (see Figure 13), depicts among other things Milton's rejection of the covenant of Mount Sinai, the moral law of the Old Testament. Significantly, this is the same monolithic law that Satan – "Newtons Pantocrator" (3:11; E98) and the "Prince" of the Newtonian "Starry wheels" (M 3:43; E97) – invokes when he sets himself up as the one true God, declaring "I am God alone / There is no other! let all obey my principles of moral individuality" (M 9:25–6; E103). Aside from indicating his desire to be the one and only God, Satan's claim that "There is no other" demonstrates that his legalism can tolerate no form of "otherness" or moral plurality. That such law is operable in Milton's heaven is apparent insofar as this heaven excludes Milton's "other," Ololon, the curiously natural "sweet River" (M 21:15; E115) who comprises Milton's divided emanation.

The manner of Milton's ultimate arrival upon Earth suggests that his earlier "ungird[ing] himself" from God's moral law also entails a symbolic release from the natural laws that maintain celestial bodies

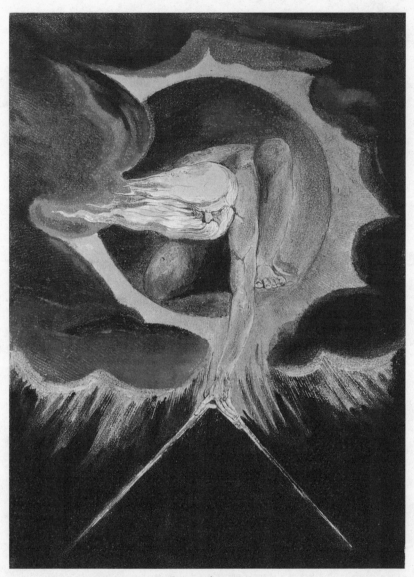

12   *Europe*, frontispiece
Courtesy of the Glasgow University Library,
Department of Special Collections

13   *Milton*, plate 13

in their "fixed destinations" upon the Satanic "Starry Wheels." Blake describes Milton's arrival thus: "Then first I saw him in the Zenith as a falling star, / Descending perpendicular, swift as the swallow or swift; / And on my left foot falling on the tarsus, enterd there" (15:47–9; E110). While Milton's descent might be attributed to earthly gravitation, this possibility seems problematic given that Milton's body subsequently enters Blake's;[17] for according to the laws of classical physics, discrete bodies may collide, but they do not merge with one another. Although he is figured as a "falling star," then, Milton has somehow escaped the Newtonian laws Blake associates with the "oceans, clouds & waters" of Theotormon's Mills. Clearly, Blake depicts Milton's arrival upon Earth in a manner suggesting an imaginative desire for emancipation from *all* forms of law, whether moral or "natural." Crucially, Milton's arrival also augurs a visionary revaluation of earthly materiality, for it causes the "Vegetable World" to appear on Blake's "left Foot, / As a bright sandal formd immortal of precious stones & gold." Far from shaking off this world as "the Dirt upon my feet No part of Me" (VLJ; E565), Blake fastens it firmly to his foot, an act that enables him "to walk forward thro' Eternity" (M 21:12–14; E115).

THE TEMPORALITY OF SATAN'S MILL

One of the foundational concerns of Newton's natural philosophy is the definition of time, and since the revisioning of temporality is one of *Milton*'s central thematic concerns, I shall devote much of this chapter's remaining discussion to a consideration of the poem's response to conceptions of time derived from or associated with Newtonian science. One of the first principles of Newton's physics is the concept of "absolute time." In the Scholium to Definition VIII of his *Principia*, Newton defines such time as follows: "Absolute, true and mathematical time, of itself, and from its own nature, flows equably without relation to anything external, and by another name is called duration: relative, apparent, and common time, is some sensible and external (whether accurate or unequable) measure of duration by the means of motion, which is commonly used instead of true time; such as an hour, a day, a month, a year" (1962, 6). To complement this notion of absolute time or duration, Newton formulates the concept of "absolute space." In contrast to "Relative space," a "movable dimension" that we apprehend according to the changing positions of bodies, "Absolute space, in its own nature, without relation to anything external, remains always similar and immovable" (ibid.). Since absolute time and absolute space "became the two fundamental quantifiable coordinates of the new Newtonian physics," so, as Charles Sherover remarks, "they entered into modern thought" (1975, 100). For his own part, Blake was offended by these new and commonly accepted conceptions of time and space, for they were abstract, mathematical, and inhuman (since they were thought to exist without relation to the sensory experience that relativizes them). Thus, in *Milton*, time and space are by no means absolutes. Indeed, when he writes that "Los is by mortals nam'd Time [and] Enitharmon is nam'd Space" (M 24:68; E121), Blake suggests that time and space should themselves be understood as *human* phenomena. Moreover, since Enitharmon is Los's Emanation, time and space are not properly separable but interrelated or "married" (Lussier 1994, 274, 276).[18] Indeed, the separation of time and space in *Milton* is itself symptomatic of the fall, since it is in the fall that whole beings become fragmented and divided from their Emanations.

This problem of the fall in Blake's myth raises the question of eternity, that extratemporal realm in which the Four Zoas who comprise Albion's being exist, prior to the fall and after their redemption in the apocalypse, in a holistic state of "mutual interchange" (J 88:5; E246). Blake's eschatological privileging of eternity has often led readers to devalue the six-thousand-year span of time constituting fallen history in Blake's mythology. Yet there is an irresolvable contradiction in Blake's late mythology, a contradiction involving the relationship between Albion and the eternal world he leaves behind when he falls. Technically, as Paul Youngquist points out, "there can be no such world, since Albion contains within his limbs *all* things temporal and eternal" (1993, 605; emphasis added).[19] Henry Lesnick addresses this problem of the relationship between eternity and time by declaring that although "eternity is extratemporal, it is manifest in time. And although it is manifest in time, it cannot logically admit of a temporal dimension; it cannot be that infinitely extended reality which precludes the existence of any other reality" (1970, 409). Recognizing that eternity is such an inapprehensible abstraction, Blake attempts to imagine it *in terms of* the mundane time in which, as Lesnick argues, "it is manifest."

Indeed, in Blake's prophetic vision, mundane time itself becomes a veritable gateway to eternity, since "periods of Space & Time / Reveal the secrets of Eternity" (M 21:9–10; E115). And if eternity's "secrets" redeem periodic or fallen time, time in some sense reciprocally redeems eternity: as Blake puts it, "Time is the mercy of Eternity; without Times swiftness / Which is the swiftest of all things: all were eternal torment" (24:72–3; E121). Time may require eternity for its redemption, but an eternity without recourse to time would itself become a kind of hell, a realm of "eternal torment." Such a hell clearly afflicts *Milton*'s Orc, whom Blake figures at one point in terms of a strange inability to participate in the cyclic orders of youth and age, life and death. Orc "incessant[ly] howls burning in fires of Eternal Youth," a strangely atemporalized state in which "Death" is denied "his appointed season when the ends of heaven meet" (29:29, 45–6; E127–8). Because Orc is out of touch with the cyclical "seasons" of time – which Blake relates to "the ends of heaven" themselves – his youth, indeed his very life, becomes cursed, resembling that of the tormented souls in Revelation who "shall ... seek death, and shall not find it; and shall desire to die, and death shall flee from them" (Revelation 9:6).[20]

My reading of a properly interdependent relationship between time and eternity in Blake's mythology has an important precedent in the criticism of Mark Lussier, who sees *Milton* as concerned with the "interplay of mind and matter" and the analogous complementarity of eternity and time (1994, 273). Such a reading remains at odds, however, with many of the extant readings of Blake's *œuvre*. According to Northrop Frye's still-influential interpretation of Blake's later prophecies, for example, there are "two poles in human thought, the conception of life as eternal existence in one divine Man, and the conception of life as an unending series of cycles in nature" (1970, 383). Unlike Erasmus Darwin, who in *The Temple of Nature* celebrates "NEWTON's eye sublime" for marking "the bright periods of revolving time" (1973b, 4.233–4), Blake, in Frye's reading, righteously rejects mundane or cyclical modes of temporality, especially the idea that humanity had its genesis in the cosmic natural cyclicity of the "Starry Wheels." As Frye would have it, humans are incapable of accepting such a vision, for its "moral and emotional implications must accompany it into the mind, and breed there into cynical indifference, short-range vision, selfish pursuit of expediency, and all the other diseases of the Selfhood, ending in horror and despair" (1970, 384). It is on the basis of such a powerful moral argument that Blake ostensibly rejects "the aura of meaningless, self-enclosed, and compulsive repetition that characterizes nature as a whole" (Frosch 1974, 161), advocating instead the Judaeo-Christian transcendentalist conception of time as a linear, teleological progression in which the spirit of truth will be gradually disclosed. Even critics who acknowledge a positively valued cyclicity in Blake's work – cyclic rhythms associated, for example, with artistic creation and eternal life[21] – contrast such temporality with the debased temporality of mere nature, the latter of whose cycles ostensibly belong only to the "World of Death" (Frosch 1974, 172). In such readings of Blake's *œuvre*, nature is quite simply and utterly the enemy of humanity and must therefore be either radically transformed or altogether transcended.[22]

There can be little doubt that Blake was suspicious of Newtonian conceptions of periodic or cyclical time. In Blake's poetry, such time provides a basis for "Satans Mathematic Holiness" of "Length: Bredth & Highth" (M 32:18; E132), since the uniform numbers gained by the analysis of planetary rotation become "a standard metric by which to measure the duration of all other things and events" (Sherover 1975, 100). Indeed, for Blake, it is impossible to "Tell of the Four-fold man, in starry *numbers fitly orderd*" (M 19:16; E114; emphasis added), for the predictive impetus of a mathematics based on prior measurement privileges "the Daughters of Memory" over "the Daughters of Inspiration" (M 1; E95) and so impedes imaginative creation. Blake states his opposition to Newton's cycloid cosmology most succinctly in an oft-quoted passage from "There is No Natural Religion" (copy b): "The bounded is loathed by its possessor. The same dull round even of a univer[s]e would soon become a mill with complicated wheels" (E2). This profound antagonism towards the mill-wheels of Newtonianism stems, I would argue, from Blake's imaginative understanding of the human need for a view of nature unconstrained by the immutable laws governing the atomistic and rigidly repetitive "*same* dull round" of Newtonian cosmology. But this antagonism does not mean that Blake rejects cyclical temporality outright. Rather, he attempts to imagine such periodicity in visionary terms, terms that in some ways anticipate the insights of today's "chaos theory" (also known as the postmodern science of complexity).

In recent years, the notion that natural cyclicity involves a rigid pattern of recurrence in which events and processes endlessly and pointlessly repeat themselves has come increasingly into question. The work of researchers like biochemist and Nobel laureate Ilya Prigogine has helped to inaugurate a new scientific and aesthetic understanding that natural phenomena, rather than invariably repeating pre-given regularities, coexist in synergetic relationships involving the creative manifestation of "true novelty" (Oelschlaeger 1991, 454n.29). In other words, scientists are now beginning to suspect that the closed or atomistic gravitational systems associated with Newtonian physics comprise, at best, only a small part of the overall makeup of the physical universe, and that most "phenomena ... are, in fact, *open* systems, exchanging energy or matter ... with their environment" in unforeseen ways (Toffler 1984, xv).[23] Today's "non-linear" fractal geometry, by attempting to model the complexity of multiple interlocking systems, profoundly problematizes the philosophical tenets supporting Newtonian mathematical science. As Jules-Henri Poincaré discovered at the beginning of the twentieth century, the equations traditionally used to calculate the gravitation of celestial bodies can be solved only when these bodies are considered in terms of a closed relational system of isolated pairs. When the mathematician attempts to add the effects of a third body, the equations are no longer solvable. The strange behaviour of non-linear equations thus suggests "that the eternal clockwork regulating the planets' orbits might come unexpectedly unsprung" (Briggs 1992, 51–2), a possibility unthinkable within the framework of classical physics. Involving as it does this radical departure from Newtonian cosmology, the science of complexity does not merely replicate the "complicated wheels" to which Blake refers in "There Is No Natural Religion."

Since reference to postmodern "chaos theory" may seem anachronistic in the context of a study of Blake, it is important to note, with Ilya Prigogine and Isabelle Stengers, that this science had its historical advent in 1811, when Baron Jean-Joseph Fourier developed, in France, a highly acclaimed mathematical model describing the propagation of heat in solids, an entropic model that contradicted Newton's thesis that time was reversible. By this time in England, moreover, Erasmus Darwin's friend and colleague, James Watt, had already perfected his steam engine, the entropic functioning of which was similarly in conflict with the efficient causality informing mechanistic appropriations of Newton's science (Prigogine and Stengers 1984, 103–4, 111). Arguably, such scientific innovations could not have been made in an historical context where an intuitive understanding of the problems and shortcomings of classical physics was not already in the air.

While Blake probably did not know (and likely would not have cared for) the technical fundamentals informing the science of complexity, the emphasis that this science places on openness and exchange between different natural phenomena suggests at least some affinity with Blake's re-visionary representation of nature in *Milton*. For in this poem, Blake formulates an imaginative alternative to the monolithic "same dull round" he associates with Newtonian cycloid cosmology and its governing laws. As I shall argue presently, the different temporal cycles Blake associates with such diverse entities as larks, wild thyme, and visionary artists entail a profound imaginative commingling of discrete entities, a commingling that in some ways prefigures the interrelationality so conceptually crucial to ecological models of earthly existence. First, however, by examining some exemplary instances of Blake's ubiquitous figuring of cycles, circles, wheels, and whirling vortices in *Milton*, I shall demonstrate some of the ways in which cyclical time, conceived imaginatively rather than mathematically, becomes what Blake will call in *Jerusalem* the "Divine Analogy" (J 85:7; E243) of an interactive and creative eternity. For whereas thinkers like Erasmus Darwin associate Newton's "bright periods of revolving time" with the discovery of nature's "latent laws" (1973b, 4.233–4; 1.1), Blake attempts creatively to imagine the same "periods of … Time" as revealing "the secrets" of an emancipated antinomian "Eternity" (M 21:9–10; E115).

SATAN'S NEWTONIAN TYRANNY

Early in *Milton*, Los calls Satan "Newton's Pantocrator," declaring that "To Mortals," Satan's "Mills seem every thing" (4:12; E98). Los's insight is important to a study of temporal cycles in *Milton*, for in Blake's poetic mythology the only rigidly repetitive processes are arguably those that are associated with, or appropriated by, Satan and his Newtonian Mills. As Morton D. Paley succinctly states, "The Mill is constantly associated with Satan because, whatever its source of power, it goes around in a circle, always returning to the same point" (1991, 191). During Blake's era, "Mortals" could hardly help but succumb to the pointless circularity of this Satanic "seem[ing]," for the model of a mechanistic, causally efficient external order was the predominant paradigm underpinning Western views of natural process.

In *Milton*, mechanism is generally consistent with what Palamabron identifies as Satanic tyranny (M 7:22; E100), for it tends, as we have seen, to presuppose an omnipotent First Mover who, in the beginning, set all things in motion under the governance of irrevocable universal laws. As deists like Hutchinson were aware, the idea of a purely mechanistic universe is the only one that can be reconciled with the orthodox conception of a wholly sovereign and omnipotent God. Surely it is such godlike sovereignty that Blake's Satan desires to appropriate when he makes "to himself Laws from his own identity. / Compell[ing] others to serve him" (11:10–11; E104). It is no mere coincidence that Blake's language here calls to mind *Jerusalem*'s model of perverse causality, the "Water-wheels of Newton": "wheel without wheel, with cogs tyrannic / Moving *by compulsion* each other" (J 15:16, 18–19; E159; emphasis added). Simply put, Newton's Water-wheels and the wheels of Satan's Mill are Blake's poetic figures for a cyclical universe fully subject to causal laws. As far as Blake is concerned, the forms of mechanism signified by Satan's Mills and Newton's Water-wheels imply equally tyrannical (if not entirely cognate) modes of oppression,[24] for each privileges a "Mathematic Holiness" of measurable "Length: Bredth & Highth" (M 32:18; E132), constructing a cosmos made all the more governable by its potentially total phenomenal predictability

– the Satanic dream and desire of much Enlightenment physical science. As commentators have long understood, such a model of the universe has dire implications for human freedom, since it forecloses all possibility of "novelty, energy, emergence, [and] progression" (Ault 1974, 97). To quote the perplexed questioning of the nineteenth-century Muggletonian astronomer Isaac Frost, if the Newtonian system is true, and "if it was so from all eternity, what hope can we have for a change?" (1846, 86).[25]

In reading *Milton*, one is tempted to identify all cyclical modes of physical movement as fully determinate, and therefore Satanic, in nature. Indeed, by "Circling Albions Cliffs in which the Four-fold World resides," Satan himself seems to become an exemplar of mechanical, cyclical movement in time.[26] But Blake, one should note, immediately underlines the *un*naturalness of Satan's "revolutionary" movement by denouncing this activity as "a fallacy of Satans Churches" (M 39:60–1; E141). Clearly, then, Satan's Mill and his Newtonian Water-wheels do not represent nature and natural process as such in *Milton*. Rather, these symbols gesture towards philosophical mechanism as a mode of governmental *discourse*, a diverse and often internally contentious body of institutionalized knowledge that simultaneously produces and disciplines nature in the ostensible process of describing its objects and the "laws" governing their existence. Ultimately, Blake's prophetic writings attempt to denaturalize mechanistic discourse by emphasizing the crucial role that mechanism plays in Satan's institutionalized theocratic effort to propagate the widespread illusion that "All Things" are "One Great Satan" (M 39:1; E140).

An early incident demonstrating the proliferative power of Satanic discourse in *Milton* occurs when Satan persuades Palamabron to exchange "stations" with him. Satan's usurpation of Palamabron's Harrow involves, on one level, an imperialist expansion and consolidation of his mechanistic tyranny. Palamabron's workers (significantly characterized as organic "living creatures," i.e., *zoa*), obviously accustomed to working to the tempo of less rigidly defined rhythms than those associated with Satan's Mill-wheels, are "madden'd like *wildest* beasts" in the wake of Satan's usurpation of the Harrow, responding with an understandable "*wild* fury" to their sudden loss of freedom under Satan's supervision (7:46–7; E101; emphasis added). Conversely, the workers of the Mills, accustomed to working to the oppressive tempo of Satan's mechanical rhythms, react to their changed circumstance under Palamabron's supervision with chaotic and carnivalesque exuberance. Los, we are told, beholds "The servants of the Mills drunken with wine and dancing *wild* / With shouts and Palamabrons songs, rending the forests green / With ecchoing confusion, tho' the Sun was risen on high" (8:8–10; E101; emphasis added). This understandable irruption of wildness and festive celebration represents the enthusiastic response of labouring prisoners suddenly freed from an oppressively regularized routine. The regimented regularity of this routine is implicit in the expectation that the workers should, at this "high" point of the Sun's diurnal round, be working at Satan's Mills and doing nothing else (8:16–17; E102).

Los blames himself for the bitter discord that results when Palamabron and Satan exchange stations. After ritualistically signalling a "solemn mourning" (8:12; E101), he declares sadly that "this mournful day / Must be a blank in Nature." In order to accomplish this strange erasure, Los asks the workers of the Harrow and the Mill to cease their work and "follow with me," adding that they may "Resume [their] labours" tomorrow. Subsequently, the workers follow Los "Wildly," and, significantly, the Mills fall "silent" (8:20–3; E102). By correlating the wildness of the workers' behaviour with the simultaneous silencing of Satan's Mills, Blake encourages his reader to imagine the temporary suspension of a paradigmatic view of nature as the realm of simple temporal recurrence. The worlds of the Harrow and the Mill, both of which have by now felt the effects of Satanic mechanism, are, it seems, temporarily freed from Satan's tyranny. Indeed, Blake goes so far as to imagine the (im)possibility of a thoroughly non-discursive nature, for Los's assertion that the day must be "a blank in Nature" suggests that nature itself will become, with the silencing of the Mills, something of a *tabula rasa*. This transformation entails a most interesting conceptual turn of events; for in John Locke's cognitive theory, it is not nature but the human mind that is originally a blank leaf or slate. Remarkably, Blake's figure of "a blank in Nature" suggests precisely the opposite: mind is not written on by nature, but nature is written on by an inherently active mind. While Lockean psychology dismantles the concept of innate ideas, thus challenging the notion of a pre-given, indwelling human "Conscience" (J 93:22; E254), Blake's poetic figure of "a blank in Nature" dismantles the common view of external nature as absolute, pre-given "reality," thus challenging the objectivity of materialist doctrine. Yet although nature's discursive slate may be wiped clean in *Milton*, it nevertheless waits to receive, at the end of Los's "mournful day" (8:20; E102), a new inscription or meaning. With the impending renewal of the conflict between Satan and Palamabron, the privilege of constructing the meaning of "nature" and the "natural" will fall to the party that successfully establishes its political hegemony.

For Blake, however, mechanism is a discursive paradigm that is not so simply suspended; and the openness of conceptual possibility implied by the "Wild[ness]" of an uninscribed or "blank" nature is all too quickly foreclosed when Enitharmon, under the influence of Los's well-meaning deception,[27] forms "a Space for Satan" and "clos[es] it with a tender Moon." This act of atomistic closure marks the sudden reappearance of Satanic mechanism: a passive Enitharmon, subject to the quasi-legal "compulsion" I described above, is suddenly "compelled to / Defend [the] Lie" (8:43–4, 47–8; E102) of Satanic innocence (8:1–3; E101). Los, as if subject to the same compulsion, follows suit. He "clos[es] up Enitharmon from the sight" of his own wrathful response to Satan's victories in Eden (9:18; E103), thus unwittingly perpetuating and consolidating the very system of atomistic closure he seeks to oppose. In the lines that follow, Satan takes this closure to its logical extreme: he legislates the anti-relational atomization of identity itself by introducing into the poem the concept of "moral individuality" governed by "Moral laws." Setting himself up as the grand exemplar of such self-enclosure, Satan announces that "I am God alone / There is no other!" (9:22–6). Appropriately, in a dramatic scene that emphatically underlines Satan's self-enclosure (but also, in its language, adumbrates its ultimate defeat), Blake represents Satan's bosom as growing "Opake against the Divine Vision," after which "a World of deeper Ulro [is] open'd, in the midst / Of the Assembly" (9:31, 34–5; emphasis added).

Blake depicts the cosmic scope and oppressive political implications of Satanic hegemony near the mid-point of *Milton*, where he offers us a glimpse of the mechanical workings of the diurnal round:

> Luvah's bulls each morning drag the sulphur Sun out of the Deep
> Harnessed with starry harness black & shining kept by black slaves
> That work all night at the starry harness. Strong and vigorous
> They drag the unwilling Orb ... (21:20–23; E115)

The insistent repetition in this brief passage of such words as "drag," "starry," "harness," and "black" reflects, at the very level of language, the notion of natural temporality as simple recurrence. At the narrative level, this pattern of linguistic repetition reflects the mechanistic philosophy to which such a notion of recurrence belongs: the Sun is conducted in its round by way of external compulsion, a compulsion most brutally emphasized by the "harness" of slavery. That such a model of natural cyclicity is perverse and oppressive is suggested by the figuration of the Sun as an "unwilling Orb" that must be dragged with the help not of free humans but of slaves who, notwithstanding their strength and vigour, are also compelled unwillingly to their task. Blake underlines the "unnaturalness" of this cosmic vision by depicting "The mountains ... & every plant that grew" as lamenting it with "wail[s]" and "solemn sighs" (21:19). In Blake's vision, in other words, the things of nature are themselves appalled by their subjection to Newtonian natural law. More hopefully, however, when the "Family / Of Eden" hears nature's lament, Providence begins – despite the fact that Los and Enitharmon can only hear this lament through the "inclos[ing]" walls of an atomized Mundane Shell (21:23–4, 28–30; E115–16).

But a note of optimism has indeed been sounded, and Blake subsequently offers us poetic depictions of processive circles and cycles that belie and attempt to challenge the Satanic vision of nature as cyclical enslavement and atomistic enclosure. In the design to plate 32 (E plate 33; see Figure 14), for example, Blake depicts the Four Zoas as interconnected circles, entities "whose Gates are opend" (34:17; E134) rather than closed. In the midst of, and intersected by, these circular entities is the Mundane Egg (a figure for the Earth itself[28]), within which appears the names of Adam and Satan. In *Jerusalem*, Blake explicitly contrasts this latter structure, which he also calls the "Mundane Shell," with Albion's Satanically petrific "frozen Altars" (J 42:78; E190), auguring a potential transformation of religious moralism that is all the more apparent when we remember that Blake depicts the egg, in *For the Sexes*, as embodying the promise of a "hatching" (E262), suggesting a mode of transcendence immanent in natural structures and in the cycle of life itself. More important, in the design we have been considering, "Miltons Track" penetrates the circular Zoas (with the notable exception of Tharmas, whose border Milton's Track nonetheless touches) and the Mundane Egg, emphasizing that the entities they depict are not atomistically self-enclosed but permeable and open.

But the image on plate 32 of the Zoas as interconnected circles is not without an accompanying textual ambivalence. When the Zoas, also called the "Family / Of Eden," recognize that Milton is in fact "the Awakener" (M 21:23–4, 33; E115–16), we are told that they

> collected as Four Suns
> In the Four Points of heaven East, West & North & South
> Enlarging and enlarging till their Disks approachd each other;
> And when they touch'd closed together Southward in One Sun
> Over Ololon ... (21:37–41; E116)

Despite their seemingly felicitous interconnection, the Zoas groan "in spirit" and are "troubled" at the thought of Milton's activity (21:43–4), for they do not realize that Milton can obtain redemption only by

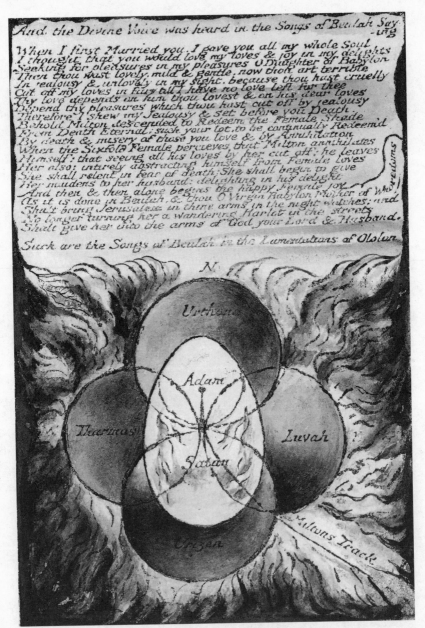

14   *Milton*, plate 32

descending into the realm of Eternal Death (Essick and Viscomi 1993, 157). One might gloss the problem here by comparing the behaviour of the Zoas in the above-quoted passage to that of *Milton's* "gorgeous clothed Flies." When these latter creatures come into contact with one another, they "touch each other *& recede*," "cross & change *& return*" (M 26:1–2,6; E123; emphasis added); and in acting thus they become, like Blake's prophesying trees, "Visions of Eternity" (26:10). With the example of these visionary flies in mind, we can understand that the problem attending the interconnection of the Four Zoas involves their failure similarly to balance the "touch[ing]" of "their Disks" with an alternating – that is, cyclical – rhythm of recession and return. By merely and only touching each other, the Zoas form the "closed" synthesis of a singular and homogeneous "One Sun," what Ololon refers to as the "unnatural refuge" (21:40, 49; E116) of a total-itarian community that cannot be open to the Other (who, in this case, is Milton himself).

Ololon is a key player in *Milton's* rethinking of natural cyclicity, and she is figured, tellingly, in terms of active circularity. On plate 34 (which in Erdman's edition directly follows the design depicting the interaction of the circular Zoas, the Mundane Egg, and Milton's Track) the Daughters of Beulah ask her: "Are you the Fiery *Circle* that late drove in fury & fire / The Eight Immortal Starry-Ones down into Ulro dark" (34:3–4; E133; emphasis added)? The realm from which Ololon has driven out these "Starry-Ones" – the "Seven Angels of the Presence" (15:3; E109) plus Milton – is Blake's Miltonic heaven, a realm that, as I argued earlier, is thoroughly circumscribed by the dictatorial thrust of an oppressive moral law. If God is understood analogically as the cosmic centre around which lesser angelic bodies move as subordinate satellites, then Ololon's act of driving out the "Starry-Ones" might be said to involve a transgression not only of the moral law but also of its physical analogues, Newton's mathe-matical "laws" of nature. However we choose to interpret it, Ololon's act is crucial to the poem's movement from moral stasis to the begin-nings of apocalyptic transformation. At a certain level, Ololon, the "Fiery Circle," also referred to apostrophically as "*O* wonder of Eter-nity" (34:7; emphasis added), dramatically embodies Blake's imagi-native revaluation of circularity and cyclicity. Indeed, her very name suggests her *revolutionary* potential in the poem: in uttering it out loud (Ol-ol-on or O-lo-lon), the round Os, in concert with the repe-tition of combined "o" and "l" sounds, enact a kind of circular revolving on the tongue, lingually gesturing towards Blake's revolu-tionary critique of physical and social self-enclosure. For as Milton's multiplicitous "Sixfold Emanation" (2:19; E96), Ololon represents the manifold contexts from which the pathological Miltonic selfhood has become severed in *Milton*; and the entire narrative thrust of the poem is towards the redemptive restoration of the complex relationality (or, one might say, ecology of being) that must define Milton's "whole" identity and, indeed, that of all beings in Blake's organic cosmos.

"THE NATURE OF INFINITY"

Perhaps more effectively than any other part of the poem, *Milton*'s famously cryptic vortex passage can shed light on Blake's revolutionary rethinking of cyclical systems. Because this complex passage is crucial to Blake's critique of Enlightenment mechanism, it will be helpful to quote it here at length:

> The nature of infinity is this: That every thing has its
> Own Vortex; and when once a traveller thro Eternity.
> Has passd that Vortex, he percieves it roll backward behind
> His path, into a globe itself infolding; like a sun:
> Or like a moon, or like a universe of starry majesty,
> While he keeps onwards in his wondrous journey on the earth
> Or like a human form, a friend with whom he livd benevolent.
> As the eye of man views both the east & west encompassing
> Its vortex; and the north & south, with all their starry host;
> Also the rising sun & setting moon he views surrounding
> His corn-fields and his valleys of five hundred acres square.
> Thus is the earth one infinite plane, and not as apparent
> To the weak traveller confin'd beneath the moony shade.
> Thus is the heaven a vortex passd already, and the earth
> A vortex not yet pass'd by the traveller thro' Eternity. (15:21–35; E109)

Arguably, critics have devoted more commentary to this passage than to any other single passage in Blake's corpus, reaching diverse conclusions concerning its ultimate meaning. For W.J.T. Mitchell, the interpretive difficulties attending our readings of the vortex passage derive from its description of abstract, extra-mundane concepts like infinity and eternity "in terms of travel through space and time and the encounter with finite things" (1970, 71). Vincent de Luca addresses this representational conundrum by arguing that the passage, as an important aspect of Blake's sublime textual practice, is deliberately designed to resist paraphrase (1991, 82), "actualiz[ing] intimations of the infinite and the eternal by detaching one from all cause-and-effect chains of corporeal existence, from time, sequential logic, and the many kinds of errant traveling" (80). Because of its emphasis on the necessary transcendence of corporeal existence, de Luca's reading is in some ways consistent with that of Stuart Peterfreund, who reads the vortex passage as restoring the primacy of mind over matter by depicting a journey "beyond the world of space and time to the place (if it can be called that) of creative consciousness" (1998, 55). While such interpretations of the vortex are illuminating, they tend to efface the crucial role that materiality continually plays in Blake's anti-dualistic apprehension of the infinite and the eternal. Far from negating the realm of time in the name of an abstract eternity, the vortex functions to bring time and eternity into dynamic interrelationship. To quote Mark Lussier, the "dual drives of the vortex, to and from eternity ... resist resolution," since, according to the "complementary dynamics" of Blakean vortical process, eternity and time or mind and matter are not entirely opposed but rather "co-present" (1994, 273). As I argued in chapter 1, Blake believed that an imaginative understanding of eternity and infinity must be sought *within* the mundane experience of time and space, since "it is impossible to think without images of somewhat on earth" (Annotations to Lavater, E600). Hence rather than dismissing the natural images Blake associates with *Milton*'s vortex (celestial bodies, cornfields, valleys, the earth itself) by advocating the need to transcend them, we would do well to consider the crucial role these images play in *enabling* Blakean imaginative enterprise.

Perhaps the most remarkable assertion Blake makes in the vortex passage is that "*every thing* has its / Own Vortex." Since the structure of a vortex involves both centripetal motion and the interactive meeting of oppositional forces (Mitchell 1978, 72), Blake's assertion suggests that each and every phenomenon can be conceptualized in terms of circular or cyclical movement in time. But Blake's vortex is not a closed structure subject only to the compulsive causality of mechanistic physics, for it can be "passd" through like a window, allowing the imaginative "traveller thro Eternity" to escape the "moony shade" of efficient-causal law and experience, literally, the "nature of infinity" – an *infinite nature* in which the enclosed space of "five hundred acres square" gives way to an "infinite plane" of possibility.[29] This plane is a site of profound interrelationship, since each integral entity inhabiting it has a vortex or gateway connecting it, via eternity, to other similarly endowed entities. Once passed, moreover, each vortex "roll[s] backward" behind the traveller, at which time it resembles *both* globular, cyclically moving bodies like the sun and the moon *and* the "human form, a friend" who inspires "benevolent" co-existence. Thus, we can see that Frye's notion that Divine Humanity and cyclical nature are Blakean polar opposites need not be axiomatic. Indeed, the journey through the vortex is followed, significantly, by numerous positively charged cyclical poetic figures. The "rising sun & setting moon" *surround* the traveller's fields and valleys. "Corn-fields" present to the traveller's gaze the nourishing produce of cyclically turning seasons, while valleys conjure up images of streams that, like *Thel's* "golden springs" (BT 3:7; E4), flow in rhythm with the hydrological cycle. In such a universe, where vortices connect myriad object-systems, the Earth is "one *infinite* plane," not the closed system or locus of the "same dull round" that so many of Blake's readers have associated with Blake's view of the material world.[30] Indeed, readers who regard natural cycles only as structures of oppressive repetition in Blake's *œuvre* might themselves be seen as "weak travellers" through the vortices of Blake's imaginative artifacts, approximating those "Mortals," mentioned above and near the beginning of *Milton*, to whom Satan's mechanical "Mills seem every thing" (M 4:12; E98).

When Milton encounters the vortex during his journey to the Earth, his experience of space undergoes a significant alteration, an alteration emphasizing the imaginative power implicit in the thinking of cyclical systems as open and interrelated rather than closed and atomistic. Passing through the vortex, Milton finds that traditional hierarchical structures are transformed. As his perspective alters, "what was underneath soon seemd above" (15:42; E110). But Blake's employment in this passage of the word "seemed" suggests that Milton's change of perspective need not be read as a simple inversion of the high and low terms constituting a traditional heaven/earth duality. As the subsequent line – "A cloudy heaven mingled with stormy seas in loudest ruin" – indicates, the formerly opposed terms of heaven and earth (the latter represented by the "stormy seas"[31]) become "mingled," not inverted. Hence the reference to "ruin" might be read to signify the destruction of a system of thought that hides heaven from human sight behind a "cloudy" veil of theological mystery.

In stark contrast to the imaginative cyclical nature he depicts in the vortex passage, Blake represents the strictly repetitive cyclicity of Enlightenment mechanistic process in terms of atomistic self-enclosure and its (un)imaginative consequences: environmental devastation and death. Early in the poem, for example, we learn that the Satanic Urizen has had his genesis in the celestial body of "a red round Globe hot burning" (3:11; E97). That the nature of Urizen's cyclically rotating globe is mechanistic rather than imaginatively dynamic is suggested by Blake's depiction of Urizen's perceptual faculties. His eyes are "Roll[ed] round into two little Orbs & closed in two little Caves" and his "petrified" ears, like *Thel's* auricular "whirlpool[s] fierce to draw creations in" (BT 6:17; E6), spiral forth "in close volutions" (M 3:14, 17–

18; E97). In these lines, Blake emphasizes the atomistic closure implicit in his understanding of Newtonian cyclical process by figuring Urizen's rolling "Orbs" as fully "closed" and encaverned and the volutions of his petrified ears as similarly "close" or closed. Urizen's sensory constitution can only result in distorted, inevitably solipsistic human percepts, sensory impressions that Blake depicts as both cosmologically generated by, and perpetuating, Newtonianism in and as a closed, literally vicious cycle in which we become what we behold by beholding (i.e., projecting upon the world) what we have already become.[32]

Urizen's perceptual makeup has dire implications both for the natural environment and its living inhabitants, implications suggested by his "Tongue of hunger & thirst" (3:22). This tongue, besides representing the insatiable appetite of Urizen's Faustian will to power, is in a sense a logical *consequence* of his Satanic-Newtonian worldview. This claim can be explained by way of a brief digression. As we saw in chapter 1, the new physical sciences (for which Urizen is in part a figure) replaced an earlier panvitalism with what Blake perceived as an all-encompassing ontology of death. Whereas panvitalism conceptualized the entire cosmos as a living organism (somewhat like the cosmic form of Blake's Ancient Man, Albion), the new sciences, highly critical of anthropomorphism, developed a panmechanistic ontology privileging, as its "model entity," pure, lifeless matter (Jonas 11, 9). We witness such a view of materiality, for example, in Galileo's discussion of the rose: "that it must be white or red, bitter or sweet, noisy or silent, and of sweet or foul odor, my mind does not feel compelled to bring in as necessary accompaniments. Without the senses as our guides, reason or imagination unaided would probably never arrive at qualities like these. Hence I think that tastes, odors, colors, and so on are no more than mere names so far as the object in which we place them is concerned, and that they reside only in the consciousness. Hence if the living creatures were removed, all these qualities would be wiped away and annihilated" (Galileo 1967, 274).[33] Following Galileo's lead, Newton similarly denigrates sensual subjective experience, removing what Galileo calls the "living creatures" (Blake's *zoa*) from his own objects of study by conceptualizing the universe primarily in terms of objective characteristics that can be measured and quantified and thus arithmetically manipulated.

For Blake, among other things, such a world-view negates human identity, reducing members of the "Divine Humanity" (i.e., *all* living things) to

Shapeless Rocks
Retaining only Satans Mathematic Holiness, Length: Bredth & Highth
Calling the Human Imagination: which is the Divine Vision & Fruition

In which Man liveth eternally: madness & blasphemy, against
Its own Qualities, which are Servants of Humanity, not Gods or Lords[.]
(M 32:14, 17–21; E131–2)

Significantly, this passage, which opposes the numerical *quantities* of scientific rationality to the imaginative *"Qualities"* of poetic "Divine Vision," follows one plate after Blake's extended poetic description of Beulah's birds and flowers (31:28–63; E130–1). In this earlier section of *Milton*, the lark's inspired song "vibrates with the effluence Divine" (31:35), while the "precious Odors" and "sweets" of Beulah's flowers derive from, and augur the return of, an expanding "Eternity" (31:46–8). Under Satan's regime of "Mathematic Holiness," however, which recognizes only "Length: Bredth & Highth" in "starry numbers fitly *orderd*" (20:16; E114; emphasis added), the imaginative "Qualities" Blake associates with the redemptive songs and scents of a subjective *"order* sweet & lovely" (31:62; emphasis added) are entirely negated. Unable to understand the world of qualities, Satan's objective order must condemn the human imagination's subjective order as "madness & blasphemy." But Blake does not wish merely to invert the dominant order of things by advocating an absolute privileging of subjective qualities over objective quantities, for such privileging would merely replace "Satans Tyranny" (32:16) of "Mathematic Holiness" with a potentially tyrannical sensuousness or subjective Holiness. Thus, Blake is careful to qualify his critique of objective, quantitative thinking by pointing out that subjective "Qualities ... are Servants of Humanity, not Gods or Lords."

Critical of any methodological tendency to separate the "living creatures," or Zoas, from the material cosmos they inhabit, Blake associates Satan, whom he repeatedly represents in terms of rock, sand, and stone (what Frye aptly characterizes as "the deadest part of the material world"; 1970, 364), with images of environmental devastation that are more than mere descriptive reworkings of traditional landscapes of hell. As he declares *in propria persona* just prior to Milton's encounter with Satan:

I ... stood in Satans bosom & beheld its desolations!
A ruind Man: a ruind building of God not made with hands;
Its plains of burning sand, its mountains of marble terrible:
Its pits & declivities flowing with molten ore & fountains
Of pitch & nitre: its ruind palaces & cities & mighty works ...
(38:15–19; E139)

While this passage can be read in terms of the contemporary philosophy of catastrophism, which understood such things as volcanic

activity and the formation of mountains as geographical conse-
quences of the ancient fall of humanity, it can also be read prophet-
ically, as a poetic warning concerning the earthly devastation that
might yet occur if humanity continues to pursue the course of discov-
ery charted by the major proponents of Enlightenment naturalism.[34]
Indeed, from our late-twentieth-century vantage point, Blake's Satan
might be seen as a prophetic personification of human-caused (but
so-called "natural") catastrophes, including the process of environ-
mental desertification.[35] An enemy of the "living waters" (5:34; E99),
the "ruind Man" of mathematical science ruins all he touches, both
buildings and open spaces, human and non-human environments,
causally *producing* the Urizenic world of "hunger & thirst" discussed
above, a world incapable of sustaining life. Hence the warning that
is part of *Milton's* prophetic message: the poem emphatically dem-
onstrates that, by embracing inflexibly mechanistic views of nature,
we inevitably arrive at Satan's desolate condition, both within and
without ourselves.

In the epilogue to *Milton* we witness a powerful alternative to the
desolate vision of human-nature relations that Satan represents and
figuratively embodies in the poem. At the end of the grand prophetic
vision that comprises *Milton*, Blake, far from enacting or advocating
an artistic transcendence of Vegetable Nature, depicts himself as
awakening from a swoon in his earthly garden, with Catherine Blake
by his side as his soul returns "To Resurrection & Judgment in the
Vegetable Body" (42:26–7; E143). With this passage, Blake shows his
readers that transcendence (here called Resurrection) can be concep-
tualized as immanent "in" Vegetable nature. Moreover, following the
example of his "gorgeous clothed Flies" who "cross & change &
return" (26:2, 6; E123), Blake, in the new arrival of his earthly return,
demonstrates his conviction that artistic creation involves a cycle: he
crosses over into vision, is *changed* by the experience, then *returns* once
more to the green and pleasant Earth that has all along supported
his mind and body in their visionary endeavour.

At this crucial point in the poem, Blake uses various poetic images
and allusions to emphasize his revisionary affirmation of natural
cyclicity as the "Divine Analogy" (J 85:7; E243) of eternal relationality
or community. He finds himself once more in his own earthly garden,
where he encounters the singing lark and the wild thyme (42:29–30;
E143), a pair of earthly creatures whose symbolic choice is particu-
larly interesting. Stuart Curran has argued that, in the symbolism of
lark and thyme, "the natural has been converted to transcendent
symbol: skylarks become angels; the scent of thyme on the heath is
an incense revealing the spiritual presence of the divine" (1986b, 113).
This kind of reading, though insightful, involves a minor problem of

misplaced emphasis: if we shift the terms of Curran's argument slightly, we might say with J.J. Garth Wilkinson (1839, xvi) that Blake, in his symbolic deployment of the lark and thyme, rather than spiritualizing nature, *naturalizes spirit*, bringing spirit out of abstraction and down to earth. It is important to remember that the lark and wild thyme are among the most earthly – one might say the most "immanent" – of England's natural creatures. Far from exhibiting in its natural growth what might be construed as an emphatic striving towards the heavens, the wild thyme is a creeping vine that is "firmly rooted in the earth" (Kauver 1976–77, 84). Despite its humble character (or perhaps because of it), this flowering herb is commonly called "Christ's Ladder," a name suggesting its symbolic status as a natural link between heaven and earth. Like the wild thyme, the lark is similarly humble yet visionary. In high contrast to such sky-dwelling birds as the eagle – a traditional poetic symbol of transcendental desire – the lark is a ground-nesting bird that builds an "*earthy* bed" (31:29; E130; emphasis added), living, as Blake reminds us, even closer to the soil than the "bright purple mantle" of the wild thyme itself (35:57–8; E136). At daybreak, however, the lark "Mount[s] upon the wings of light into the Great Expanse" of the sky (31:32), a movement suggesting that this bird functions, like the thyme, to symbolize a connection *in* nature between heaven and earth. Perhaps emulating Christ's example in St Matthew's gospel, Blake asks his reader to derive a valuable spiritual lesson from the birds of the air and the wildflowers of the field (Matthew 6:26–8).[36] Arguably, Blake's symbolic choice of the lark and wild thyme as his visionary counterparts in *Milton* involves not a transcendental negation of earthly nature but an affirmation of the "holiness" that is a fundamental property of all Blakean life.

To return to the theme of temporality, it is important to note with Frye that the lark is "the early-rising bird" of the returning day, and that the wild thyme is "the early-flowering plant of the returning spring" (1970, 355). As respective harbingers of new diurnal and seasonal beginnings in nature, these creatures together represent the complex *inter*relationality of cyclical processes when they are understood imaginatively and holistically. Their presence in Blake's garden suggests that the completion of the poet's own visionary cycle in *Milton* involves Blake in a commingling with other new beginnings in a natural cycle of returning days embraced within a larger cycle of returning seasons. And the result of this commingling, it must be emphasized, is by no means a static return of the Same. On the contrary, this garden scene represents a meeting of human and natural entities who become implicated like the wheels *within* wheels of

Ezekiel's vision and *Jerusalem's* Eden (J 15:19–20; E159), each containing and modifying something of the other according to the emanative principle of "mutual interchange" (J 88:5; E246). And it is because of this interchange that Blake's garden becomes in *Milton* what Curran has most aptly called "a reservoir of infinite potentiality" (1986b, 176).

Some additional commentary on the lark will help to clarify this claim; for at the level of Blake's imaginative poetics, this bird exemplifies the mutual interchange that occurs when cyclical processes mingle in the natural world. As Blake tells us, the lark's

> little throat labours with inspiration; every feather
> On throat & breast & wings vibrates with the effluence Divine
> All Nature listens silent to him & the awful Sun
> Stands still upon the Mountain looking on this little Bird
> With eyes of soft humility, & wonder love & awe ... (M 31:34–8; E130–1)

Here the lark, whose song, as I have noted, augurs the beginning of another diurnal round, has the power to *influence* the cycle it announces and in which it participates: the "awful Sun," no longer an "unwilling Orb" enslaved by the economy of mechanistic compulsion described above, "Stands still" at the sound of the lark's voice, which affects, indeed, "All [of] Nature." We might interpret the message the lark's song imparts by considering, in addition to the Sun's emancipated response, another environmental context of its utterance: as Blake tells us, "Just at the place to where the Lark mounts, is a Crystal Gate" (35:61; E136). If this gate, like its counterpart in the imaginative vortex, marks the way out of necessity and enclosure in the self-centred systems constituting the "Starry Wheels" of Newtonian cycloid cosmology, then the lark's song signifies, and marks the threshold of, an alternative emancipatory cyclicity: the apocalyptic cyclicity of "Divine Analogy" (J 85:7; E243). (In Blake's post-apocalyptic eternity, all things continue imaginatively to exist and act in rhythm with "the Planetary lives of Years Months Days & Hours"; J 99:3; E258). Finally, Blake articulates a bond of poetic and visionary fellowship with the lark by associating this representative of the natural world, whose "little throat labours with inspiration" (31:34), with material acts of inspired poetic creation, hence with the cycle described above that constitutes the inspired poet's visionary endeavour.

The wild thyme's role in the poem is similarly complex. Although Blake returns at the end of his visionary quest to his own *domestic* garden, the *wild* thyme's presence there suggests that this enclosed garden, rather than adumbrating the "absolute civilization" of Frye's

Eden (1970, 389), incorporates *within* its domesticity something of the chaotic "wildness" of non-domesticated nature – a wildness that crucially modifies the domestic context. Blake tells us, moreover, that "The Wild Thyme is Los's Messenger to Eden, a mighty Demon" whose "presence in Ulro dark" is "Terrible deadly & poisonous" (35:54–5; E136). The wild thyme is certainly an enemy of Ulro, for the very existence of Ulro, the realm of rigidly mechanistic temporality and therefore of "Eternal Death," is threatened by the kinds of temporal excess and creaturely alterity that "wildness" represents. David Erdman has suggested, indeed, that the wild thyme's very name rings in Blake's poem "with a prophetic pun" (1969, 431), which I would interpret as a poetic gesture towards the "wild" temporality I have been attempting to describe in this chapter. Such time involves not the linearity of Christian teleology nor the closed and rigidly repetitive cyclicity of Newtonian mechanism but an expansive and complex interrelated system of cycles, the multifaceted temporal structure characterizing Blake's alternative vision of nature, "the nature of infinity."

4 *Jerusalem*'s Human Ecology

And it was commanded them that they should not hurt
the grass of the earth, neither any green thing, neither any tree;
but only those men which have not the seal of God in
their foreheads.

(Revelation 9:4)

CRITICISM, NATURE, AND *JERUSALEM*

It is a commonplace in Blake studies to consider *Jerusalem* the poetic
culmination of Blake's anti-natural philosophy, a philosophy that had
not yet attained its mature or fullest expression in the earlier epics.
In a discussion of Blake's generic practice, Stuart Curran notes that
Milton marks the last time in the poet's career that Blake "writes
poetry of natural description whose beauty is ravishing" (1986b, 113).
Since critics often regard *Jerusalem* as the continuation and culmina-
tion of a single epic beginning with *Milton*,[1] its comparative eschewal
of a pastoral vision in favour of a more emphatically apocalyptic
vision lends some credence to the notion that Blake's attitude
towards the material world was becoming increasingly antipathetic.
As Harold Bloom points out, there "is no equivalent in *Jerusalem* to
the wonderful vision of a natural world being redeemed by the work
of Los that we are given in the closing plates of the first book of
Milton." What Blake's final epic supposedly shows us instead is
nature viewed unequivocally as "the delusive nightmare-world of
the Ulro" (Bloom 1963, 365–6), the nightmare world of Hell itself
(Deen 1983, 218).[2]

Such a reading of nature in *Jerusalem* involves what I see as an
oversimplification of a complex problem. By demonstrating in this
chapter some of the ways in which nature and ideology are intri-
cately related in *Jerusalem*, I shall offer a more equivocal reading of
the poem's representation of nature. It is important to note, first of

all, that Blake's critique of the relationship between nature and ideology is itself multifaceted and sometimes contradictory. On occasion, for example, Blake deploys an essentialist poetics, establishing a critical distinction between the things of nature themselves and the ideological or practical uses to which they are put by humans. Bath's status in *Jerusalem* is a case in point. As I argued in the introduction, Blake depicts Bath in at least two contrasting ways: on the one hand, he envisions it as a geographical wonder "Whose springs are unsearchable & knowledg infinite," and it is primarily in this "natural" guise that Blake praises Bath as the "mild Physician of Eternity" (J 41:1–2; E188); on the other hand, Blake condemns Bath as "Legions" (37:1; E183), since its popularity as a spa involved human appropriations of its natural healing powers for various and questionable self-interested ends. Blake's implicit critique of Bath's human appropriation is an essentialist one insofar as it suggests that a "real" and "natural" Bath exists apart from or prior to the interests of those who use its space for profit or illicit pleasure. In this instance, as in numerous others, Blake's critique is quite simply not a deconstructive one; rather, to quote Jacques Derrida, it is "pre-deconstructive," for it is grounded in an "ontology of presence as actual reality and as objectivity" (1994, 170). This is by no means to deny the political efficaciousness of the pre-deconstructive aspect of Blake's critique. As Derrida himself admits, a pre-deconstructive philosophy need not be seen as "false, unnecessary, or illusory" (ibid.). If nothing else, an ontology of presence can function as an enabling political *strategy*; for by attempting to conceptualize the things of nature as they might be said to exist apart from human practices, we can begin to imagine some critical distance from those practices. From such an imaginative and critical vantage point, we may begin, perhaps, to reassess and reconfigure our relationship to the non-human environment.

Blake is, however, ultimately suspicious of his own strategic invocations of presence, in which he invites us to imagine nature in "objective" or "extra-discursive" terms. Perhaps this suspicion stems in part from his inability to trust in a doctrine of objectivity during an age in which the objective discourse *par excellence* was that of mechanistic science. For Blake, as I have argued previously, this discourse was not disinterested and objective but thoroughly political, helping to produce and promote an enslaved human and non-human world by naturalizing and perpetuating established modes of religious and legal authority. There are thus crucial moments in *Jerusalem* wherein Blake seems entirely to eschew an ontology of presence, as when he depicts nature's very "congeneration" as a consequence of Albion's and Luvah's struggle for "dominion" over the body of Vala.

As we have seen, the circumstances surrounding this overtly political incident suggest that, for Blake, power relations function in part to *produce* "the vast form of Nature" (J 43:77–81; E192–3).

Moments like this one are relatively rare in Blake's late poetry. Ultimately neither a strict essentialist nor a consistently rigorous deconstructionist, Blake often formulates views of nature that combine, in a rather unsettling manner, both ontological and discursive or deconstructive modes of poetic critique. The best instance of such a combination occurs in *Milton* where, in the midst of Satanic strife, Los declares that "this mournful day / Must be a blank in Nature" (M 8:20–1; E102). In this passage, as we have seen, Blake's metaphorical language encourages us to imagine nature itself as a kind of *tabula rasa*, formerly written upon by human discourses but now temporarily liberated from such linguistic imposition. The major philosophical implication of this passage is seemingly primitivist in tenor: Los erases the totality of nature's cultural inscriptions, until nature stands naked in its extra-discursive purity. Yet what can be the *nature* of such a nature? Certainly, as a "blank," this strange figure signifies no apprehensible identity and thus no ontological presence. Blake's revisionist allusion to the concept of the *tabula rasa* thus tantalizes us with the possibility of accessing an extra-discursive nature, only to present us, ironically, with a troubling *absence*. At moments like this one, the seeming essentialism that often haunts Blake's vision of nature reveals itself as provisional, the strategic prelude to a radical critique of an authoritative objectivity that, as I argued in my introduction, can all too easily be invoked to support dogmatic understandings of nature as regulatory standard or norm.

Because of its strong antinomian or anti-legalistic tendencies, Blake's critique of regulative authority is often idealistic and seemingly founded upon a primitivist understanding that, beneath the subjective accretions of corrupting social influence, lies an authentic and undistorted social "reality." Consider, for example, Blake's remarks concerning institutional corruption in *Jerusalem*, wherein he differentiates true Art, Liberty, and Religion from their constructed semblances or politically interested representations. Midway through the poem's second chapter, Los refers in seemingly credal antinomian fashion to the various productions of "Law" as "Swelld & bloated General Forms." For Los, such forms are insidious, involving "A pretence of Art, to destroy Art: a pretence of Liberty / To destroy Liberty. a pretence of Religion to destroy Religion" (J 38:19, 30, 35–6; E185). These lines demonstrate Blake's occasional tendency to view institutional ideology in terms of "false consciousness." Because orthodoxy largely controls the social mechanisms of interpretation, it can paradoxically define Art, Liberty, and Religion in ways that are actually destructive of these things. Blake is pointing here, in other words, to the ways the discursively constructed "preten[sions]" of orthodoxy become normalized or naturalized in the social world as destructive realities.

On the same plate in *Jerusalem*, Blake suggests that the complex realm of nature is subject to similar modes of distortion. By deploying destructive practices that produce and support false forms of Art, Law, and Religion, Albion's sons, Scofield and Kox, "accumulate / A World in which Man is by *his* Nature the Enemy of Man" (38:51–2; E185; emphasis added). Scofield's and Kox's world is the self-interested realm of the Ulro, a realm that is quite simply the material world of much Blake criticism (cf. Damon 1988, 416). For many of Blake's readers, it is this realm – the world of nature itself – which stultifies and corrupts its human inhabitants (as Blake seems to suggest later in the poem when he writes of "A World where Man is *by Nature* the enemy of Man" [49:69; E199; emphasis added]). And yet, to essentialize the Ulro in this particular way is to efface *Jerusalem*'s critique of the role human ideology plays in the conceptual construction or production of materiality itself. By failing to grasp Blake's political critique of nature's *regulative* conceptual function in the social world, many readers persist in seeing *Jerusalem* as philosophically hostile to the material world "itself." Such a view not only distorts the central political concerns of Blake's great epic; it entails a critical devaluation of nature that might, to borrow the poet's own rhetorical formulation, be characterized as "a pretence of Nature to destroy Nature." But the Ulro, we must remember, gestures not only towards the material world but also and perhaps primarily towards human self-interest, the anti-relational solipsism that shapes the fallen Albion's view of the world and its living creatures. In the ensuing discussion, therefore, I shall focus on Blake's representations of the relationships between and among humanity, "nature," and the "natural" in *Jerusalem* in order to query the role that such self-interest plays in Blake's philosophy of human-nature relations.

Blake's opposition to extreme forms of human self-interest or self-enclosure is well known. Indeed, *Jerusalem*'s central action recounts the simple tale of Albion's withdrawal from dynamic relationality, his fall into solipsism, and his ultimate renovation as a fully integrated, resocialized human being. Albion's reunion with Jerusalem, his Emanation, is crucial to his renovation, for it is only through a mingling of Emanations that humans may encounter one another without violence. As Los tells Enitharmon,

When in Eternity Man converses with Man they enter
Into each others Bosom (which are Universes of delight)
In mutual interchange. and first their Emanations meet
Surrounded by their Children. if they embrace & comingle
the Human Four-fold Forms mingle also in thunders of Intellect
But if the Emanations mingle not; with storms & agitations
Of earthquakes & consuming fires they roll apart in fear
For Man cannot unite with Man but by their Emanations
Which stand both Male & Female at the Gates of each Humanity[.]
(88:3–11; E246)

This passage describes the social interactions that continually occur within Albion's unfallen eternal form. Albion may in this state be a whole and integral entity, but he should not be understood as a homogeneous primal unity, for he is composed of Zoas, or personified faculties, that continually "converse" with one another "In mutual interchange" through the "comingl[ing]" of their Emanations. As David L. Clark defines it, "the emanation is a trope for the possibility of relationship itself, for the principle of adjoining which inscribes entities in the web of difference" (1994, 186). And yet, if the Emanation tropes a *fundamental* relationality – a relationality existing *prior* to Albion's fall into division and difference – the gendered language Blake uses to describe this dynamic is, as Clark remarks (ibid.), troublesome; for although Los declares that the Emanations "stand *both* Male & Female at the Gates of each Humanity," he subsequently characterizes their mutuality as a mode of "Brotherhood" (J 88:14). Hence while *Jerusalem* continually highlights the importance of relationality – which is a fundamental concept of ecology – it often does so in questionably gendered terms, privileging a seemingly masculinist primal mutuality while depicting the adverse consequences of the fall primarily in the plight of its eponymous heroine, the feminine Emanation Jerusalem. Thus, to a certain extent, *Jerusalem's* critique of self-interest and solipsism – implicit in its poetic emphasis on the necessary commingling of entities – seems inadvertently to reinscribe aspects of the anti-relational dynamic it attempts to oppose.[3]

I shall examine this problem of gender and its relationship to *Jerusalem's* philosophy of nature presently, in my discussion of Vala's function in Blake's mythology. For the moment, I must emphasize that relationality is by no means a purely human phenomenon in *Jerusalem*. This point is an important one; for any attempt to enclose ourselves within the category of humanity by drawing an oppositional limit between humanity and non-human nature entails a grand denial of difference: at the very least, the logic supporting such a stance inevitably homogenizes the multiplicitous entities forced to occupy each side of the oppositional divide.[4] It is significant, then, that *Jerusalem*'s figurative language often associates the human Emanation's function with the earthly or natural landscape. Blake chooses, for example, to figure the failure of emanational "comingl[ings]" between humans in terms of environmental cataclysm: "if the Emanations mingle not," Los declares, then "with storms & agitations / Of earthquakes & consuming fires they roll apart in fear" (88:6, 8–9; E246). While Blake invokes a violent nature to metaphorize the catastrophic consequences of emanational failure, he invokes a peaceful natural landscape to depict the successful and felicitous commingling of Emanations. In the opening lines of *Jerusalem*'s first chapter, for instance, the Saviour presents the poem's ideal of the holistic interrelationship of all entities in curiously natural terms: "I am in you and you in me," he declares, "mutual in love divine: / Fibres of love from man to man thro Albions pleasant land" (4:7–8; E146). In his commentary on this passage, Harold Bloom argues that "imaginative fibres ... must bind man to man if England is to be liberated from the vegetative fibres that form the chains of selfhood and jealousy" (1963, 369). While Bloom has a point here, the opposition he establishes between "imaginative" and "vegetative" fibres is ultimately difficult, perhaps even impossible, to sustain. Quoting Edwin Clarke, Nelson Hilton points out that the very word "fibre" (derived from the latin *fibra*) came into the English language to signify "a basic unit of animal and plant life" (1983, 80). Although Blake certainly asks us imaginatively to rethink the conceptual meaning of "fibre" in *Jerusalem*, it is not clear that he wishes or is able to eradicate the biological and natural aspect of its reference. If Hilton's argument is correct, Blake deploys the term in order to establish a verbal *connection* between the human and vegetable realms (81). Indeed, while one may be able provisionally to differentiate "imaginative" from "vegetative" fibres in Blake's work, one would find it exceedingly difficult to defend the view that the former fibres refer only to humanity while the latter refer to a natural realm essentially opposed to it. Crucial to the present argument, rather, is the peculiar fact that in the opening lines of *Jerusalem*'s first chapter the Saviour conceptualizes "Albions pleasant land" as the primary *locus* of love's dynamic of human interconnection, indeed as the very corporeal medium "thro" which love's imaginative "fibres" perform their redemptive function of joining "man to man" (J 4:7–8).

In the lines directly following the Saviour's pastoral evocation of Albion's land, however, *Jerusalem*'s tonal register abruptly changes.

Suddenly, we learn that "In all the dark Atlantic vale down from the hills of Surrey / A black water accumulates." Subsequent to this ominous transformation of the landscape, moreover, the Saviour declares that "the Divine Vision is darkend" (4:9–10, 13; E146). By hiding his "Emanation lovely Jerusalem / From the vision and fruition of the Holy-one" (4:16–17), Albion has rejected the emanative "Fibres of love" that connect Eternity's human inhabitants one to another, thrusting his "pleasant land" into an "accumulat[ing]" darkness (and auguring, one should note, the self-divided world of Ulro, which, as we saw above, will subsequently be "accumulated" in the poem by Scofield and Kox [38:51–2; E185]). According to Blake's cosmological vision, this correlation of the human incapacity for love and the darkened vision of the natural environment is entirely logical, for Albion represents in Blake's mythology not only humanity but England's material landscapes as well. Indeed, Albion's condition exemplifies Blake's notion that a direct correspondence exists between internal and external realities, for Albion can undergo no emotional, intellectual, or psychological alteration that does not also affect all aspects of his physical geography. Thus, one major symptom of Albion's "souls disease" and its darkening of the "Divine Vision" (4:13) is the "darkend" appearance of England's terrain (4:9–10), a terrain, one might say, whose transformation prophesies the possibility that Albion's fall will result in the "dark-end" of Non-Entity.

Significantly, Blake's reference in *Jerusalem* to "Albions pleasant land" recalls the opening lyric to *Milton*, wherein Blake locates the building of "Jerusalem, / In Englands green & pleasant Land" (M 1:14–15; E96). Although this lyric suggests that the building of Jerusalem must foundationally incorporate "greenery," such a thesis has rarely been advanced by Blake's most prominent readers. Alluding to *Milton*'s opening lyric in his discussion of *Jerusalem*, Northrop Frye argues, for instance, that the New Jerusalem must *replace* "Englands green & pleasant Land" in order to be actualized. For Frye, quite simply, England must "turn its green and pleasant land *into* Jerusalem" (1970, 392; emphasis added); since the effort "to restore the New Jerusalem in (not to) England" (396) would contradict his thesis that the city of God must be the site of "absolute civilization" (389). One of the great problems with this aspect of Frye's archetypal reading is its presupposition that Blake's own syntax in *Milton*'s opening lyric is erroneous and must be altered by the reader in the process of interpretation.

Although his work is strewn with absolutist rhetoric, Blake can be wary of absolutes; and a glance at various aspects of *Jerusalem* will show that the relationship he constructs between nature and culture in this poem does not partake of an absolute dichotomy opposing non-human and human being or natural process and human cultural activity. To be sure, at the bottom of *Jerusalem*'s title page design (see Figure 15) Blake depicts the fallen Jerusalem as a "vegetated" entity whose human form is imprisoned in "the Sleep of Ulro" (4:1; E146).[5] Above this figure to the left, the newly awakened Jerusalem looks down at her sleeping self with an expression of utter dismay, suggesting that she now recognizes the harmfulness of her earlier vegetated state. In her fully awakened state, at the top of the page, however, Jerusalem resembles not a typical human angel but a human-insect hybrid whose wings are tinted, significantly, in gorgeous green.[6] On the same plate, moreover, the colour green provides a background for the letter "i" in Albion's name, establishing yet another iconographic correspondence between human selfhood (the "I") and the green world of nature. Hence in the design comprising the poem's very title page, we begin to see that both Albion and Jerusalem, Blake's respective representatives of Selfhood and Emanation, need not be understood as strictly human or cultural entities.

Like Albion and Jerusalem, Blake's Christ embodies both culture and nature – the realms of "vision *and* fruition" (4:17; E146; emphasis added) – in the poem. In chapter 2, for example, we are told that Christ "is all in all, / In Eden: in the garden of God: and in the heavenly Jerusalem" (34:24–5; E180). Later, we discover similarly that "every Human Vegetated Form in its inward recesses / Is a house of ple[as]antness & a garden of delight Built by the / Sons & Daughters of Los in Bowlahoola & in Cathedron" (73:50–2; E229). In each of these passages natural process, inhabiting the tended space of the garden, accompanies the more overt cultural constructions of the house and the city. And although the garden refers to a domesticated landscape (as opposed to the chaotic wilderness of "unconquered" nature), Blakean cities are by no means opposed to natural processes. As Los declares in the final chapter, "The land is markd for desolation & unless we plant / The seeds of Cities and of Villages in the Human bosom / Albion must be a rock of blood" (83:54–6; E242). Los's reference to the planting of seeds figures the genealogy of "Cities & Villages" in organic terms, suggesting the need for humans to build civilization in ways that are continuous with, rather than strictly opposed to, processes of biological growth. Far from positing a strict dichotomy between nature and humanity (by which the oppositional limits of Frye's "absolute civilization" would be delineated), Los's remarks warn us that a dichotomized view of these two realms will destroy England, transforming Albion into "a rock of blood." Two plates later, Los speaks again of the necessity to "plant ... / The Seeds [of cities] ... in the bosom of Time & Spaces womb / To spring up

15   *Jerusalem*, plate 2
Yale Centre for British Art, Paul Mellon Collection

for Jerusalem" (85:27–9; E244). These lines suggest that the successful building of Jerusalem will not be accomplished by a rejection of nature or natural processes. To quote Peter Otto, the *entire* universe of Los and Enitharmon "is the ground necessary for visionary expansion" (1991, 27). In the ensuing discussion, I shall explore the conceptual and material territory of this necessary "ground."

ALBION'S FALL AND THE FALL OF NATURE

If *Jerusalem* offers its readers a tantalizing glimpse of Albion's unfallen condition in the Saviour's early reference to "Fibres of love from man to man thro Albions pleasant land" (4:8), this glimpse is merely retrospective, for the verb tense of the Saviour's subsequent question – "Where hast thou hidden thy Emanation lovely Jerusalem / From the vision and fruition of the Holy-one?" (4:16–17) – reveals that Albion's fall has occurred prior to this moment in what Morton Paley calls "the anterior myth" (1983, 199). The fall, which sets the stage for virtually all other events in the poem, is in a sense unimaginable; for if, on a cosmic level, Albion's limbs contain "all things in Heaven & Earth" (plate 27; E171), then his human form embodies *both* Eternity and time, making his fall from Eternity illogical or self-contradictory. Reading this problem as an aspect of *Jerusalem*'s textual instability, Paul Youngquist remarks that, with the fall, the "One Being identical with all things appears not to be identical with himself" (1993, 605). This insight is important, for it sheds light on the problem of anthropomorphism in *Jerusalem*. On the one hand, as I argued in chapter 1, Blake's anthropomorphic cosmology – his notion that all things are integral human particulars of Albion's cosmic human form – enables the conceptualization of an environmental ethics in which each and every thing must be granted the respect and dignity that traditional Judaeo-Christianity tends to reserve exclusively for humans. With Albion's fall out of relationship and into solipsistic self-enclosure, on the other hand, this ethical anthropomorphism becomes somehow inoperable. No longer identical with himself but internally divided, Albion begins to engage in oppressive acts of anthropomorphic projection, denying the particular alterity of the natural realm by colonizing it in terms of his now solipsistic sense of self-identity.

Albion's first significant act of self-projection occurs in his opening dialogue with Christ. This encounter is important, because it provides a template for all subsequent self/other interactions in the poem prior to Blake's redemptive apocalypse. Crucially, since Albion's limbs contain all things temporal and eternal, his dialogue with the Saviour must in some sense be enacted internally. Thus, Albion's seemingly blasphemous notion that Christ is nothing but a "Phantom of the over heated brain" (4:24; E146) is, in a sense, an accurate assessment of his circumstance; for Christ is indeed a part of his own intellectual (not to mention physical) being. Albion fails, however, to understand that Christ's existence and his own are of a piece. His newly embraced phantasy of an externalized Christ is mirrored in his subsequent encounters with all entities (whether human or non-human), for every thing he meets is, properly speaking, an aspect or projection of his own self.

Interestingly, Albion's notion of the "separateness" of non-human entities seems to have played a decisive role in his fall, at least as he describes this incident in a crucial retrospective gesture towards the anterior myth:

We reared mighty Stones: we danced naked around them:
Thinking to bring Love into light of day, to Jerusalems shame:
Displaying our Giant limbs to all the winds of heaven! Sudden
Shame siezd us ... (24:4–7; E169)

It is important to note here that Albion's "Sudden / Shame" directly follows his construction of the "winds of heaven" as separate viewing spectators of his giant dance. Indeed, he repeats this anthropomorphism four plates later when he declares similarly that "all / These hills & valleys are accursed witnesses of Sin / I therefore condense them into solid rocks" (28:8–10; E174). As in *Paradise Lost*, the fall of nature in *Jerusalem* seems to be coincident with or a consequence of the fall of humanity. Yet Albion's remarks in each of these passages suggest that nature's fall, rather than involving an ontological transformation of the material world itself (as in so many of the world's mainstream religious mythologies[7]), is perceptually based upon an act of anthropomorphic projection. From Albion's human standpoint, the *idea* that the things of nature are separate gazing "witnesses" of his behaviour unaccountably entails a "Sudden" self-reflexive understanding of that behaviour as sinful. Concomitantly, according to Albion's logic, the things of nature, having participated in his sin via their ostensible witnessing, become "accursed." Los's statement, later in the poem, that "the accursed things were [Albion's] own affections" (42:3; E189) is highly significant in this regard. Repeating the word "accursed," this statement, explaining Albion's act of "Brooding on [the] evil" of "others" (42:2, 1), recalls Albion's earlier accusation against the things of nature, where his own sense of shame causes him to view these things as evil "witnesses." In Blake's mythology, the anthropomorphism implicit in this notion of "witnessing" founds the original devaluation or fall of nature, whose non-human entities, as we shall see, become explicitly separated from humanity in the wake of Albion's dancing display of "Giant limbs." Later in the poem, the Spectre rejoices in this "Giant dance," for this entity, who "has no Emanation but what he imbibes from decieving / A Victim" (65:58–60; E217), is the product of the very conceptual separation of entities that makes possible the anthropomorphic "saming" of non-human nature, an act that aggrandizes the Selfhood by painting the external world entirely in its own colours.

After condensing the "accursed" "hills & valleys" into "solid rocks," Albion's anthropomorphic colonization of non-human entities gathers momentum:

> He sat by Tyburns brook, and underneath his heel, shot up!
> A deadly Tree, he nam'd it Moral Virtue, and the Law
> Of God who dwells in Chaos hidden from the human sight.
> (28:14–16; E174)

Subsequently, this tree shoots "into many a Tree," a disturbing growth the narrator refers to as "an endless labyrinth of woe! / From willing sacrifice of Self, to sacrifice of (miscall'd) Enemies / For Atonement" (28:19–21). In light of the pathetic fallacies discussed above, we must examine Albion's relationship to this "deadly Tree" most carefully; for after his encounter with this tree and his parenthetically highlighted act of "miscalling" (wherein Albion mistakenly identifies his friends as "Enemies"), Albion misnames his twelve sacrificial altars of "rough unhewn rocks" "Justice, and Truth" (28:21–3). This set of obvious misidentifications raises the likelihood that Albion's earlier identification of the tree as "Moral Virtue" is similarly misguided. The tree, in short, is not a poetic representative of a natural world that has somehow insidiously contaminated Albion's being. On the contrary, it has been anthropomorphically colonized by Albion's divided psyche, and its misnaming as "Moral Virtue" is symptomatic of Albion's own "souls disease" (4:13; E146). It is appropriate, then, that Blake should represent the fallen Albion's penchant for anthropomorphic projection (the sacrificial "saming" of externalized entities) as part of his misguided effort to achieve a homogenizing "At-one-ment."

Blake depicts the relationship between Albion's anthropomorphism and his fall most succinctly in the design to plate 19 (see Figure 16). Lying "on the ground in pain & tears" (18:46; E163), the

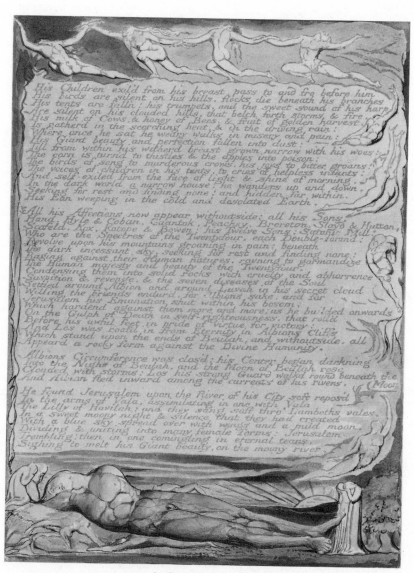

His Children exil'd from his breast pass to and fro before him
His birds are silent on his hills. flocks die beneath his branches
His tents are fallen; his trumpets, and the sweet sound of his harp
Are silent on his clouded hills, that belch forth storms, & fire
His milk of Cows, & honey of Bees, & fruit of golden harvest,
Is gatherd in the scorching heat, & in the driving rain:
Where, once he sat he weary walks in misery and pain:
His Giant beauty and perfection fallen into dust:
Till from within his witherd breast grown narrow with his woes:
The corn is turnd to thistles & the apples into poison:
The birds of song to murderous crows, his joys to bitter groans!
The voices of children in his tents, to cries of helpless infants!
And self-exiled from the face of light & shine of morning,
In the dark world a narrow house! he wanders up and down,
Seeking for rest and finding none: and hidden far within,
His Eon weeping in the cold and desolated Earth.

All his Affections now appear withoutside; all his Sons,
Hand, Hyle & Coban. Guantok, Peachey, Brereton, Sl[oy]d & Hutton,
Scofeld; Kox, Kotope & Bowen; his Twelve Sons; Satanic Mill:
Who are the Spectres of the Twentyfour, each Double-formed:
Revolve upon his mountains groaning in pain: beneath
His dark incessant sky, seeking for rest and finding none:
Raging against their Human natures, ravning to garmandize
The Human majesty and beauty of the Twentyfour.
Condensing them into solid rocks with cruelty and abhorrence
Suspicion & revenge, & the seven diseases of the Soul
Settled around Albion and around Luvah in his secret cloud
Willing the friends endurd, for Albions sake, and for
Jerusalem his Emanation, shut within his bosom:
Which harden'd against them more and more; as he builded onwards
On the Gulph of Death in self-righteousness. that roll'd
Before his awful feet, in pride of Virtue for victory:
And Los was roofd in from Eternity in Albions Cliffs
Which stand upon the ends of Beulah, and withoutside, all
Appeard a rocky form against the Divine Humanity.

Albions Circumference was closd; his Center began darkning
Into the Night of Beulah, and the Moon of Beulah rose
Clouded with storms: Los his strong Guard walkd round beneath the
And Albion fled inward among the currents of his rivers. (Moon

He found Jerusalem upon the River of his City soft repos'd
In the arms of Vala, assimilating in one with Vala
The Lilly of Havilah: and they sang soft thro' Lambeths vales,
In a sweet moony night & silence that they had created
With a blue sky spread over with wings and a mild moon,
Dividing & uniting into many female forms: Jerusalem
Trembling; then in one commingling in eternal tears,
Sighing to melt his Giant beauty, on the moony river.

16   *Jerusalem*, plate 19
Yale Centre for British Art, Paul Mellon Collection

fallen Albion has literally crushed two other creatures in the process
of his fall. Although these creatures appear to be human, the figure
to the left has a distinctively birdlike head; and the limbs of both
figures appear to be rooting themselves into the soil beneath them.
These oddities of representation – in which human entities are not
entirely differentiated from the non-human beings inhabiting or com-
prising their environment – can be read in two possible ways. On the
one hand, the design suggests that Albion's fall has resulted in the
animalization or vegetation of humanity (a possibility that I shall
examine in detail later in this chapter). But given Albion's numerous
acts of pathetic fallacy in *Jerusalem*'s text, we might also see this
design as enacting in visual terms the process of anthropomorphic
projection, which violates the integrity of the non-human "other" by
defining it in terms of the human "same." By taking on human char-
acteristics, Albion's animals and vegetations become monstrous, per-
haps even "accursed." Understood in such a light, this design draws
a correlation between Albion's fall and his self-centred view of
nature, a correlation emphasizing the potentially deadly violence of
his anthropomorphic tendencies.

These tendencies are especially interesting in light of Blake's rep-
resentation in *Jerusalem* of the familial relationship existing between
Albion and geographic phenomena. On plate 36, the very valleys,
hills, and rivers of Albion's landscape express this relationship in a
touching lament: "Albion is sick! said every Valley, every mournful
Hill / And every River: our brother Albion is sick to death" (36:11–
12; E182). At this point in the poem, we learn that the "hills & val-
leys" (whom Albion earlier denounces as "accursed witnesses of
Sin") are actually his own siblings. Albion's falling out with these
members of his family is symptomatic of an important change in his
condition following the "Giant dance," a change that can be under-
stood by attending to the narrator's comments concerning Christ's
behaviour in relation to Albion. For after Albion turns away from
"Universal Love," the "mild ... Saviour" follows him,

Displaying the eternal Vision! the Divine Similitude!
In loves and tears of brothers, sisters, sons, fathers, and friends
Which if Man ceases to behold, he ceases to exist ... (34:7, 10, 11–13)

In the wake of his dance, Albion "ceases to behold" his brothers, the
geographical forms that mourn his fall. Beholding instead his own
"accursed" and distorted anthropomorphic construction of these
entities, Albion loses all sight of "the eternal Vision" displayed in
their "loves and tears." Thus, according to the Saviour's logic, Albion

"ceases to exist." In a context emphasizing the interrelationship of all earthly entities, such a development is entirely logical, for "the self, like the cell, has no being at all outside [its] environmental context" (Nash 1989, 159). Considering Albion's dilemma with this insight in mind, we can understand that his denial of relationship with the familial things of nature is also and simultaneously a denial of the self, a denial whose immediate consequence is a fall into the shadowy realm Blake refers to as "Non-Entity" (J 5:51; E148).

Albion, it must be noted, is aware of a connection between his self-described pathology and the plights of his family members, both human and non-human. As he declares in a touching lament,

> Shame divides Families. Shame hath divided Albion in sunder!
> First fled my Sons, & then my Daughters, then my Wild Animations
> My Cattle next, last ev'n the Dog of my Gate. the Forests fled
> The Corn-fields, & the breathing Gardens outside separated
> The Sea; the Stars: the Sun: the Moon: drivn forth by my disease ...
> (21:6–10; E166)

Albion's shame, based on a presumably unprecedented subject/object division in his self-conception, causes all things externalized by this division actively to "flee" from him and from his oppressive anthropomorphic practice. This turn of events suggests that Albion's process of withdrawal manifests itself, as it were, bi-directionally. While his shamed psyche retreats repressively into itself, the geography and "Wild Animations" that comprise his physical makeup flee in an external, outward direction. It is in this sense that Albion himself is "divided ... in sunder."

Mirroring Albion's pathology, Albion's cities and their inhabitants become "sick to death" (66:68; E219).[8] In an attempt to resolve this dilemma, "Wales & Scotland" send

> the Dove & Raven: & in vain the Serpent over the mountains.
> And in vain the Eagle & Lion over the four-fold wilderness.
> They return not: but generate in rocky places desolate.
> They return not; but build a habitation separate from Man.
> (66:67, 70–3; E219)

The significantly "four-fold" character of the wilderness in this passage contrasts sharply with Albion's less than four-fold state (a state symptomatic of the falling out that has occurred among the Four Zoas comprising his internal being). This contrast suggests that such wilderness – nature not yet colonized by Albion's acts of anthropomorphic projection – might play an important role in restoring fallen humanity to the wholeness of its prelapsarian condition. In the human/animal division that it ultimately depicts, however, this passage recalls God's promise to Noah that "the fear of you and the dread of you shall be upon every beast of the earth, and upon every fowl of the air, upon all that moveth upon the earth, and upon all the fishes of the sea" (Genesis 9:2). Although the articulation of this unprecedented circumstance directly precedes God's promise to establish a "cosmic covenant" (Northcott 1996, 168) between himself, humanity, and literally "every living creature" (Genesis 9:8–16), it is nevertheless significant that God forecasts the more immediate dissolution of humanity's currently harmonious relationship with the non-human world in the context of his reaffirmation of human "dominion" over nature, a dominion originally granted to Adam and Eve in the prelapsarian context of Genesis 1:28–30 (Nash 1989, 89). In the postlapsarian world, it would seem, human dominion takes on an increasingly malevolent aspect, as animals come to "fear" and "dread" their human lords. The point I wish to make here is that, from the non-human perspective that Blake constructs in the wake of Albion's fall (and to which he rather heretically attributes some agency in his presentation of the animals' refusal to cooperate with the human designs of Wales and Scotland), Albion's anthropomorphisms entail an oppressive domination of nature, one that the animals choose to reject even at the cost of perpetuating the "separation" grounding the very anthropomorphic practice that oppresses them.

Albion's penchant for pathetic fallacy, it must be emphasized, affects not only externalized nature but also his own sense of self-identity. On plate 43, for example, we learn that "Albions Reactor" "hath compelld Albion to become a Punisher & hath possessd / Himself of Albions Forests & Wilds!" (43:11, 16–17; E191). Since all things are ultimately parts of Albion's identity in *Jerusalem*, Albion's Reactor should be seen as an externalized aspect of his own divided selfhood. Thus, Albion "reacts" to his own pathetic fallacy – that which "possess[es]" his "Forests & Wilds" – by (mis)naming externalized entities and (mis)identifying their motivations. Reacting, in other words, to his own affected notion that such things as hills and valleys have witnessed his ostensible sin, Albion "Punish[es]" these things by conceiving of them as "accursed." Such behaviour is akin to that which characterizes Hegel's concept of the "unhappy consciousness," which, to quote Judith Butler, "berates itself constantly, setting up one part of itself as a pure judge aloof from contradiction and disparaging its changeable [i.e., physical] part as inessential, although ineluctably tied to it" (1997, 46). As we have seen, Albion is profoundly "tied to" the things of nature by the familial bond he shares with them; but he attempts to disavow this bond by retreating into his atomized psyche. Wishing, moreover, that Vala could weave for him "a chaste / Body over [his] unchaste Mind" (21:11–12; E166), he implies that his corporeal aspect – the entire body of nature – is of questionable chastity. Although he also condemns his mind as "unchaste," Albion's very ability to pass such a judgment on his physical or appetitive being implies his belief that an aspect of his divided consciousness retains the necessary chastity or purity required to evaluate its ostensibly unchaste part.

The fragmentation of Albion's consciousness has important consequences for his understanding of the physical "nature" of his pathology:

> The disease of Shame covers me from head to feet: I have no hope
> Every boil upon my body is a separate & deadly Sin.
> Doubt first assaild me, then Shame took possession of me
> Shame divides Families. Shame hath divided Albion in sunder!
> (21:3–6; E166)

According to Frye, Albion's "boils and plagues represent the physical misery of the state of nature," which is itself "the source" of his pathology (1970, 361). Given Albion's atomistic understanding of his condition, however, it is more likely that his pathology associates him not with Frye's vaguely essentialist "state of nature" but with the Enlightenment's paradigmatic *construction* of nature in its all-pervasive adaptations of Newton's science; for during the eighteenth century, many thinkers, including Blake, all too quickly identified Newton's undefined "particles" with Democritean, Lucretian, or Epicurean "atoms" (Bronowski 1960, 36). In short, because Albion is unable in his pathological self-division to conceptualize his "disease" in holistic terms, he must see each of his boils as "a separate ... Sin." Viewed thus atomistically, each symptomatic boil would need to be treated in isolation for Albion to be successfully restored to health. Needless to say, at such a rate (that is, without some kind of gestalt intervention) a comprehensive cure for his condition would be all but impossible. Reflecting his strange affliction, Albion's universe itself becomes atomized in deistical mechanistic fashion, as all phenomena become "separated" from his giant form, externalized or "drivn forth," as he subsequently puts it, "by my disease" (21:9–10).

In *Jerusalem*, Albion's efforts to deny the multiplicity of connections existing between the self and its definitive contexts (both social and environmental) produces the Spectre of analytic reasoning. In the second chapter of copies A, C, and F, for example (the order of which Erdman's edition follows), Albion's "Spectrous / Chaos" (29:1–2; E175) appears directly in the wake of his "building A Strong / Fortification against the Divine Humanity" (28:25–6; E174), that cosmic body which, as we saw in chapter 1, provides the morphological basis of Blake's panvitalistic and anti-atomistic organicism. The Spectre's status as "the Reasoning Power / An Abstract objecting power," causes it, significantly, to become "A murderer of its own Body" (10:13–14, 12; E153). To the extent that Albion's body includes the natural world itself, it is appropriate that his renovation is preceded by his falling into "the Furrow," where he is "Plowed in among the Dead" (57:13–14; E207); for this event adumbrates Albion's necessary reunion with his earthly aspect, the material part of himself that has been "murdered" by his abstract and atomistic reasoning power.

The "Reasoning Power," Blake declares, is "An Abstract objecting power, that Negatives every thing" (10:13–14; E153). According to the epistemology of contemporary physical science, in Blake's view, "every thing" outside of the reasoning mind is "Negative[d]," objectified, that is, as the "not-me." Since, as Blake never tires of proclaiming in *Jerusalem*, the human subject "becomes what it beholds,"[9] the mind itself inevitably becomes an object of its own objective reasoning processes. This is why, in the wake of Albion's self-imposed exile, it is not only the "Earth" that is "desolated" (19:16; E164) but Albion's own subjectivity: "All his Affections," we are told, "now appear withoutside" (19:17). As Blake describes this transformation two plates earlier, abstraction is a form of "Envy Revenge & Cruelty / Which separated the stars from the mountains: the mountains from Man / And left Man, a little grovelling Root, outside of Himself" (17:30–2; E162). When the paradigmatic reification of an object-world or objectified nature is taken to its logical conclusion, humanity becomes, in short, "separated from [its] subjective self, objectivized and alien, to be manipulated as any other objects in the universe" (Doskow 1982b, 64). It is in this sense that the Spectrous Newtonian Satan – an aspect of Albion's own externalized affections – produces "A World where Man is *by Nature* the enemy of Man" (49:69; E199; emphasis added).

It is perhaps paradoxical to conclude that one of the products of Enlightenment thought is a denial of the very subjective processes that give rise to it; but as many commentators have remarked, mechanistic materialism has never been able adequately to account for the existence of the human mind. In *Jerusalem*, virtually all of Blake's references to the human brain point towards this problem; and it is likely that Blake's obsession with vegetative fibres involves his intellectual

resistance to contemporary thinking regarding the "fibrillous" struc-
ture and makeup of the human brain (Hilton 1983, 81). A brief discus-
sion of contemporary neuroscientific theory will help to clarify this
point. During the late seventeenth century, the renowned neurophys-
iologist Thomas Willis, whose work profoundly influenced John
Locke's theory of cognition, in a sense glorified the human brain by
arguing unprecedentedly that it (and its associated system of nervous
fibres) was the *only* seat of the soul (G.S. Rousseau 1976, 144). In an
age of increasing objectivity and scepticism, however, the soul's divin-
ity began to lose ground to the processes characterizing its physiolog-
ical being; and by 1796 Joseph Priestley was able to argue that this
crucial aspect of human identity was merely and only "an activity of
the brain and the nervous system" (Crehan 1984, 290). In *The Four
Zoas*, Blake's Tharmas arguably invokes this neurophysiological
denial of the human soul when he asks Enion "Why wilt thou Exam-
ine every little fibre of my soul / Spreading them out before the Sun
like Stalks of flax to dry" (4:29–30; E302). Here, not only are the soul's
"fibres" atomistically individuated, objectified, and externalized; at
the poetical level their exposure to the light of scientific scrutiny
effaces divinity: they are spread out "before the Sun," in the sense that
they are given priority *over the Son* who is for Blake the soul's Saviour.

Blake emphasizes the violence implicit in such an objectification of
human consciousness when he speaks in *Jerusalem* of the brain being
"cut round beneath the temples shrieking" (58:7; E207; see also 66:64;
E219). Foreshadowing the logical conclusion of this objectifying pro-
cess, Blake writes that "The Twelve Daughters in Rahab & Tirzah
have circumscribd the Brain / Beneath & pierced it thro the midst
with a golden pin" (67:41–2; E220). To the extent that Rahab and
Tirzah personify the Baconian "womb of nature" (Bacon 1860, 4:100),
this passage suggests that physical science's "penetration" of an
objectified feminine nature leads to the penetration (or "piercing") of
the masculine brain that perpetrates this act. As far as Blake's thor-
oughgoing poetical critique is concerned, objective science turns
every thing into an object, not excluding the mind and soul of the
scientist who practises it. Dennis Lee summarizes this process suc-
cinctly in his commentary on the rise of modern-day neurobiology,
which takes the human brain as its *object* of study. Traditionally, Lee
points out, consciousness has been understood as "valuative and
qualitied"; but objective studies of the brain problematize this
assumption, offering instead "value-free equations for the behaviour
of the cortical synapses." From the standpoint of neurobiology, con-
sciousness is merely "a subjective interpretation we have mistakenly
projected onto the brain, but which has finally floated clear of its

object." As with Blake's object-brain "pierced ... thro the midst with a golden pin," there is, for Lee, "only one conclusion open to consciousness" in the wake of recent brain theory: "consciousness is dead" (Lee 1977, 52–3).

Blake would have agreed most heartily with the terms of Lee's argument: the notion that an objective view of nature destroys the mind of the objectifying reasoner is ubiquitous in *Jerusalem*. The design to plate 62 (see Figure 17) – depicting a "brazen (not a living) serpent ... bound on [Albion's] head like an instrument of torture" (Erdman 1974, 341) – demonstrates this dynamic most dramatically. On plate 43, Blake twice figures "the vast form of Nature" as a serpent (43:76, 80; E192–3). Recalling this poetic figuration, we can interpret the brazen serpent binding Albion's head on plate 62 as an iconographic figure for the objectified form of nature itself. Albion's objective epistemology not only kills the serpent nature (hence its brazen rather than living form in the design); it also tortures and threatens ultimately to destroy Albion's own consciousness by negating his subjective interiority. That Albion has interiorized the objectified world around him is apparent in the similarity between his own eyes and the external peacock-feather eyes that encircle the brazen-serpent outline around his head. If we interpret the small human figure at the bottom of the plate as an image of Albion in his original naked form, we can better understand the fallen Albion's dilemma. As he confronts his own objectified image in the form of the tortured giant whose head has been circumscribed by the epistemology of his object world, Albion becomes what he beholds. That Albion's pathology has both social and ecological ramifications is suggested by the menacing flames rising up the page; for these flames threaten to engulf and consume both of the human forms in the design *and* the green turf upon which they stand. Thus, the violence implicit in Albion's objectifying acts of anthropomorphism has come full circle, threatening to destroy not only the things of an externalized nature but his own individualized being as well. Because such destruction has implications for our understanding of Vala's function in *Jerusalem*, we would do well at this point to investigate Vala's character as Blake unfolds it in the poem's text and designs.

VALA, PATRIARCHY, AND THE POLITICS OF NATURE

Partly through conceptual oversimplification and the critical need to deploy a convenient taxonomical shorthand, Vala has inspired the rebuke and disdain of generations of Blake scholars. Traditionally,

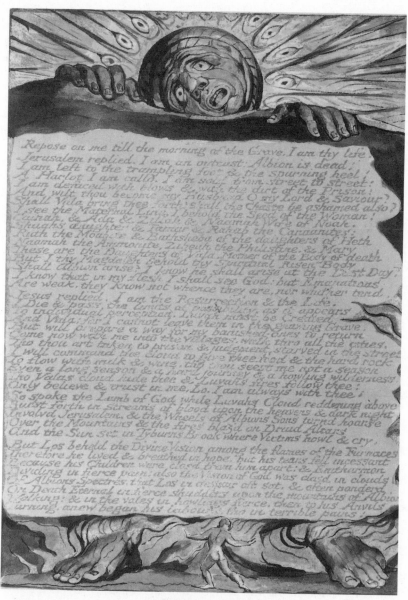

Repose on me till the morning of the Grave. I am thy life
Jerusalem replied. I am an outcast: Albion is dead!
I am left to the trampling foot & the spurning heel!
A Harlot I am calld. I am sold from street to street:
I am defaced with blows & with the dirt of the Prison!
And with thou become my Husband O my Lord & Saviour?
Shall Vala bring thee forth! shall the Chaste be ashamed also?
I see the Maternal Line, I behold the Seed of the Woman!
Cainah, & Ada & Zillah & Naamah Wife of Noah.
Shuahs daughter & Tamar & Rahab the Canaanites:
Ruth the Moabite & Bathsheba of the daughters of Heth
Naamah the Ammonite, Zibeah the Philistine, & Mary
These are the Daughters of Vala, Mother of the Body of death
But I thy Magdalen behold thy Spiritual Risen Body
Shall Albion arise? I know he shall arise at the Last Day!
I know that in my flesh I shall see God: but Emanations
Are weak. they know not whence they are, nor whither tend.

Jesus replied. I am the Resurrection & the Life.
I Die & pass the limits of possibility, as it appears
To individual perception. Luvah must be Created
And Vala; for I cannot leave them in the gnawing Grave.
But will prepare a way for my banished-ones to return
Come now with me into the Villages. walk thro all the Cities.
Tho thou art taken to prison & judgment, starved in the streets
I will command the Cloud to give thee food & the hard rock
To flow with milk & wine, tho thou seest me not a season
Even a long season & a hard journey & a howling wilderness!
Tho Vala's cloud hide thee & Luvah's fires follow thee!
Only believe & trust in me, Lo. I am always with thee!

So spoke the Lamb of God while Luvahs Cloud reddening above
Burst forth in streams of blood upon the heavens & dark night
Involved Jerusalem. & the Wheels of Albions Sons turnd hoarse
Over the Mountains & the fires blaz'd on Druid Altars
And the Sun set in Tyburns Brook where Victims howl & cry.

But Los beheld the Divine Vision among the flames of the Furnaces
Therefore he lived & breathed in hope. but his tears fell incessant
Because his Children were closd from him apart: & Enitharmon
Dividing in fierce pain: also the Vision of God was closd in clouds
Of Albions Spectres, that Los in despair oft sat, & often pondered
On Death Eternal in fierce shuddrings upon the mountains of Albion
Walking: & in the vales in howlings fierce, then to his Anvils
Turning, anew began his labours, tho in terrible pains

17   Jerusalem, plate 62

Yale Centre for British Art, Paul Mellon Collection

Vala has been defined in essentialist terms as a personification of "nature" itself: she is, to cite a handful of examples, "nature on earth" (Frye 1970, 263), "the laws of nature" (Damon 1988, 430), "the possessive love of a fixed natural order" (Bloom 1963, 378), "purely physical nature ... control[ling] the world in which she exists" (Doskow 1982b, 19), and "nature wanting to be all in all" (Hagstrum 1973, 112). What is especially curious about such critical evaluations of Vala's character (most explicitly so in the last two definitions I have cited) is the degree of agency casually attributed in Vala's name to the realm of nature she ostensibly symbolizes. Far from being a cultural cipher, an empty signifier subject to contested and arbitrary productions of meaning, Vala is, for numerous critics, an insidious force controlling the world, actively "wanting to be all in all." Thus, Jean H. Hagstrum argues that Vala, in the guise of "the dominant Female Will," "extends her sway from nature to philosophy, which she naturalizes into mechanism, and to religion, which she naturalizes into deism" (1973, 112). Or, as Minna Doskow's more comprehensive formulation would have it, "Nature's destructiveness ... expands to include the destructiveness of material institutions, penal codes, civil laws (courts), wars (armies), civil institutions, and nations, as well as the closest human relationships (families), and all human expression (tongues)" (1982b, 127). In both of these arguments (which are in many ways representative of discussions of the Vala-nature nexus in Blake's work), an active Vala wilfully contaminates the cultural realm (which must thus be on its guard against her imposition) and not vice versa.

If we begin to approach Vala from a generic perspective, however, we can see that her textual status is subject to some significant conventional constraints. This aspect of Vala's generic status can be clarified by a brief discussion of William Hayley's 1782 *Essay on Epic Poetry*, which, as Joseph Wittreich has demonstrated (1972, *passim*), influenced Blake in important ways. Understanding, with numerous of his contemporaries, that the English epic required renovation, Hayley asserted that the dualism of "Heaven and Hell" had been exhausted as an epic structural principle; thus, he urged England's poets to invent a "new" epic mythology (5:268). A glance at Blake's late epics demonstrates Blake's ultimate agreement with such a prescription. In *The Four Zoas, Milton,* and *Jerusalem*, he largely replaces the Heaven/Hell opposition of the Christian epic with that of Eternity/Nature, personifying nature as the female character Vala. In a sense, then, Blake condemns nature *in advance* by making Vala occupy the structural space attributed to Satan or Hell in influential epics like *The Divine Comedy* and *Paradise Lost*. And yet we would do well to consider Vala's character in light of Blake's famous critique of *Paradise Lost* in *The Marriage of Heaven and Hell*; for by dismantling Milton's epic Heaven/Hell dualism in this text, Blake inadvertently encourages his readers to question the structurally similar Eternity/Nature dualism that haunts his own epics, and thus to revalue what he revealingly calls, in his annotations to Swedenborg, "meer Nature or Hell" (E605).

There is much evidence in *Jerusalem*, moreover, that Vala, far from being an essentialist symbol of an insidious realm of "nature" per se, is, like the energetic Satan of *Paradise Lost*, very much a construct of the institutionalized discourses that name her and define her significance. Among the most important of these discourses is that of contemporary science: Jerusalem's "Shadow," Blake writes, "is Vala, builded by the Reasoning power in Man" (39:40; E187). Vala is thus the product of Albion's unimaginative, analytical Spectre; since elsewhere in the poem Blake identifies the Spectre as "the Reasoning Power in every Man" (J 54:7; E203). As we have seen, the Spectre personifies a form of cognition belonging to the epistemology and methodology of mechanistic natural philosophy. Thus, Albion's Spectre exclaims, "Am I not Bacon & Newton & Locke[?]" (54:17). Clearly, as the relationship between Vala and the Spectre suggests, Vala is no extra-cultural "given" and, therefore, no independent external agency: she is a *model* of nature "builded" or produced by Enlightenment natural philosophy.

More than this, Vala is the product of institutionalized religion and its self-serving conceptions of nature. Significantly, it is the Sons of Albion – among the most untrustworthy narrators in the poem – who explicitly identify her as "Babylon the City of Vala" and "the Goddess Virgin-Mother," declaring that "She is our Mother! Nature!" (18:29–30; E163). And it is Albion, that imposer of phantasy upon externalized entities, who asks Vala "art thou not Babylon? / Art thou Nature Mother of all!" (30:8–9; E176). As Karl Kiralis remarked in a study published over forty years ago, these identifications of Vala as Mother Nature are "fallen ... conception[s] of her and not, as some critics have assumed, [her] basic meaning." Thus, Kiralis correctly concludes, "*Nature* is not an adequate description of Vala" (1961, 105). More accurately – and the difference is crucial – Vala personifies Western humanity's discursive conceptions of the natural world. In *Jerusalem*, these conceptions are consistently coloured by the various deployments and contestations of politics and power.

The con-fusion of "nature" and religious politics in the construction of Vala's identity is most apparent when, as we are told, Albion's Sons "took their Mother Vala, and ... crown'd her with gold: / They namd her Rahab, & gave her power over the Earth" (78:15–16; E234). Critics often interpret Vala's identification as Rahab as part and parcel of Blake's condemnation of nature, for Rahab, in the New Testament, is "Mystery, Babylon the Great, the mother of harlots and abominations of the earth" (Revelation 17:5). As we have seen, such a reading of Vala's character associates her with a natural world that colonizes and corrupts human spirituality, literally inventing, in the process, deism, or "natural religion." But Vala's role as Rahab is problematic: like her identification as Mother Nature, it is the result of an act of naming, a product of social discourse rather than an "objective" attribution of some pre-given essence. Vala's association with religious hegemony is apparent in the design to plate 32 (E plate 46; see Figure 18), where Blake juxtaposes Vala with St Paul's Cathedral, his symbol for the oppressive politics of state religion.[10] In this design, Vala's dark veil extends upward from the darkness of a heavily shadowed St Paul's, whose base, disappearing into total blackness, is imagistically disconnected from Albion's earthly shore below. This design suggests that the metaphor of Vala's (or Rahab's) veil has for its tenor not nature "itself" but rather the traditional veil of the Old Testament's inner temple of orthodoxy. Symbolically, in Blake, this veil functions as a kind of theological prophylaxis, separating a distant and mysterious sky-God from direct human contact and so justifying Priesthood's mediative intervention into human spiritual affairs. Thus, Vala's threatening gesture in this design – her reaching out to cover Jerusalem with her dark veil – signifies not "natural" oppression but the violence implicit in an institutionally sanctioned denial of human spiritual liberty.

That Vala functions conceptually to justify the violence of religious orthodoxy in *Jerusalem*'s fallen patriarchal society is apparent in her association with religious warfare on plate 22. Once again, however, we must be chary of "naturalizing" this association by blaming its existence on the realm of nature, for *Jerusalem*'s text represents Vala's role in religious warfare as a product of her cultural conditioning. Recounting the events of her childhood, for example, Vala tells Albion that Jehovah and his son Cush placed her in a "golden Ark" at the head of "his Armies." Vala's subsequent assertion that "The flesh of multitudes fed & nouris[h]ed me in my childhood / My morn & evening food were prepard in Battles of Men" (22:4–7; E167) suggests that her mature identity is the very product of the warlike relations she experienced during her formative years. Arguably, Jehovah and Cush make use of Vala to naturalize and thus support their political crusade, setting her up as a sexual reward designed to provoke and "sustain" the male warrior in his "glorious combat & the

18   Jerusalem, plate 32
Yale Centre for British Art, Paul Mellon Collection

battle & war" (45:65; E195). Later in the poem, after Jerusalem's long lamentation (which begins at 78:31), Blake offers us a telling description of Vala in her warlike context: "Beside [Jerusalem] Vala howld upon the winds in pride of beauty / Lamenting among the timbrels of the Warriors: among the Captives / In cruel holiness" (80:8; E236). Vala, having been glorified since her childhood by Jehovah's male warriors, might be excused here for her display of "pride" and "cruel holiness." Indeed, her howlings and lamentations (which are offered, interestingly enough, in a non-partisan way to "Warriors" and "Captives" alike) suggest that, despite her having grown to adulthood, she remains victimized by the violence that surrounded her during a youth spent amidst the "Battles of Men." Hence the nature that Vala comes to symbolize can be understood as a product of religious discourse and its attendant ideological crusade. All in all, the circumstances surrounding Vala's predicament in *Jerusalem* suggest that material nature is not responsible for the production of religious warfare; on the contrary, Vala's upbringing demonstrates that religious warfare helps to produce and "naturalize" a certain Hobbesian understanding of nature as a battleground of hostile relations between and among living entities.

Like her youthful identity, which is limited by the role she must play as a feminine icon of patriarchal warfare, Vala's mature identity tends to be defined by the various roles she must assume in a male-centred economy of social relations. In the postlapsarian world, Vala is Albion's bride; as we have seen, however, Albion comes to think of her as his Mother, nature. Thus, as critics like Brenda S. Webster (1983, 276) and Morton Paley (1983, 196–9) have pointed out, Albion's pathology is symptomatic of an Oedipal crisis whose accompanying guilt engenders and perpetuates his hostility towards her. But one can also trace Albion's hostility to a much more mundane but no less significant material circumstance of Vala's existence: in the male-centred social economy characterizing Albion's fallen world, she inevitably becomes, like all women, an important object of exchange. Since both Albion and Luvah claim Vala as their own (she is Albion's wife and mother, but she is also Luvah's wife, emanation, and daughter), Vala becomes embroiled in a conflict of ownership that culminates in an acrimonious battle for "dominion" over her body (43:61–2; E192).[11] Although Blake's attitude towards gender was problematic, as many of his references to an insidious "Female Will" would suggest, his representation of Albion's and Luvah's battle over the feminized body of nature in some ways prefigures late-twentieth-century eco-feminist insights correlating the cultural domination of nature and oppression of women.

By the end of the eighteenth century, the notion that the body of nature was a female one was well established. As I mentioned in my introduction, Francis Bacon helped scientifically to modernize this ancient view by presenting science as a systematic endeavour to penetrate the "womb of nature" in order to discover "many secrets of excellent use" (1860, 4:100). The intrusive violence of Bacon's metaphorical language is implicit, as is the instrumental logic of his intent when he refers to the "use" to which nature's secrets might be put by the masculinist scientist. Interestingly enough, Bacon denies the rapacity of this undertaking by defining the scientist's relationship to nature in terms somewhat reminiscent of the courtly love tradition: "the empire of man over things depends," he argues, "wholly on the arts and sciences. For we cannot command nature except by obeying her" (4:114). By attempting to understand and obey the laws of feminine nature, Bacon suggests, the masculine scientist will be able to court and subdue her with the sanction of her full consent. More sceptically, one might argue that this strategy of ostensible obedience will enable the rapacious scientist to remove nature's veil without direct coercive force, by convincing her that she retains full agency in the affair.

In *The Four Zoas*, if not so obviously in *Jerusalem*, this notion of nature as consenting feminine lover is highly questionable; for Vala is shown in the Second Night to be coerced by, rather than to command, nature's laws. Appearing "among the Brick kilns," where she is "compelld / To labour night & day among the fires," Vala laments her condition and that of her fellow labourers:

O Lord wilt thou not look upon our sore afflictions
Among these flames incessant labouring, our hard masters laugh
At all our sorrow. We are made to turn the wheel for water
To carry the heavy basket on our scorched shoulders, to sift
The sand & ashes, & to mix the clay with tears & repentance
...
Furrowd with whips, & our flesh bruised with the heavy basket[.]
(FZ 31:4–8, 14; E320–1)

The wheel Vala is forced to turn in this passage is the Newtonian water-wheel, one of Blake's metaphors for the efficient-causal cyclicity he sees as a fundamental characteristic of mechanistic science. As I argued in chapter 3, the water-wheel partakes of the antinomian symbolism of the "Everlasting Gospel" (J 27; E171), in which water signifies the epoch of Mosaic legalism from which, in Blake's view, humanity has been liberated by the blood of Christ. Blake, I have argued, associates Newton with water throughout his *œuvre* in order to emphasize his aversion to a scientific discourse that locates static and immutable "laws" in nature itself. To the extent that Vala symbolizes nature, her enforced turning of "the wheels for water" and her carrying of "the heavy basket" (perhaps, in this context, a water container) in *The Four Zoas* suggests not an entity who oppressively *wields* natural law but one who has been violently subjected to its dictates. From this standpoint, natural philosophers like Bacon and Newton – those men who "discover" or formulate nature's laws – can be seen as the "hard masters" who laugh at Vala's condition; for in Blake's view they are the ones whose legalistic doctrines have enslaved nature by inscribing determinate law indelibly into the very structure of the universe. That Blake chose not to transpose this passage from *The Four Zoas* into the text of *Jerusalem* suggests that, as his mythology developed, his attitude towards Vala became less sympathetic. Nevertheless, we catch in *Jerusalem* a glimpse of Vala's enslaved condition when she briefly invokes the oppressive water-wheels of the dark Satanic Mill:

> the slave groans in the dungeon of stone.
> The captive in the mill of the stranger, sold for scanty hire.
> They view their former life: they number moments over and over;
> Stringing them on their remembrance as on a thread of sorrow.
> (20:15–18; E165)

Both Vala's reference to the "mill" and her representation of time as a series of moments the slave must mathematically "number" are direct poetic invocations of the mechanistic processes Blake associated with Newtonian science. That Vala goes on to correlate this human enslavement with her own "griefs" (20:20) suggests the existence of a discrepancy between her "proper" identity and her textual status as the personification of a legalistically inscribed nature.

Vala's invocations of the slave "in the dungeon of stone" and the "captive in the mill" are particularly interesting given that Blake later represents Jerusalem herself as a victim of both of these forms of imprisonment: she is "closd in the Dungeons of Babylon," where she is forced to labour "at the Mills" (60:39, 41; E210). In order to comfort Jerusalem in her captivity, the Divine Voice dramatizes Blake's revisionist rendition of the story of Joseph and Mary:

> She looked & saw Joseph the Carpenter in Nazareth & Mary
> His espoused Wife. And Mary said, If thou put me away from thee
> Dost thou not murder me? Joseph spoke in anger & fury. Should I

Marry a Harlot & an Adulteress? Mary answerd, Art thou more pure
Than thy Maker who forgiveth Sins & calls again Her that is Lost
Tho She hates. he calls her again in love. (61:3–8; E211)

To quote Morton Paley's succinct summary, this passage reflects
Blake's "lifelong hostility to the doctrine of the Virgin Birth, with its
concomitant exaltation of celibacy and its condemnation of sensual
enjoyment" (1983, 134). To Paley's insight I would add that Blake's
hostility to this doctrine reflects, in a more general sense, his distaste
for its implicit transcendentalist devaluation of material existence
(since without such existence the earthly experience of sensual enjoy-
ment would be impossible). Let me clarify this point by discussing
briefly the sexual politics informing the passage quoted above. Blake's
critics tend to read the reconciliation between Joseph and Mary in
terms of the former's ultimate forgiveness of the latter;[12] such a read-
ing, however, is partial in its implicit male-centredness. For true rec-
onciliation to occur, Mary must also forgive her husband for his false
assumption of purity (J 61:6), as Jehovah's subsequent address to
Joseph plainly suggests: "this is the Covenant / Of Jehovah: If you
Forgive *one-another*, so shall Jehovah Forgive You" (61:24–5; E212;
emphasis added). In Blake's view, God's covenant is always a rela-
tional one, just as it is in the ecological theology of Richard J. Clifford
and Michael S. Northcott, whose readings of the Bible stress the all-
inclusive ethical dynamics informing God's promised bond with the
created world and its diverse community of living beings.[13] Since
Blake's theology continually emphasizes the integral role of forgive-
ness in the attainment of redemption, his invocation of "the Covenant
/ Of Jehovah" indicates the need for a relational, *mutual* forgiveness
between Mary and Joseph. As Blake's figurative language suggests, the
realization of this mutual forgiveness has important consequences not
only for the earthly parents of Jesus but for the natural world as well:

Then Mary burst forth into a Song! she flowed like a River of
Many Streams in the arms of Joseph & gave forth her tears of joy
Like many waters, and Emanating into gardens & palaces upon
Euphrates & to forests & floods & animals wild & tame from
Gihon to Hiddekel, & to corn fields & villages & inhabitants
Upon Pison & Arnon & Jordan. (61:28–33)

This passage prefigures the central assumption of postmodern eco-
feminist discourse by establishing a palpable connection between the
domination of nature and the oppression of women. Because patri-
archal morality tends to categorize women in terms of a questionable

Wife/Harlot binary opposition (61:3–6; cf. 57:8–9), Joseph feels justified in subjecting Mary to his self-righteous moralizings. In such a context, Mary's Emanations – comprising a rich world of gardens, palaces, forests, cornfields, and so on – remain significantly locked inside her. With the dismantling of Joseph's unjust moral economy, however, these repressed Emanations spring forth in splendid diversity. Of course, insofar as this emanational dynamic suggests that patriarchal morality functions to repress an "authentic" feminine identity, it partakes of the sort of essentialism that advocates of deep ecology claim to see in the writings of various ecofeminist scholars.[14] However, Mary's unrestrained identity, when it finally reveals itself, is by no means reductively "natural"; for Mary emanates a complex array of natural *and* cultural entities and artifacts. Significantly, this release of Emanations (Blake's trope for the relational commingling of integral beings) allows Mary and Joseph to commingle in a newfound spirit of mutuality, a spirit implied by the mingling of their mutual tears of joy (61:14, 29).

Much earlier in the poem, Albion confronts Vala by invoking a moral economy of gender relations virtually identical to the one Joseph attempts to enforce upon Mary prior to his reconciliation with her. After describing his own diseased condition – a pathology brought on by "Shame" (21:3; E166) – Albion tells Vala that "All is Eternal Death unless you can weave a chaste / Body over an unchaste Mind! Vala! O that thou wert pure!" (21:11–12). Given Albion's habit of projecting aspects of his self-conception onto others in the poem, we can assume here that Albion has projected his own impure self-image onto Vala, so that she becomes yet another externalized object of his "Shame." At any rate, Albion's negative assessment of Vala's morality – implicit in the complaint "O that thou wert pure!" – is highly questionable, for one assailed by the impurity of shame is hardly fit to judge the purity of others. As we have seen, Albion's "disease" of shame causes his family members, "Wild Animations," cattle, forests, cornfields, gardens, and celestial bodies to become "separated" from him and to flee his presence (21:7–10). The reconciliation of Mary and Joseph adumbrates the impending apocalyptic resolution of this crisis of separation as animals, forests, cornfields, gardens, and other phenomena are liberated from the governance of a moral code that oppresses women *and* the feminized object world, keeping both of them separate from "Man." With the transformation of sexual relations implicit in Blake's doctrine of *mutual* forgiveness, the female, no longer circumscribed by the politics of patriarchy, becomes expansive and multiplicitous, emanating a world of harmoniously coexistent natural and cultural phenomena. One might say that Mary's freedom and the freedom of the material world are of a piece.

The implicit critique of patriarchy underpinning Mary's questioning of Joseph's moralistic Wife/Harlot dichotomy can helpfully illuminate Vala's predicament in *Jerusalem*'s fallen male-centred universe. In particular, Vala's references to heterosexual love and marriage can inform our understanding of Blake's conception of nature's subjection to the androcentric cultural realm, because they expose the dynamics of female commodification in an economy of patriarchal exchange. Recounting a parable "of old," Vala indicts the ruthless instrumentalism of patriarchal marriage in the boldest terms:

> Set your Son before a man & he shall take you & your sons
> For slaves: but set your Daughter before a man & She
> Shall make him & his sons & daughters your slaves for ever!
> And is this Faith? (45:51–55; E195)

Vala's closing question here is obviously rhetorical, for she is only too well aware of the ramifications of female exchange in a world where marriageable daughters become the mercenary instruments of masculinist self-interest. Unlike Jerusalem, however (who, as "Liberty," refuses willingly to participate in such an economy of male/female relations – 45:44), the enslaved Vala emphatically asserts her status as Albion's wife, declaring "Albion is mine! Luvah gave me to Albion" (45:50). These two declarations, it must be noted, are mutually contradictory, for although Vala affirms her right to possess Albion, she subsequently admits that Luvah has already given *her* "to Albion," an act that concretizes her status as an object of exchange and ownership. As in the scene where Albion and Luvah battle for "dominion" over Vala's body (43:61–2; E192), this exchange is an aspect of patriarchal power politics. As a commodified object of masculinist desire, Vala becomes, in short, the pivotal point around which the political "strife of Albion & Luvah" (45:55; E195) turns.

Vala's conflicted position *vis-à-vis* Albion and Luvah crucially informs her narrative function in *Jerusalem*. Consider, for example, the horror she expresses earlier in the poem when she declares of Albion: "I have looked into the secret Soul of him I loved / And in the dark recesses found Sin & can never return" (22:14–15; E167). Although this speech has been interpreted as an inadvertent self-condemnation on Vala's part,[15] it can be productively read in feminist terms as the articulation of a political dilemma. In a patriarchal regime, feminine identity is necessarily male-centred, since the "properly" feminine woman must define herself in subordinate relation to the dominant male, the father or husband who "possesses" her. Thus, for the indoctrinated female, the initial realization that the male's "secret Soul" harbours "Sin" comes as a profound psychological shock, shattering the ideological notion of man as woman's natural superior, the normative assumption to which Vala "can never return" as a result of her newfound knowledge. Albion's subsequent confession – "I have erred! I am ashamed! and will never return more" (23:16; E168) – confirms Vala's perception of his sinful condition, suggesting, perhaps, that the state to which Albion can "never return" also involves the problem of identity in a patriarchal regime that ultimately enslaves *both* "sons & daughters" (45:54; E195).

Like the hills and valleys that comprise Albion's geography, the externalized Vala is a derivative emanation of Albion's fractured being, and she is thus subject to, and adversely affected by, his psychic conflicts and impositions. This derivative and subordinate aspect of Vala's identity becomes especially apparent on plate 43, just prior to the congeneration of nature, in the remarkable passage where the self-deluded Albion falls down to worship his own Shadow:

> Albion walkd on the steps of fire before his Halls
> And Vala walkd with him in dreams of soft deluding slumber.
> He looked up & saw the Prince of Light with splendor faded
> Then Albion ascended mourning into the porches of his Palace
> Above him rose a Shadow from his wearied intellect:
> Of living gold, pure, perfect, holy: in white linen pure he hoverd
> A sweet entrancing self-delusion a watry vision of Albion
> Soft exulting in existence; all the Man absorbing! (43:33–40; E191–2)

It is tempting here to associate the rising Shadow with Vala (who is explicitly identified in the text as Jerusalem's "shadow" [12:19; E155; 45:41; E195]), and thus to blame Vala for Albion's bizarre behaviour in this passage. Since Vala walks with Albion "in dreams of soft deluding slumber," we might see Albion's "self-delusion" (which Blake also describes as "Soft") as a product of Vala's "natural" or corporeal influence. We must remember, however, that the Shadow derives from Albion's "wearied intellect," not from Vala's. Hence the reference to Albion's "self-delusion" raises the likelihood that Vala's "dreams of soft deluding slumber" are aspects of Albion's projection onto Vala of his *own* state of mind. Albion's ability to influence Vala can be seen in the similarity of their responses to the rising of the Shadow:

> Albion fell upon his face prostrate before the watry Shadow
> Saying O Lord whence is this change! thou knowest I am nothing!
> And Vala trembled & coverd her face! & her locks were spread on the
> pavement ... (43:41–3; E192)

In this passage, Vala exactly reproduces Albion's behaviour, falling, as he does, "prostrate" before the Shadow (a position implied by the spreading of her "locks ... on the pavement"). Clearly, she does not *cause* Albion's actions but *reacts* to them in a manner suggesting that she is, like the golden shadow, a kind of mirror-image of, or projection from, Albion's own selfhood. The result of Albion's projectional world-view is a fading of the Prince of Light's "splendor" and an "Idolatrous" worshipping of his own Shadow (43:35, 46), processes symbolizing a fading or denial of relationality and a concomitant falling into solipsism.

The extent of Albion's self-idolatry is shocking. Addressing his Shadow, the fallen man declares:

If thou withhold thine hand; I perish like a fallen leaf:
O I am nothing: and to nothing must return again:
If thou withdraw thy breath. Behold I am oblivion. (43:50–2)

If the Shadow symbolizes Albion's self-conception or ratio – not the insidious influence of nature but an anthropomorphic projection "from his wearied intellect" – then, because the Prince of Light (the antidote to this vision) has already "faded" (43:37, 35), the Shadow's withdrawal will indeed cause Albion to become as "nothing": neither light nor shade. In the design to this plate (Copy E, plate 29; see Figure 19), Albion's address to the Shadow is juxtaposed against an image, in the right-hand margin, of a pair of human forms – probably those of the prostrate Albion and Vala – which appear to be disintegrating, losing their outlines of identity. Clearly, as the image suggests, Albion worships his own selfhood in a way that negates both masculine and feminine identity. That this negation adversely affects the realm of nature is suggested by his subsequent behaviour; for as Luvah descends to confront Albion, the latter "turn[s] his back on Vala" (43:57). Strangely enough, it is at this point that the struggle for "dominion" over Vala's body begins.

As I demonstrated above in my discussion of a contemporary neuroscience that "pierces" Albion's object-brain with a "golden pin," objective modes of understanding "nature," when they are exclusively privileged, have adverse implications for human conceptions of self-identity. By constructing an objective universe of dead matter, Blake argues, we effectively murder ourselves, for we "become what we behold." This strange "return of the repressed" informs Blake's construction of that bugbear, the "Female Will." According to Damon, the "Female Will ... is evil," for when "the Individual is divided, the Emanation has a will of her own, which acts in opposition to her

Then the Divine Vision like a silent Sun appeard above
Albions dark rocks: setting behind the Gardens of Kensington
On Tyburns River, in clouds of blood: where was mild Zion Hills
Most ancient promontory, and in the Sun, a Human Form appeard
And thus the Voice Divine went forth upon the rocks of Albion

I elected Albion for my glory; I gave to him the Nations,
Of the whole Earth. He was the Angel of my Presence: and all
The Sons of God were Albions Sons: and Jerusalem was my joy.
The Reactor hath hid himself thro envy. I beheld him.
But you cannot behold him till he be reveald in his System
Albions Reactor must have a place prepard: Albion must Sleep
The Sleep of Death, till the Man of Sin & Repentance be reveald.
Hidden in Albions Forests he lurks: he admits of no Reply
From Albion: but hath founded his Reaction into a Law
Of Action, for Obedience to destroy the Contraries of Man
He hath compelld Albion to become a Punisher & hath possessd
Himself of Albions Forests & Wilds! and Jerusalem is taken.
The City of the Woods in the Forest of Ephratah is taken!
London is a stone of her ruins; Oxford is the dust of her walls!
Sussex & Kent are her scatterd garments: Ireland her holy place:
And the murderd bodies of her little ones are Scotland and Wales
The Cave of the Caverns are the smoke of her consummation
The Nations are her dust! ground by the rolling wheels
Of her lordly conquerors, her palaces levelld with the dust
I come that I may find a way for my banished ones to return
Fear not O little Flock I come! Albion shall rise again.

So saying, the mild Sun inclosd the Human Family.

Forthwith from Albions darkning locks came two Immortal Forms
Saying We alone are escaped. O merciful Lord and Saviour,
We flee from the interiors of Albions hills and mountains!
From his Valleys Eastward, from Amalek Canaan & Moab:
Beneath his vast ranges of hills surrounding Jerusalem.

Albion walkd on the steps of fire before his Halls
And Vala walkd with him in dreams of soft deluding slumber.
He looked up & saw the Prince of Light with splendor faded.
Then Albion ascended mourning into the porches of his Palace
Above him rose a Shadow from his wearied intellect:
Of living gold, pure, perfect, holy: in white linen pure he hoverd
A sweet entrancing self-delusion a watry vision of Albion
Soft exulting in existence; all the Man absorbing!

Albion fell upon his face prostrate before the watry Shadow
Saying O Lord, whence is this change! thou knowest I am nothing!
And Vala trembled & coverd her face! & her locks were spread on the pavement

We heard astonishd at the Vision & our hearts trembled within us:
We heard the voice of slumberous Albion, and thus he spoke,
Idolatrous to his own Shadow words of eternity uttering:

O I am nothing when I enter into judgment with thee!
If thou withdraw thy breath I die & vanish into Hades
If thou dost lay thine hand upon me behold I am silent:
If thou withhold thine hand; I perish like a fallen leaf:
O I am nothing: and to nothing must return again:
If thou withdraw thy breath, behold I am oblivion.

He ceasd: the shadowy voice was silent: but the cloud hoverd over their heads
In golden wreathes the sorrow of Man: & the balmy drops fell down.
And lo! that son of Man that Shadowy Spirit of mild Albion:
Luvah descended from the cloud; in terror Albion rose:
Indignant rose the awful Man, & turnd his back on Vala.

We heard the voice of Albion starting from his sleep:

Whence is this voice crying Enion! that soundeth in my ears?
O cruel pity! O dark deceit! can love seek for dominion?

And Luvah strove to gain dominion over Albion
They strove together above the Body where Vala was inclosd
And the dark Body of Albion left prostrate upon the crystal pavement,
Coverd with boils from head to foot: the terrible smitings of Luvah.

Then frownd the fallen Man, and put forth Luvah from his presence
Saying, Go and Die the Death of Man, for Vala the sweet wanderer
I will turn the volutions of your ears outward, and bend your nostrils
Downward and your fluxile eyes englobd roll round in fear,
Your withering lips and tongue shrink up into a narrow circle,
Till into narrow forms you creep: take Vala the Goddess
That they learn what is to absorb the Man, you Spirits of Pity & Love.

They heard the voice and fled swift, as the winters setting sun.
And now the human blood foamd high, the Spirits Luvah & Vala,
Went down the Human Heart where Paradise & its joys abounded
In jealous fears & fury & rage & thunders roll round their fervid feet:
And the vast form of Nature like a serpent playd before them
And as they fled in folding fires & thunders of the deep.
Vala shrunk in like the dark sea that leaves its slimy banks.
And from her bosom Luvah fell far as the east and west.
And the vast form of Nature like a serpent rolld between,
Whether of Jerusalems or Valas ruins congenerated we know not:
All is confusion: all is tumult: & we alone are escaped.
So spoke the fugitives: they joind the Divine Family, trembling.

19   Jerusalem, plate 29
Yale Centre for British Art, Paul Mellon Collection

consort" (1988, 447). While Damon's insight is a good one (for objectified nature does indeed take on a kind of agency in Blake's myth when, as it were, it objectifies the human in turn), his positing of the Female Will as an essential locus of evil in Blake's myth is questionable, for as *Jerusalem* repeatedly demonstrates, the Female Will is originally a construct of Albion's self-delusive anthropomorphic activity: "O Albion," Los asks, "why wilt thou *Create* a Female Will?" (30:31; E176; emphasis added). Eight lines later, Los reformulates this important question in a telling manner: "Is this the Female Will O ye lovely Daughters of Albion. To / Converse concerning Weight & Distance in the Wilds of Newton & Locke[?]" (30:39–40; E177). Los's questions have a related twofold function. On a grammatical level, first of all, the change from the indefinite article in Los's first question (where he refers vaguely to "*a* Female Will") to the definite article in his second (where he speaks more concretely of "*the* Female Will") suggests a strange consolidation of the entity in question, a suspiciously sudden slippage from mere hypothesis to naturalized fact or given knowledge. In the space of a few lines, in short, the Female Will – Albion's own phantasmagoric "Creat[ion]" – becomes, like Vala's realm of external nature, an identifiable *object*. Los's reference to Newton and Locke, moreover, associates this objectified Female Will with – indeed identifies it as a production of – masculine objective science: the epistemology and methodology of Albion's self-division. Thus, the Female Will is a kind of fiction and not an essential category in Blake's mythology. While I do not wish to apologize for the sexism implicit in Blake's identification of this construct *as female*, I would argue that any consideration of Vala's role as a major representative of the Female Will must take into account the latter's discursive aspect, or Blake's critique of the ideological production that is nature will be. misunderstood as a simple denunciation of the material world as such.

Admittedly, my reading of Vala's character and role in *Jerusalem* is a sympathetic one, placing perhaps a dangerous degree of trust in the validity of her own "autobiographical" narrative and its implicit critique of various modes of discursive authority. To this extent, my interpretation may be at odds with Blake's own intentions. Indeed, Morton Paley insightfully calls two of the speeches I have drawn on to support my reading of Vala's oppression (20:12–20 and 22:1–15) "false-elegiac speeches," arguing that their nostalgia and analytic logic offer proof of their unjust imposition on the reader's sympathy. "Like the Satan of the early parts of *Paradise Lost*," Paley concludes, "Vala is made all the more dangerous by her ability to elicit such a [sympathetic] response" (1983, 192–3). Paley's point is an important one, for there are a number of passages in *Jerusalem* where Blake seems overtly to denounce Vala and her activities. Nevertheless, Vala's utterances comprise some of the most dynamic and energetic poetry in all of *Jerusalem*; and their implicit critique of patriarchal science and established gender roles is certainly consistent with the common critical view that Blake was an opponent of "tyranny in all its guises" (Lorraine Clark 1991, 10). Indeed, the rhetorical power of Vala's poetry, along with the poignant insights it offers into her enslaved condition under patriarchy, suggests the appropriateness of the analogue Paley draws between Blake's Vala and Milton's Satan. If Blake was not intentionally championing Vala's cause, perhaps he was of Vala's party without knowing it.[16]

BLAKE'S POLYPUS, MILTON'S CHAOS, AND THE DANGERS OF "DEEP ECOLOGY"

In 1739 Trembley's discovery of the polyp, or freshwater hydra, caused something of a sensation in Europe's scientific community. Neither vegetable nor animal but displaying characteristics of both, the polyp caused many taxonomists no small degree of intellectual perplexity and discomfort. In some circles, the question whether this creature was a plant or an animal continued to be debated from the time of its discovery until the end of the century (Hilton 1983, 88). For other thinkers, however, the polyp (whose existence had been predicted by Liebniz prior to its actual discovery) was celebrated as "the long-sought missing link" between the plant and animal kingdoms (Lovejoy 1953, 233). Conceived, in other words, as a transitional entity joining disparate orders of being, the polyp's existence supported the much-touted hypothesis that the natural creation loathes a vacuum. Rather than seeing in this creature a monstrous violation of established categories, deistical naturalists like Bonnet tended to celebrate it as living proof of God's goodness as reflected in the exuberant fullness or plenitude of his creation.

But the characteristics and behaviours of this freshwater zoophyte also made it a rather disturbing creature. For one thing, it was monstrous in aspect, having at one end of its body a mouth surrounded by a multitude of appendages resembling tentacles. While the naturalist George Sandys referred to these appendages as "feet," his contemporary, Henry Baker, called them "arms" (Hilton 1983, 88) – a minor disagreement, to be sure, but one that underlined the taxonomical confusion the creature's existence already tended to inspire. Moreover, as Sandys noted, the polyp had a "ravenous" appetite – and a rather frightful manner of satisfying it. Waving its many appendages in what Baker termed a "mill-like" motion, the creature generated a current powerful enough to draw in its numerous and helpless prey.[17] Arguably, Blake has such a model of predation in mind when he describes Satan's "Heart" as having "numerous branches varying their motions" to draw in "the unfortunate contemplator / Who becomes his food" (J 29:21–4; E175). Although Blake never uses the term "polyp," the behaviour of his monstrous Polypus, like that of Satan, seems modelled, to a great extent, upon the predatory habits of that recently discovered creature, but with a crucial difference. In his *Attempt toward a Natural History of the Polype* (1743), Baker noted that, upon being bitten, the polyp's prey would succumb to instant death. In Blake's mythology, however, the Polypus's human prey is by no means so mercifully killed. As we shall see, the Polypus assimilates humans into its body very much alive, but in a manner that robs them of all autonomy or ability to resist this absorption. Thus, Blake's Polypus symbolizes a kind of death-in-life, the nightmare state Blake refers to as "Non-Entity."

As fascinating to contemporary scientists as its predatory manner were the biological polyp's reproductive patterns and prolific regenerative capacity. "Those who have attended to the habits of the polypus," Erasmus Darwin writes, "affirm, that the young ones branch out from the side of the parent like the buds of trees, and after a time separate themselves from them" (1803, 1:384). Something of this notion likely informs Blake's representation of "Albion's Tree" (a synonym for the Polypus), which is able to shoot "into many a Tree! an endless labyrinth of woe!" (28:19; E174). In the following passage we can see that a similar model of regeneration also informs Blake's construction of "the Great Selfhood / Satan," who has

> a white Dot calld a Center from which branches out
> A Circle in continual gyrations. this became a Heart
> From which sprang numerous branches varying their motions
> Producing many Heads three or seven or ten, & hands & feet
> Innumerable at will ... (29:19–23; E175)

In Blake's myth, the procreative capacity of this hydralike entity, the Satanic Selfhood, is all the more frightening given its ability to multiply itself "Innumerabl[y] *at will*." If its predatory habits make this horrific creature a representative of the "Devouring Power" (29:24), its reproductive capability suggests that it simultaneously belongs to the contrary Blakean category of the "Prolific" (MHH 16; E40). For Blake, as we shall presently see, such confusion of contraries has disturbing implications for both human and non-human beings.

Another aspect of the biological polyp's regenerative capacity finds a particularly disturbing application in Blake's mythology: as eighteenth-century biologists observed, one might cut the polyp into innumerable pieces; but, far from killing the creature, such dismemberment would cause it to proliferate, since each severed segment would itself become a complete living polyp (Miner 1960, 198–9n.1). Arguably, Blake draws on these notions of the polyp's indestructibility and excessive proliferation in the construction of his Polypus. After Los envisions the Sons of Albion enrooting themselves "In every Nation," becoming "a mighty Polypus growing / ... over the whole Earth" (J 15:3–5; E159), for example, his own sons "Stand round him cutting the Fibres from Albions hills / That Albions Sons may roll apart over the Nations" (15:23–4). This act, probably intended to resist the onslaught of the predatory Polypus, causes it instead to proliferate even further, as we see when Reuben, one of its victims, "enroots his brethren in the narrow Canaanite / From the Limit Noah to the Limit Abram" (15:25–6). Because the Limits Noah and Abram are temporal, signifying, respectively, the postdiluvian and antediluvian epochs (Paley 1991, 153), the Polypus is potentially able to colonize "the whole Earth" not only in the present but across all time as well. Its proliferation, then, is truly fearful: the "mighty Polypus" threatens to assimilate *all* diverse life forms, both past and present, into identical aspects of its own homogeneous form.

This brief analysis of the relationship between Blake's Satanic Polypus and the biological polyp, as understood by contemporary science, should suggest something of the former's complexity as a poetic figure in *Jerusalem*. Perhaps it is partly because of the seemingly obvious relationship between figure and the biological aspect of its reference, however, that critics have tended to interpret the Polypus's significance in questionably reductive and essentialist terms. According to the dominant critical viewpoint, this creature symbolizes the "material[ity] ... of Generation" (Curran 1985a, 25), "the vegetated life at its blindest and most helpless" (Bloom 1963, 411), and that which life itself becomes as Vala "extend[s] her iron hand" across Blake's mythical world (Otto 1991, 181–2). In *Milton*, to be sure, Blake posits a one-to-one relationship between the Polypus and the Ulro, the latter of which the poem explicitly defines as "a vast Polypus / Of living fibres down into the Sea of Time & Space" (34:24–5; E134). But, as I have been arguing in different contexts throughout this study, we should be wary of essentializing Blake's poetic figures in too reductive a manner. Although the poet's references to "living fibres" and "the Sea of Time & Space" lend support to the common view that he uses the Polypus to denounce material existence itself, I shall argue, instead, that the Polypus functions in Blake's myth to highlight the problems implicit in a *particular* contemporary under-standing, or discursive manifestation, of such existence.

In *Jerusalem*, it must be noted, Los imagines the Polypus in its first explicit textual appearance as "growing / From Albion over the whole Earth" (15:4–5; E159; emphasis added), not from the whole Earth over Albion. In other words, Los's "awful Vision" of the Polypus (15:5) – his prophetic warning concerning the monstrous colonization that *might* occur on Earth if humans fail to take immediate corrective action – suggests that Albion's pathology will potentially contaminate the entire material realm, "the whole Earth" whose very wholeness pre-cedes the existence of the "growing" Polypus. But how, exactly, does the Polypus come into existence in the first place? Blake's reference to Los's "awful Vision" contains a clue that can help us to formulate an answer to this question. In *Milton*, Los calls the Polypus "No Human Form but only a Fibrous Vegetation / A Polypus of soft affections with-out Thought or Vision" (24:37–8; E120). Los is able to see this monster in *Jerusalem* only because he is capable of "Vision," that which, as the passage from *Milton* plainly states, the Polypus itself lacks. For Blake, I would argue, *all* those who lack vision are as incapable of seeing the Polypus as it is of seeing itself (or reflecting on its own existence) – hence the social necessity of the prophet. Because most people, being fallen prophets (M 24:75; E121), cannot identify it, the Polypus is decid-edly dangerous. Indeed, humanity's lack of vision is precisely that which engenders the Polypus in the first place. In the strictest terms, then, Stuart Curran is wrong to speak of "those who have *accepted* the material Polypus of Generation" (1986a, 25; emphasis added); for such a comment implies a degree of agency or choice lacking in the non-visionary human of Blake's mythology. The Polypus, much more insid-ious than Curran's comment suggests, denies and co-opts all human intention. This is why, in a discussion of Satan's "Devouring Power," Blake speaks of "the unfortunate contemplator" who, quite unwit-tingly, becomes the Polypus's "food" (J 29:23–4; E175).

How do humans lose the capacity for vision that would enable them to recognize, evade, and combat the threatening Polypus? Once again, the problem is discursive and multifaceted, having its origin in the human social world rather than in the realm of materiality per se. The Polypus that "grow[s] / From Albion over the whole Earth" is also identified in the text as Albion's Tree, that which, as we have seen, Albion anthropomorphically names "Moral Virtue, and the Law / Of God who dwells in Chaos hidden from the human sight" (28:15–16; E174). For Blake, dogma such as that which provides the basis for "Miltons Religion" (M 22:39; E117), with its Puritanical construction of an absolutely distant Sky-God, itself produces the Polypus, which, like Milton's God, is "hidden from the human sight" (though not from imaginative "Vision"). Blake's reference to the "God who dwells in Chaos" recalls, furthermore, Milton's chaotic atoms in *Paradise Lost*. In Milton's cosmogony, chaos is a region of "Eternal anarchy" marked by "endless wars" and "confusion," where "Hot, Cold, Moist, and Dry, four champions fierce / Strive … for mastery, and to battle bring / Their embryon atoms" (1992, 2:896–900). These atoms, the strangely insubstantial materials of Miltonic Creation, are obviously different from the atoms associated with Newton; but for Blake at least, any difference between them is largely insignificant: both Miltonic and Newtonian atoms belong to, and originate from, "the Atheistical Epicurean Philosophy of Albions Tree" (J 67:13; E220),[18] that atomistic branch of classical philosophy that contributes to the human construction of the Polypus.

In a famous passage from *Paradise Lost*, Milton figures chaos as a state of warfare wherein atoms gather "around the flag / Of each his faction, in their several clans" (1992, 2:900–1). In Blake's view, this military metaphor is apt indeed. Becoming what they behold, those who advocate an atomistic model of existence themselves behave like Milton's atoms, inevitably pursuing warlike relations with all entities they happen to encounter. Albion's Sons are a case in point. The second appearance of the Polypus in *Jerusalem* directly follows their own factional activities, in which they build "Castles" and "strong Fortifications" in order to conduct corporeal warfare (J 18:38–42; E163). In addition, the Polypus's "Emissaries / In War," Hyle and Coban, go forth from and return to the Polypus "Like Wheels from a great Wheel reflected in the Deep," wheels that rend "a way in Albions Loins" (18:41–4). These obvious poetic references to Newton's mill-wheels associate Newtonian atomism with the warfare of Miltonic chaos, demonstrating Blake's view that such atomism is merely another manifestation of "the Atheistical Epicurean Philosophy of Albions Tree" (67:13; E220), one of the execrable discourses responsible for the creation of the threatening Polypus.[19]

A consideration of the full passage in which Blake's reference to Epicureanism occurs will clarify the relationship between the Polypus and the important figure of the fibre in *Jerusalem*. Blake writes that Rahab and Tirzah "drew out from the Rocky Stones / Fibres of Life" in order "to Weave" bodies for humans, both male and female:

They cut the Fibres from the Rocks groaning in pain they Weave;
Calling the Rocks Atomic Origins of Existence; denying Eternity
By the Atheistical Epicurean Philosophy of Albions Tree
Such are the Feminine & Masculine when separated from Man
They call the Rocks Parents of Men, & adore the frowning Chaos[.]
(67:3–4, 11–15; E220)

The "Fibres of Life" that Rahab and Tirzah cut "from the Rocks" are synonymous with the "Fibres of love," which, as we have seen, perform the emanational and life-affirming function of joining "man to man thro Albions pleasant land" (4:8; E146). By cutting these all-important fibres, Rahab and Tirzah foreclose all possibility of inter-subjective commingling, which can occur only through the meeting of our "Feminine & Masculine" principles – those "Emanations / Which stand both Male & Female at the Gates of each Humanity" (88:10–11; E246). In their unsevered state, the fibres in question point towards a dynamic holism in which all things are mutually and integrally interrelated; but when they are "cut ... from the rocks" and "separated from Man," they become abstract atomic units, aspects of the solipsistic warfare that characterizes all process in Milton's "frowning Chaos." Once again it is important here to differentiate (albeit not without a certain essentialism) things from the inscriptions they receive in Blake's writing; for the Rocks from which Rahab and Tirzah extract their "Fibres of Life" are not *in fact* "Atomic Origins of Existence" or primordial "Parents of Men" – they are merely "call[ed]" or named as such. By reiterating his reference to the act of "Calling" in relation to these Rocks, Blake emphasizes the linguistic constructedness of a philosophical atomism that, by separating matter (the Rocks underlying Albion's green and present land) from the ethical principles that animate it ("Life," love, or spirit), tends to universalize violent modes of social relations.

Blake reveals the results of Rahab's and Tirzah's acts of atomistic dissection later on the same plate:

> Tirzah sits weeping to hear the shrieks of the dying: her Knife
> Of flint is in her hand: she passes it over the howling Victim
> The Daughters Weave their Work in loud cries over the Rock
> Of Horeb! still eyeing Albions Cliffs eagerly siezing & twisting
> The threads of Vala & Jerusalem running from mountain to mountain
> Over the whole Earth: loud the Warriors rage in Beth Peor
> Beneath the iron whips of their Captains & consecrated banners
> Loud the Sun & Moon rage in the conflict: loud the Stars
> Shout in the night of battle & their spears grow to their hands
> With blood, weaving the deaths of the Mighty into a Tabernacle
> For Rahab & Tirzah; till the Great Polypus of Generation covered
>   the Earth ... (67:24–34)

The brutal violence pervading this passage is nothing short of appalling. In a universe where the very stars and satellites engage in bloody battle, and where spears "*grow*" as if naturally "to their hands," it is only natural that human "Warriors" would behave similarly and that "the whole Earth" would become a bloody battleground. Blake's attribution of such violence to an atomistic materialism and its cosmogony is implicit in his allusion to *Paradise Lost*, for the "consecrated banners" around which all things "rage in ... conflict" recall the battles that rage "around the flag[s]" of "faction" in Milton's anarchic, atomistic chaos (1992, 2:900–1). Ultimately, one should note, the "Fibres of Life" that Rahab and Tirzah weave are themselves ironically named. Since these fibres have been atomistically (and dualistically) severed from their relational contexts and the material loci of their earthly manifestations, they become *deathly* fibres, the atomic units with which the Daughters of Albion weave "the deaths of the Mighty into a Tabernacle / For Rahab & Tirzah; till the Great Polypus of Generation covered the Earth" (J 67:33–4; E220).

The misnaming of these fibres is important, for in many ways the Polypus functions as a travesty or parody of the holistic relationality which is a definitive yet ultimately irreducible or undefinable trait of Blakean "Life."[20] The Polypus, as Albion's Tree, alludes ironically to Christ's new reign in *Paradise Regained*, which, Milton prophesies, "shall be like a tree / Spreading and overshadowing all the earth" (1992, 4:147–8). But whereas the Christocentric theology of *Paradise Regained* emphasizes redemptive love and a sociality based on mutual forgiveness, thus displacing the terrifying theological legalism informing *Paradise Lost* (Wittreich 1978, 68), Blake explicitly names Albion's Tree after the "Law" of "Moral Virtue" (J 28:15; E174), the Law that Moses received upon Mount Sinai, "the Rock / of Horeb" (67:26–7; E220). As we have seen, such Law is for Blake a principle of separation rather than connection, for like the symbolic veil of the inner temple, it functions to keep God "hidden from the human sight" (28:16; E174) and so separated from human contact.

At a certain level, however, the Polypus does indeed represent communal interconnection; but this is a pathological conception of community, one that implies not the dynamic interrelationality of integral entities but the non-differentiation of the heteronomous condition. On plate 18, Blake traces the Polypus's genealogy to something like a foundational negation of difference: "Soon Hand mightily devour'd & absorb'd Albions Twelve Sons. / Out from his bosom [grew] a mighty Polypus, vegetating in darkness" (18:39–40; E163). The Polypus emerges, significantly, directly out of Hand's act of devouring and absorbing his brothers, an act that destroys their individuality or particular outlines of identity. In the design to this plate (see Figure 20), Blake depicts three naked forms falling down the right-hand margin, forms providing a marginal gloss to the events recounted in the textual narrative.[21] This series of descending and

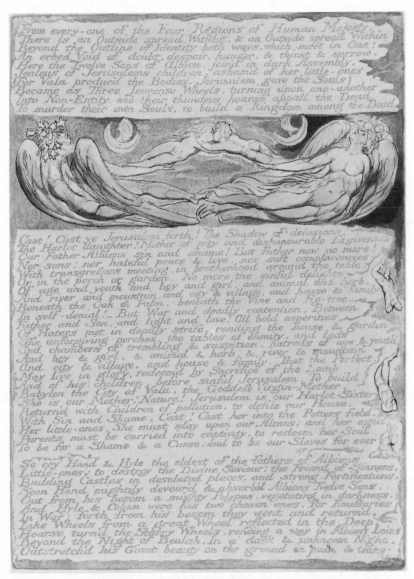

From every-one of the Four Regions of Human Majesty,
There is an Outside spread Without, & an Outside spread Within
Beyond the Outline of Identity both ways, which meet in One:
An orbed Void of doubt, despair, hunger, & thirst & sorrow.
Here the Twelve Sons of Albion, joind in dark Assembly,
Jealous of Jerusalems children, ashamd of her little-ones
(For Vala produced the Bodies, Jerusalem gave the Souls)
Became as Three Immense Wheels, turning upon one-another
Into Non-Entity, and their thunders hoarse appall the Dead,
To murder their own Souls, to build a Kingdom among the Dead.

Cast! Cast ye Jerusalem forth! The Shadow of delusions!
The Harlot daughter! Mother of pity and dishonourable forgiveness
Our Father Albions sin and shame! But father now no more!
Nor sons, nor hateful peace & love, nor soft complacencies
With transgressors meeting in brotherhood around the table,
Or in the porch or garden. No more the sinful delights
Of age and youth and boy and girl, and animal and herb,
And river and mountain, and city & village, and house & family,
Beneath the Oak & Palm, beneath the Vine and Fig-tree.
In self-denial!—But War and deadly contention, Between
Father and Son, and light and love! All bold asperities
Of Haters met in deadly strife, rending the house & garden
The unforgiving porches, the tables of enmity, and beds
And chambers of trembling & suspition, hatreds of age & youth
And boy & girl, & animal & herb, & river & mountain
And city & village, and house & family. That the Perfect,
May live in glory, redeemd by Sacrifice of the Lamb
And of his children, before sinful Jerusalem. To build
Babylon the City of Vala, the Goddess Virgin-Mother.
She is our Mother! Nature! Jerusalem is our Harlot-Sister
Returnd with Children of pollution, to defile our House,
With Sin and Shame. Cast! Cast her into the Potters field.
Her little-ones, She must slay upon our Altars; and her aged
Parents must be carried into captivity, to redeem her Soul
To be for a Shame & a Curse, and to be our Slaves for ever

So cry Hand & Hyle the eldest of the fathers of Albions
Little-ones; to destroy the Divine Saviour; the Friend of Sinners,
Building Castles in desolated places, and strong Fortifications.
Soon Hand, mightily devour'd & absorb'd Albions Twelve Sons,
Out from his bosom a mighty Polypus, vegetating in darkness,
And Hyle & Coban were his two chosen ones, for Emissaries
In War, forth from his bosom they went and returnd.
Like Wheels from a great Wheel reflected in the Deep.
Hoarse, turnd the Starry Wheels, rending a way in Albions Loins
Beyond the Night of Beulah. In a dark & unknown Night,
Outstretchd his Giant beauty on the ground in pain & tears:

20   Jerusalem, plate 18

Yale Centre for British Art, Paul Mellon Collection

seemingly headless human figures (perhaps the same individual in various stages of physical and intellectual dissolution) points to the loss of identity that occurs when one is assimilated by the Polypus. Blake emphasizes the appalling consequence of this assimilation by means of a gradual decrease in the inking of the figures' outlines as they fall towards the bottom of the page. Indeed, the outline of the third figure in this descending series is hardly inked at all, so that it seems to blend with some vegetation growing up the right-hand margin of the plate. Upon close inspection, one can detect what appears to be the remains of a fourth naked form near the bottom of the plate, directly to the right of lines 41 through 43 (and, significantly, just below the seeming birth of the Polypus on line 40). This fourth form, the outline of which is not inked at all, looks (to quote Blake's *Descriptive Catalogue* of 1809) like "a cloudy vapour or a nothing" (E541), suggesting that, in the encounter with the Polypus, the individual human loses all autonomous identity.

Blake adumbrates this fall into heteronomy in the opening lines of the same plate, where he articulates his view of the relationship between human subjective interiority and the external object-world as it was understood by the scientific naturalism of his day.

> From every-one of the Four regions of Human Majesty,
> There is an Outside spread Without, & an Outside spread Within
> Beyond the Outline of Identity both ways, which meet in One:
> An orbed Void of doubt, despair, hunger, & thirst & sorrow.
> Here the Twelve Sons of Albion, join'd in dark Assembly ...
> (18:1–5; E162)

This passage describes the danger of the heteronomous condition, the state in which the "Outline of Identity" becomes blurred and the integrity or individuality of the entity is lost. Such a crisis stems from the excessive privileging of objectivity implied by the repetition of the word "Outside" in the second line of the passage. The first instance of this word would need to be changed to "Inside" (so that the passage would read, "There is an Inside Spread Without, & an Outside spread Within") if some kind of balanced interchange between subjective interiority and external cosmos were to be achieved. As it stands (with the "Outside" spread both "Without" *and* "Within") human subjectivity is overwhelmed by the "Outside" or objective universe, with the consequence that this same universe holds no place "Within" it for the human subject. The overarching presence of an "Outside" thus generates "doubt, despair, hunger, & thirst & sorrow" *within* the human entity. This all-pervasive "Outside" is the reality of the Polypus itself; and the "dark Assembly" that conjoins Albion's Sons in pathological, hyper-holistic community (18:5) augurs the coming – or is itself a manifestation – of the Polypus that devours and absorbs them near the end of the same plate (18:39–40).

Because it negates the difference of other entities in its acts of devouring and absorption, the Polypus belongs to the Blakean category of the Hermaphrodite, that confused state in which subject and object "seem to come together, but in such a way that the distinctions between the two are obliterated" (Frosch 1974, 83–4). This mode of subject-object relationship is analogous to the "fourth similitude" Michel Foucault delineates in his study of pre-Enlightenment epistemology: that of "the play of *sympathies.*"²² To clarify the relationship between the Polypus and this mode of identification, it will be helpful to quote an excerpt from Foucault's discussion: "Sympathy is an instance of the *Same* so strong and so insistent that it will not rest content to be one of the forms of likeness; it has the dangerous power of *assimilating*, of rendering things identical to one another, of mingling them, of causing their individuality to disappear – and thus of rendering them foreign to what they were before" (1994, 23–4). To counteract this drive towards sameness, Foucault continues, "sympathy is compensated for by its twin, antipathy" (24). In *Jerusalem*, the human who has been absorbed by the Polypus is a victim of the creature's excessive "sympathy," which is why Blake characterizes the Polypus in terms of "soft affections," the pity that "divides the soul" (M 24:38, E120; 8:19, E102). A human who overemphasizes the importance of the "Outside" (at the expense of the "Inside," that is, subjective interiority and its processes of intellection), as we saw above, creates the necessary conditions for such an absorption. In short, too much identification with the external world can, in Blake's thought, lead to a harmful annihilation of the identifying self. Such a conclusion is seriously at odds with the environmental ethics of such prominent eco-philosophers as Arne Naess. One of the founders of the "deep ecology" movement, Naess advocates an ethic of human "identification" with all life, a mode of relationship entailing "an extension of sympathy that reaches so far and becomes so constant that the self loses any desire to differentiate between itself and the world" (Pite 1996, 362).²³ In *Jerusalem*, as my analysis of the Polypus thus far should suggest, such a degree of identification entails a holistic totalitarianism that actually forecloses ethical possibilities; for from a Blakean standpoint, ethics can be thought and practised only in the context of a relational interaction between *integral* entities, each of which retains its own minute particularity, or difference, in the process of social interaction.

This is not to suggest that Blake privileges antipathy over its contrary, the "similitude" of sympathy. Rather, he emphasizes the need vigilantly to maintain a *balance* between these two modes of identification. Such balance is implicit in the Blakean concept of the "Outline of identity," also called the "bounding line" (DC; E550). In Blake's visual art and poetry, this necessary outline protects the entity's integrity and autonomy by maintaining its difference from other entities. Taken to an extreme, however, the bounding line defining one's minute particularity can give way to "strong Fortifications" (J 18:38; E163; see also 28:25–6; E174) or "stone walls of separation" (J 90:12; E249), impenetrable barriers that foreclose the possibility of communal relations by preventing the mutualistic commingling of Emanations. Blake's privileged line, therefore, is not fixed or static. While it defines the entity within its proper boundaries, it also "bounds" in the sense that it "leaps" and "jumps," performing what Blake calls, in his *Descriptive Catalogue*, "infinite inflexions and *movements*" (E550; emphasis added). In other words, the "bounding line" is moveable and porous, strong enough to define an entity in the context of its own minute particularity but flexible enough to prevent atomism or solipsism by accommodating sociality and the commingling of difference.[24]

One of Blake's descriptions of the Polypus in *Milton* illustrates most succinctly the necessity of maintaining a balance between these contraries of identity and difference (or sympathy and antipathy):

> were it not for Bowlahoola & Allamanda
> No Human Form but only a Fibrous Vegetation
> A Polypus of soft affections without Thought or Vision
> Must tremble in the Heavens & Earths thro all the Ulro space
> Throw all the Vegetated Mortals into Bowlahoola[.] (M 24:36–40; E120)

To appreciate the importance of this passage to an adequate understanding of the Polypus, one must first define those strange and complex figures Bowlahoola and Allamanda. As the site where "the various Classes of Men are all markd out determinate" (M 26:37, 39; E123), Bowlahoola is a space in the Blakean cosmos where *distinctions* are made. The same can be said of its physiological function. As "the Stomach in every individual man" (M 24:67; E121), Bowlahoola breaks food down into its component particulars for digestion by the physical body. Allamanda, on the contrary, is "the nervous system ... the apparatus for giving and receiving communications" (Damon 1988, 17). Hence it enables sympathetic *connections* to be made between individuals. Similarly, as "Commerce" on "Earth" (M 27:42; E125),

Allamanda ideally functions as a mode of social relationship, enabling the physical and ideational exchanges that occur between different entities. Summarizing these differences between Bowlahoola and Allamanda, Mark Bracher argues that the former is the analytic power (which breaks complex relationships or entities down into their minutely particular components) while Allamanda is the synthetic power (which establishes connections between discrete entities) (1985, 167). An overabundance of the analytic power (Bowlahoola) leads to an atomized, fragmented world view and thus to a fractured world. Conversely, too much synthetic power (Allamanda) causes dissociation or a fall into non-entity as the individual identifies too closely with the totality of its environmental stimuli. In Blake's mythology, both analytic and synthetic powers are necessary to the maintenance of a balanced sense of selfhood, one that can relate sympathetically with other beings without losing its individual integrity or the minute particularity of its being.

Milton's references to Bowlahoola and Allamanda suggest that an overabundance of synthetic power (Allamanda) enables the proliferation of the monstrous Polypus and the connective tissues comprising its "Fibrous Vegetation." Thus, the Polypus is a figure for the indissociate human, the product of pathological sympathy or totalitarian community. Such a human is not intentionally malevolent in its actions (hence its seemingly harmless "soft affections"). But its lack of a differentiating "Thought or Vision" inevitably entails a self-directed violence that destroys the integrity of its being. Entirely the product of sympathy or synthesis, in other words, the entity characterized by an excess of Allamanda becomes a "Vegetated Mortal" having no particular identity and knowing no self-difference. Therefore, Blake associates it on the same plate with a "Web of Death" (24:36; E120) rather than one of life. The solution to such indissociate human identity is to "Throw all the Vegetated Mortals into Bowlahoola" (24:40),[25] where, subjected to a balanced restoration of the analytic power, the harmful vegetative syntheses caused by an overactive Allamanda will be broken down, enabling these entities to reassert an appropriate degree of individuality.

In the hyper-sympathetic state symbolized by the Polypus, the human is, somewhat paradoxically, unable to assert any genuine sympathy for other entities comprising and inhabiting its natural and social environments. To a certain extent, this problem is perceptually based. Immediately prior to the appearance of the Polypus on plate 66 of *Jerusalem*, we learn that human "perceptions" have been "dissipated into the Indefinite." Subsequently those mortals who have been

assimilated to the Polypus "look forth" into the world only to discover
that all things inhabiting their field of vision are now obscured:

> the Sun is shrunk: the Heavens are shrunk
> Away into the far remote: and the Trees & Mountains witherd
> Into indefinite cloudy shadows in darkness & separation.
> By invisible Hatreds adjoind, they seem remote and separate
> From each other; and yet are a Mighty Polypus in the Deep!
> (66:47–54; E219)

Implicitly, this passage represents poetically Blake's critique of the
primitivism that he and contemporaries like Mary Wollstonecraft
associated with Rousseau. For Blake, the primitivist notion that
humans must rid themselves of their "cultural" conditioning in order
to access an uncorrupted state of "nature" is ultimately harmful, both
to humanity and to the natural world. In short, excessive communion
or sympathetic "identification" with nature (as I argued above in my
reference to Arne Naess's "deep ecology") does not bring Blakean
humanity into a closer relationship with the external cosmos; on the
contrary, it causes the "heavens" to become "far remote" (like the
abstract sky-God who governs them), while at the same time
"wither[ing]" trees, mountains, and all other earthly forms. Far from
bringing humans into communion with the totality of their cosmic
environment, the Polypus of natural sympathy enacts their "separa-
tion" from it – and from each other. This separation, as I have been
arguing, is part and parcel of the heteronomous condition, an indis-
sociated state accompanied by the darkening and withering of *both*
subjects and objects – a process foreclosing the very possibility of
differential relations. To quote from Mary Wollstonecraft's famous
critique of Rousseauvian "primitivism," the Polypus symbolizes a
"ferocious flight back to the night of sensual ignorance" (1982, 53).

Earlier in *Jerusalem*, a similar crisis of perception and identity
occurs. Associated both with the process of "vegetation" and with
the appearance of the Polypus (the two of which figures are clearly
related), this crisis has adverse social *and* ecological ramifications.

> The Gigantic roots & twigs of the vegetating Sons of Albion
> Filld with the little-ones are consumed in the Fires of their Altars
> The vegetating Cities are burned & consumed from the Earth:
> And the Bodies in which all Animals & Vegetations, the Earth & Heaven
> Were contained in the All Glorious Imagination are witherd & darkend.
> (49:10–14; E198)

It is important to note that Blake uses "vegetation" in two distinct senses in this passage. When he writes of the "Bodies" of "Animals & Vegetations," the word refers to the botanical phenomena of nature, actual organic vegetations that are damaged and destroyed by the cultural activities of Albion's Sons. That Blake values these vegetations most highly is apparent in the relationship he posits between their physical "Bodies" and the "All Glorious Imagination." When Blake describes Albion's Sons and their "Cities" as "vegetating," however, the concept is negative and so represented in terms of violence and destruction. Because of this human form of "vegetation" – which implies the same lack of "Thought or Vision" characterizing the state of the Polypus – the non-human forms of plants and animals, once "contain in the All Glorious Imagination," are "witherd & darkend"; and human cities "are burned & consumed" in a fiery holocaust. Once again, Blake associates these forms of environmental and social destruction with the "narrowed perceptions" characterizing the emergence of the "Polypus of Death" (49:21, 24). For Blake, quite simply, the human and vegetable realms must remain integral and distinct, for they are the loci of irreducibly different forms of existence. The blurring of the bounding line that both joins and separates these realms leads, in Blake's vision, not to heightened inter-species communion (as Naess's deep ecology would have it) but to the destruction of both human and non-human phenomena (cities *and* wild places, human *and* non-human beings, Heaven *and* Earth). For Blake, in other words, the human desire to return to nature, to achieve "oneness" with its glorious animal and vegetable forms, entails the possibility of a pernicious "vegetating" that ultimately destroys "the little-ones," the Minute Particulars defining both identity and difference.

The figure of the vegetative human is ubiquitous in *Jerusalem*, where it is often explicitly associated with the Polypus. Immediately prior to the latter's first appearance in the poem, for example, Blake depicts Albion's son Scofield as "Vegetated by Reubens Gate" (15:2; E158). This passage recalls a similar incident on plate 11, wherein "Scofield is bound in iron armour! / He is like a mandrake in the earth before Reubens gate: / He shoots beneath Jerusalems walls to undermine her foundations!" (11:21–3; E154). Blake associates Scofield with the mandrake for good reason. As the English physician Sir Thomas Browne pointed out in the seventeenth century, "the ancients ... generally esteemed [the mandrake] narcotick or stupefactive, and it is to be found in the list of poisons set down by Dioscorides, Galen, Ætius, Ægineta" (1968, 315). Browne's remark can illuminate our understanding of Scofield's function in *Jerusalem*, for, as a "Vegetated" human mandrake, Scofield exists in a stupefactive or poisoned state. Hence it is likely that he undermines the foundations of Jerusalem – thus destroying his only hope of liberty from such a state – without fully realizing what he is doing. It is interesting to note with Browne, moreover, that the ancients also regarded the narcotic mandrake as "a philter or plant that conciliates affection" (316), for this aphrodisiac effect suggests something of the seductive nature of the Polypus, whose "soft affections" enable it to transform unwitting men like Scofield into human vegetations.

The mandrake's well-known traditional association with human fertility is also relevant to this discussion. The "common conceit," as Thomas Browne points out, is that the biblical "Rachel requested these plants [from Leah] as a medicine of fecundation, or whereby she might become fruitful" (313). This association certainly informs the function of the Polypus – that prolific maker of human mandrakes – in Blake's epic poetry. As we have seen, eighteenth-century commentators were fascinated by the regenerative capacity of the freshwater polyp; and Blake's Polypus, in its almost infinite ability to propagate itself, incorporates and exaggerates this characteristic. By undermining Jerusalem's foundations, Scofield's activity as the Polypus's mandrake offspring threatens drastically to proliferate the human vegetative condition, enlarging the Polypus's domain from the entire realm of time and space to that of Eternity itself (since Jerusalem is, at one level of its figural signification, the Eternal or Heavenly city). With Albion's cosmic form entirely assimilated to the proliferating, colonialist Polypus, all hope of human liberty (which is Jerusalem) would be destroyed.

What is less well known about the mandrake is that its medicinal application "provokes the menstrous flows, and procures abortion" (316). Undoubtedly, Blake's mandrake-making Polypus symbolically incorporates this association, for it is simultaneously a figure for fecundation *and* abortion, a contradictory entity "at variance with Itself / In all its Members" (J 69:6–7; E223). Significantly, this reference to the Polypus's internal discord directly follows its representation as a cancer of the womb.[26] In what is perhaps *Jerusalem*'s most frightful image, Blake recounts a scenario in which "all the Males combined into One Male & every one / Became a ravening eating Cancer growing in the Female / A Polypus of Roots of Reasoning Doubt Despair & Death" (69:1–3). These lines explicitly associate the Polypus with androcentric activity. At one level, its cancerous growth stems from contemporary scientific endeavour and its particular modes of objective "Reasoning." For Blake, modern science's Baconian penetration of nature's "womb," far from encouraging a propagation of life, is a rapacious act that turns creation itself into a monstrosity, the "ravening eating" Polypus of "Death." At a more mundane level, the Sons' colonization of the female body represents the negative implications for female subjectivity of a social economy wherein women are forced to interiorize a harmful male-centred mode of identity, one that is not diverse in its minute particularity but thoroughly homogeneous (as Blake implies in his reference to the Satanic "One Male").[27] At any rate, the negation of diversity implicit in the figure of the "One Male" culminates in a condition of "infernal bondage" (69:9) both for females *and* for males, a condition in which identity can only be destructively "at variance with Itself" (69:6). The resultant form – like "the Misletoe [that] grows on the Oak" (one of Blake's numerous analogues for the Polypus) (66:55; E219) – cannot ultimately survive its own activity, for it parasitically destroys the very body or host that supports its existence.

The figure of the male Polypus as a virulent cancer growing in the "womb of nature" suggests something of the patriarchal aspect of its manifestation in *Jerusalem*. Just prior to its second explicit appearance in the text, the Sons of Albion, in a perverse parody of Eternal "Brotherhood" (88:14; E246), unite to condemn the female Emanation Jerusalem, declaring their intention to build in her stead "Babylon the City of Vala." Subsequently deifying Vala as "the Goddess Virgin-Mother," they loudly proclaim her to be "our Mother! Nature!" (18:28–30; E163). This act of naming serves a twofold purpose. By declaring themselves the offspring of a deified Nature, they are at once able to sacralize *and* to naturalize their building of Babylon and the divisive politics of Babylonian warfare that would destroy Jerusalem. Moreover, by proclaiming their mother a virgin, the Sons usurp divinity, setting themselves up as self-righteous Christs, attempting thus "to destroy" the *real* "Divine Saviour; the Friend of Sinners" (18:37). The Sons' various activities are obviously contradictory. Although they identify themselves as Mother Nature's offspring, the very products of "nature's womb," the Sons negate their mother's reproductive role – not to mention their own related corporeality – by insisting on her virginal chastity. This self-contradictory discursive activity produces a deathly cancerous, inevitably self-destructing monstrosity: "a mighty Polypus, vegetating in darkness" (18:40). While Blake represents the Polypus as a kind of vegetable, the fact that it vegetates "in darkness," beyond the reach of creation's life-giving light, suggests that it is not a "natural" vegetation at all. Rather, it is the product of a complex power struggle, a struggle whose misguided human combatants construct and deify "nature" for explicitly political purposes. That such activity is at odds with the interests of nature "itself" (and so by no means "natural") is made apparent on the plate immediately following, where we witness an ecological devastation: the alteration of climate; the destruction of crops, domesticated animals, and human children; and the ultimate production of a "desolated Earth" (19:1–16; E163–4). Since one of Blake's greatest desires was to inspire the building of Jerusalem in England's green and pleasant land, we might see in the Polypus a dire prophetic warning, a Blakean admonition articulated in the hope of averting such desolation.

Coda:
Blake's Apocalypse, Druidism, and the Humanization of Nature

Where shall we take our stand to view the infinite & unbounded
Or where are human feet for Lo our eyes are in the heavens
(Blake, *The Four Zoas*)

Like many people of my generation, I was inundated during my formative years by media reports concerning real or scientifically predicted ecological disaster. Gazing outraged, perplexed, or merely stupefied at the television screen, I watched as a succession of broken oil tankers vomited their toxic cargoes onto shoreline habitats; I consumed graphic tabloid accounts and documentaries describing the adverse social and environmental consequences of a number of highly publicized chemical and radiation leaks; I heard interminable stories of drought and famine, species loss, massive clear-cut logging operations, nuclear weapons testing, global warming, ecological terrorism, and a host of other unthinkable occurrences. Consequently, I was horrified by the violence that humans seemed continually to perpetrate on each other and on the natural environment, and I found myself becoming increasingly sceptical about the value of humanity, which seemed not the pinnacle of earthly being (as I had been taught in grade school) but the very bane of the planet. Like so many young people, in short, I began in the face of seemingly insoluble environmental crisis – not to mention the frustrating appearance of governmental and corporate quietude – to cultivate a sense of scorn for humanity, believing that I much preferred plants and animals to humans, and even telling myself that the Earth would be a better place if humans simply followed the dinosaurs into the oblivion of extinction.

In retrospect, I attribute these impulses to the frustrations and hubris of my disgruntled adolescence; and although my concerns for the well-being of the natural world are today unabated, I am relieved to note that I long ago stopped harbouring such unproductive anti-human sentiments! Thus I am troubled whenever I hear the (sometimes justifiable) charge of misanthrope levelled at contemporary environmentalist critique (I'll resist detailing the ways I shudder at the dismissive epithet "tree-hugger," and all the sly meanings it inevitably encodes). Where lies the truth? While an environmentalist focus upon the anthropocentric arrogance of traditional humanism is in many ways justifiable, one must also admit that the ecocentric privileging of nature *over* humanity involves a certain arrogance of its own, especially where such privileging fails to acknowledge the human difficulties and suffering that some forms of proposed environmentalist policy must entail, including, among other things, the dislocation of peoples, the loss of jobs, and the eradication of various cultural customs and ways of life.[1] For better or worse, I have sought in this study to find some common ground between socially and environmentally oriented ways of reading Blake's still-relevant poetry, attempting to understand how the poet's equivocal philosophy of nature illuminates his discourse on *human* strife and redemption. Since I believe it is a great error to perceive environmental and social modes of critique as exclusive and incompatible pursuits, and since I must at every turn acknowledge the ultimate inescapability of my own particular cultural humanity, I realize that some thinkers (especially those who wish to locate environmental ethical value in nature itself rather than in humanistic or anthropomorphic discourses on nature) will have much reason to object to my discussion of Blake's distinctively human-centred environmental poetics.

Speaking from experience, I find such possible objection entirely understandable: when I first attempted to struggle through a reading of Blake's *œuvre*, I was highly suspicious of the poet's philosophical emphasis upon the "human form divine," distrusting especially the anthropocentric character of his ostensibly redemptive apocalypse. But I also noticed that the poems themselves seemed to anticipate and sanction my suspicions by questioning their own human-centred textual biases. As I have argued throughout this study, Blake's work, despite its heterogeneous scope, shows us how self-interested modes of discursive practice lead inevitably to the philosophical devaluation, physical domination, and ultimate desolation of the Earth, its ecosystems, and its living creatures, both human and non-human. In *The Book of Thel*, the protagonist's conditioned obsession with human-centred discourses of hierarchy and use-value cause her destructively to instrumentalize her environment and its non-human inhabitants, allowing her in turn to be manipulated as a gendered instrument of the self-interested and inequitable pursuits of a naturalized patriarchy.

In *Milton*, Satan's legal code of human morality (in both its religious and naturalistic forms) appals all living things, reducing humans to docile automatons and the cosmos itself to a vast and lifeless machine. Finally, in *Jerusalem*, we witness the devastating consequences that follow Albion's self-centred anthropomorphic practices, the andro-centric feminization of nature, and even the all-too-human effort to identify sympathetically with the totality of nature itself. Now if, in each of these poems, human conceptions of nature are largely the *cause* of nature's devaluation and downfall, can the humanization of nature that occurs in *Jerusalem*'s apocalypse (98:44; E258) be trusted as an appropriate resolution to this most pressing problem?

One can begin to answer this question by considering a passage from Elizabeth Barrett Browning's *Aurora Leigh* (1856), for although this poem was published thirty-six years after Blake completed *Jerus-alem*, its anthropomorphic philosophy of human-nature relations is at times remarkably similar to Blake's. For Barrett Browning, as for Blake, a certain kind of anthropomorphic activity seems a necessary prereq-uisite to a workable environmental ethic. As her female protagonist, the poet Aurora Leigh, so succinctly states,

> A tree's mere firewood, unless humanised –
> Which well the Greeks knew when they stirred its bark
> With close-pressed bosoms of subsiding nymphs,
> And made the forest-rivers garrulous
> With babble of gods. (5:95–9)

This passage recalls Blake's well-known reference in *The Marriage of Heaven and Hell* to the "ancient Poets," who also humanize their environment by

> animat[ing] all sensible objects with Gods or Geniuses, calling
> them by the names and adorning them with the properties of woods,
> rivers, mountains, lakes, cities, nations, and whatever their
> enlarged & numerous senses could percieve. (MHH 11; E38)

For both Blake and Barrett Browning, poetic anthropomorphism pre-vents a purely utilitarian approach to the natural world. When the things of nature are deified via human imaginative intervention, they become sacred and articulate, like the prophesying trees Blake's *Milton* presents as "Visions of Eternity" (M 26:7–10; E123). If Hans Peter Duerr's assertion that "people do not exploit a nature that speaks to them" (1985, 92) is correct, such a humanization of nature might be seen as ecologically and ethically efficacious.[2] At any rate, for Blake and Barrett Browning, it is when natural entities are *deh*u-manized that they become nothing more than exploitable resources or "raw materials": no longer the sacred loci of human-projected deity, trees become "mere firewood," masts for the fleets of imperialist navigation or grist for the dark and ominous mills of a burgeoning capitalist industrialism.

In Blake's view, as I have argued, such instrumentalization of nature is particularly insidious, extending beyond the object world to the perceiving subjects of that world, who inevitably "become what they behold." Blake describes this process of objectification implicitly in *The Marriage of Heaven and Hell*. While the ancient poets are busy imbuing the world's "sensible objects" with a multitude of particularized "mental deities," other more general, less poetical, discursive impulses come into play,

> Till a system was formed, which some took advantage of & enslav'd the vulgar by attempting to realize or abstract the mental dieties from their objects: thus began Priesthood.
> Choosing forms of worship from poetic tales.
> And at length they pronounced that the Gods had orderd such things.
> Thus men forgot that All deities reside in the human breast.
>
> (MHH 11; E38).

While it is possible to argue that the ancient poets are complicitous with an oppressive Priesthood, creating the systemic conditions necessary to its formal institution through acts of anthropomorphic animation, one should note that Priesthood is nevertheless for Blake a "new" social phenomenon: it *begins* directly in the wake of concerted attempts to "abstract the mental dieties from their objects." If, according to Barrett Browning's overt logic, such abstraction mercilessly instrumentalizes the natural world, it also in Blake's view "enslav[es] the vulgar," turning not only common people but creative poets themselves into unwitting instruments of the self-interested and self-ordained interpretive élite Blake refers to as "Priesthood."

In *Jerusalem*, Blake declares that the *original* Priesthood is in fact a Druidic manifestation: since, according to his anglocentric theology, "'All things Begin & End in Albions Ancient Druid Rocky Shore,'" the Old Testament Patriarchs – "Abraham, Heber, Shem, and Noah" – must themselves have been "Druids" (J 27; E171). This revisionist view of biblical history (which Blake likely inherited through the work of English antiquarians like Jacob Bryant and Edward Williams[3]) complicates and problematizes Blake's anthropomorphic environmental ethic, for the Druids, far from regarding trees as mere firewood, were a primitive race of nature worshippers who "held the oak sacred, and worshipped in oak groves, cutting the rare mistletoe with a golden knife" (Damon 1988, 108). In Blake's mythology, however, the Druid sacralization of nature remains dangerous for a couple of crucial reasons. To revisit the *Marriage of Heaven and Hell*, although the Druidic Priesthood does not "abstract the mental deities from their [natural] objects," it attempts just as problematically "to realize" (11; E38) these projected deities, actualizing them as *inherent* properties of the external world by granting them an objective or "real" existence in nature per se. Like its close cousin "abstraction," this Blakean process of "realization" causes humans to forget that nature's sacredness is, from the standpoint of human understanding, always and inevitably a distinctively human production. "Thus," Blake declares, "men forgot that All deities reside in the human breast" (11; E38). By denying or negating the human poetic origin of nature's deification, Blake's Druidic Priesthood engages in a species of ecocentric spiritual misanthrope: attributing divinity *to* nature – and, concomitantly, denying its residence in human being – they sever a fundamental spiritual human-nature connection.

Such a process of human-nature severance sheds light on the Druidic nature of Albion's fall in *Jerusalem* from an interactively balanced fourfold unity of constituent Zoas into the divisive and dismal state of Eternal Death. Near the end of the poem, just as the process of cosmic renovation begins, an appalled Brittannia (Vala and Jerusalem finally reunited) explains the "murder" of the divine humanity as nothing other than an aspect of ritualized Druidic misanthrope:

> O pitious Sleep O pitious Dream! O God O God awake I have slain
> In Dreams of Chastity & Moral Law I have Murdered Albion! Ah!
> In Stone-henge & on London Stone & in the Oak Groves of Malden
> I have Slain him in my Sleep with the Knife of the Druid O England[.]
> (J 94:22–5; E254)

Brittannia's self-accusatory words must be weighed most carefully. Her explicit references to Druidism are particularly significant, for in Blake's mythology the nature-loving Druids actualize the misanthropic underpinnings of their nature worship by basing their religion on the ritualized practice of human sacrifice (Fisher 1961, 38–9). According to Blake, Druidism thus anticipates ascetic modes of Christian religious belief, which negate human corporeal or sensual existence by advocating a false "Chastity," including an accompanying prophylactic separation of humanity and divinity. What is more, the depiction of Druidic practice in Blake's *œuvre* suggests that

Druidism also prefigures the arrival of Enlightenment physical sci-
ence, whose objective methodology in a sense sacrifices humanity by
attempting to expunge from the cosmos all anthropomorphism, all
subjectivity, all traces of the vital human form that provides both the
macrocosmic and microcosmic bases of Blake's universe. Hence in
the fallen world of *Jerusalem*, Blake characterizes both ancient Druid-
ism and contemporary physical science in terms of a deadly analyt-
ical Reason (66:3; E218). Such similarity enables us to see Brittannia's
sacrificial knife as a forerunner of the real or figurative scalpel of the
Enlightenment an-atomist, who, murdering to dissect, reduces whole
living creatures to their inanimate component parts. Crucially, since
everything is ultimately human in Blake's imaginative cosmos, Brit-
tannia's Druidic slaying of Albion, once accomplished, would render
all entities inert and dead, like the "pure" and lifeless matter that
Enlightenment science privileges as its model conceptual entity.

Given Blake's understanding of the anti-human nature of Druid
and Druidic practices, we can begin to appreciate the appropriateness
of Albion's behaviour when he awakens to the sound of Brittannia's
confession:

> The Breath Divine went forth over the morning hills Albion rose
> In anger: the wrath of God breaking bright flaming on all sides around
> His awful limbs: into the Heavens he walked clothed in flames
> Loud thundring, with broad flashes of flaming lightning & pillars
> Of fire, speaking the Words of Eternity in Human Forms ...
> (J 95:5–9; E255)

Albion, behaving much like the Christ of the Parousia or Second
Coming (Paley 1983, 231), directs his wrath against the "Druid Spec-
tre" (J 98:6; E257), progenitor of the epistemic practices that have
functioned to negate his own human being. Having become in his
newly risen state a champion of intellectual rather than corporeal
warfare, Albion chooses for his weapon not the deadly "Sword of
Steel," so decried in antinomian theological writing (Reeve and
Muggleton 1760, 9–10), but human language, the creative stuff of
intellectual exchange and poetry itself. As he speaks out against the
violence of Druidic misanthrope, Albion reaffirms his formerly
despised humanity in the strongest of terms, his "Words of Eternity"
themselves becoming manifest as living, breathing "Human Forms."
In the wake of this inspired intellectual activity, Blake prompts his
readers to envision, from an explicitly earthly standpoint, an apoca-
lyptic transformation of the mechanized natural world.

> Thou seest the Sun in heavy clouds
> Struggling to rise above the Mountains. in his burning hand
> He takes his Bow, then chooses out his arrows of flaming gold
> Murmuring the Bowstring breathes with ardor! Clouds roll around the
> Horns of the wide Bow, loud sounding winds sport on the mountain brows
> Compelling Urizen to his Furrow; & Tharmas to his Sheepfold;
> And Luvah to his Loom ... (J 95:11–17; E255)

In this passage, we witness the Sun's imitation and adaptation of Albion's actions. As we have seen, the latter "rose / In anger: the wrath of God breaking bright flaming on all sides around / His awful limbs." Following this exemplary behaviour, the Sun also "Struggl[es] to rise," after which, in close imitation of Albion's "flaming" wrath, "He ... chooses out his arrows of flaming gold." This act "Compell[s]" the three truant Zoas – Urizen, Tharmas, and Luvah – to rejoin the faithful Urthona (who is Los), resuming their respective stations at furrow, sheepfold, and loom. But the Sun's exerted force, far from signifying the blind "compulsion" Blake repeatedly associates in *Milton* with Newtonian physical law, compels the Zoas to join in an active and creative *intellectual* combat in "Wars of mutual Benevolence" and "Wars of Love" (J 97:14; E256).

Blake emphasizes the natural world's emancipation from the compulsive forces of Newtonian physical law in his subsequent poetic depiction of the concerted actions of "the Sun & Moon." These orbs, formerly symbols of a determinate and therefore oppressive celestial mechanism, are now, in their altered condition, able to "lead ... the Visions of Heaven & Earth" forward towards Blake's emancipatory antinomian Eternity. Three plates later, following the Sun's exemplary activity, the Four Zoas, taking up their own Bows, prepare to launch flaming "Arrows of Intellect" at the "Druid Spectre" itself. Rather than opposing or lamenting the impending destruction of nature-worshipping Druidism and its particular vision of the natural world, the things of nature respond to the Zoas' warlike behaviour just as they had earlier responded to the Sun's similarly wrathful activity:

> Murmuring the Bow-string breathes with ardor. Clouds roll round the horns
> Of the wide Bow. loud sounding Winds sport on the Mountains brows:
> The Druid Spectre was Annihilate[.] (J 98:4–6; E257)

Uniting to annihilate the Druid Spectre, humanity (represented by Albion and his constituent Zoas) and nature (represented by the sun, moon, clouds, and wind) do not destroy rational science in Blake's apocalypse. Freeing science, rather, from what Blake saw as its Druidic enthralment, they create the conditions necessary for its ultimate reunion with the poetic arts from which it had formerly been severed. Hence "Bacon & Newton & Locke," previously Blake's deathly parody of the holy trinity, are not destroyed or banished but grammatically conjoined to the living human trinity of "Milton & Shakspear & Chaucer" (98:9). With the annihilation of the Druid Spectre, Priesthood and its rigidly codified systems of thought are replaced by the intellectual agency and mutuality implied by Blake's intersubjective ideal of "Mental Fight." This ideal recuperates the Enlightenment by affirming a necessary mode of critical rationality; but it tempers this rationality by uniting it with the self-reflexive, creative, and spiritual impulses Blake identifies with art and poetry. To quote *The Four Zoas*, the result of this union is "sweet Science" (51:30; E334), Blake's ultimate vehicle of "imaginative redemption" (Greenberg 1983, 117).

With this turn of events in mind, we can understand that Blake's overt disdain for Druidism need not be seen as a sign of disdain for all material or natural existence. Far from being a product of nature per se, Druidism implies for Blake a particular mode of discursive practice, a violence contemporary society perpetrates upon the material world in its efforts to apprehend and contain the latter's irreducible alterity. This aspect of Blake's *social* critique helps to explain what I have called the pre-deconstructive double vision informing his deployment of poetic figures whose referents are to some extent "natural." Consider, for instance, Blake's poetic depiction of the oak, the Druidic tree in whose "Groves" Brittannia claims to have slain Albion. While the oak's association with the violence of human sacrifice suggests the negative aspect of its metaphorical role in *Jerusalem*, its figurative function in Blake's *œuvre* is, in an overall sense, ambivalent and unsettled. To begin with, the oak functions in much of the early poetry as a poetic figure for Blake's positively valued state of Innocence. Since "The Ecchoing Green" (E8) provides a particularly germane case in point, it will be helpful here to reproduce this brief *Song of Innocence* in its entirety:

The Sun does arise,
And make happy the skies.
The merry bells ring
To welcome the Spring.
The sky-lark and thrush,
The birds of the bush,
Sing louder around,
To the bells chearful sound.

While our sports shall be seen
On the Ecchoing Green.

Old John with white hair
Does laugh away care,
Sitting under the oak,
Among the old folk,
They laugh at our play,
And soon they all say.
Such such were the joys.
When we all girls & boys,
In our youth-time were seen,
On the Ecchoing Green.

Till the little ones weary
No more can be merry
The sun does descend,
And our sports have an end:
Round the laps of their mothers,
Many sisters and brothers,
Like birds in their nest,
Are ready for rest;
And sport no more seen,
On the darkening Green. (SIE; E8)

In this deceptively simple poem, human and non-human beings coexist in a spirit of harmonious mutual interchange: "The sky-lark and thrush, / The birds of the bush, / Sing louder" in direct response to the human music produced by the "merry" churchbells, whose melodic ringing, far from negating natural process, celebrates it by "welcom[ing]" the returning spring. By the end of the poem, this imaginative sense of mutual human-nature interchange is, in a manner of speaking, literalized, as Blake likens the innocent children, resting in the safety of their mothers' laps, to weary "birds in their nest." Significantly, at the very centre of the poem's harmonious all-encompassing community is "the oak," under whose sheltering branches the "old folk" gather in cheerful, laughing witness of the day's life-affirming activities. Far from being associated with Druidic violence, the oak of "The Ecchoing Green" is a potent figure of Blakean Innocence and the benevolent plenitude of inclusive cosmic community.

As Brian John succinctly remarks, however, "Experience will pervert [the oak] into a Druidic Emblem" (1974, 26). Thus, in the highly fraught political contexts of *Jerusalem*'s narrative, Blake associates the oak not with the ideality of a plenitudinous Innocence but with "the Patriarch Druid" and the misanthropic extremes of human sacrifice (J 98:48–51; E258). But this figurative relationship cannot ultimately prevail even in a patently non-innocent poem like *Jerusalem*. Since in popular culture the oak was commonly associated with England itself, it follows that the renovation of Albion-England must involve a renovation of Albion's major poetic figures. Such a process likely informs Blake's statement in *Jerusalem* that "As the Misletoe grows on the Oak, so Albions Tree [grows] on Eternity" (66:55; E219), since the parallelism of this passage correlates the oak with Blake's highly valued Eternity, the "home" of the Unfallen Albion, while correlating the Druidic mistletoe with Albion's Tree, the monstrous Polypus that threatens to assimilate and destroy Albion and all things inhabiting his all-inclusive cosmic form. While these correlations (which in a sense liberate the oak from its ancient Druidic signification) might seem unfair to the mistletoe's biological referent, they are nevertheless politically appropriate, for mistletoe is a parasitic entity that sustains itself by destroying other beings (just as in Blake's mythology the Druidic religious system sustains itself via the scapegoatism implicit in formalized rituals of human sacrifice; Fisher 1961, 38). As a naturally occurring phenomenon, biological parasitism – like other forms of natural predacity – points towards a major problem inherent in any unqualified valorization or celebration of nature, not the least because it can be invoked conceptually to sanction or "naturalize" analogous forms of human "parasitic" violence.[4] Ultimately, by removing "the whole Druid Law ... away" (J 69:39; E223), Blake's antinomian Jesus dismantles *discursive* appropriations of nature that function to support and justify violent modes of social relationship, freeing Albion from the grip of the Polypus and his animated oak from the deadly embrace of its Druidic mistletoe.

Incidentally, in a discussion of the antinomian "Everlasting Gospel," Blake attempts to prove his thesis that the Old Testament patriarchs "were Druids" by calling this state of historical affairs something that "the Druid Temples (which are the Patriarchal Pillars & Oak Groves) over the whole Earth witness to this day" (J 27; E171). Unfortunately, from our vantage point at the turn of the twenty-first century, we must take Blake's own word as an affirmation of this historical "truth"; for if oak groves existed across "the whole Earth" in Blake's time, their numbers have long since been decimated. In North America, for example, vast expanses of oak savanna, which early European settlers derogatively termed "oak barrens," covered an estimated thirteen million hectares of land. Today, in the wake of massive industrial clearcutting, less that 0.02 percent of these original forested areas remain (Burns and Reidy 1996, 4, 13). It is sad but hardly surprising that so many of the world's great oak groves have finally succumbed to the violence they were once made to signify as symbols of Druidic sacrificial practice.[5]

With these sobering insights in mind, let us reconsider Brittannia's remarks concerning the role she has played in the Druidic slaying of the giant Albion (J 94:22–5; E254). After assuming complete responsibility for Albion's murder, Brittannia condemns herself in patently stereotypical terms, crying "O all ye Nations of the Earth behold ye the Jealous Wife." These gendered self-deprecatory words are, however, ultimately undermined as Brittannia goes on inadvertently to acknowledge that Albion's murder, far from having been carried out by herself alone, was conducted in the context of a highly politicized social milieu: in the line that concludes her confession of murder, she reveals that "The Eagle & the Wolf & Monkey & Owl & the King & Priest were there" (94:26–7). The grammatical conjoining in this passage of non-human entities to "King & Priest" suggests, at one level, that Blake is "animalizing" the latter, denouncing "King & Priest" – and the social institutions they represent – as less than human or less than humane. At another level, however, this same conjoining suggests that the animals in the passage have been tied to or bound by the same forms of institutionalized power that relentlessly oppress Brittannia's constituents, Vala and Jerusalem, after Albion's fall and prior to his apocalyptic renovation in *Jerusalem*. Indeed, the ultimate positioning on the plate of "King & Priest" (consistently representatives of legal and hierarchical tyranny in Blake's antinomian-influenced philosophy) suggests that the systems of authority they represent, and not Brittannia, have been responsible for Albion's death.

This political scenario becomes especially significant given *Jerusalem*'s explicit critique of social hierarchy. Midway through the poem, for example, the Eternals, discussing their relationship to "the Dead" of the Ulro, articulate an unequivocal distaste for hierarchical social structures. "To be their inferiors or superiors we equally abhor," they declare. "Superior, none we know: inferior none: all equal share / Divine Benevolence & joy" (55:7–9; E204). If, as the Eternals plainly state, Eternity refuses to countenance the inequities of social hierarchy, then presumably the kinds of political conflict that rage around Vala's body during the course of the poem will be eradicated by the apocalypse, especially including those modes of conflict associated with or produced by discourses allowing humans "dominion" over each other and over non-human others. At any rate, as *Jerusalem*'s apocalypse gathers momentum, Blake presents the reader with a list of animals that is significantly altered in constitution: the "King &

Priest" who accompany the animals listed in Brittannia's confession are here conspicuously absent. On plate 98, Blake tells us that he has "heard Jehovah speak"

> Terrific from his Holy Place & saw the Words of the Mutual Covenant Divine
> On Chariots of gold & jewels with Living Creatures starry & flaming
> With every Colour, Lion, Tyger, Horse, Elephant, Eagle Dove, Fly, Worm,
> And the all wondrous Serpent clothed in gems & rich array Humanize
> In the Forgiveness of Sins according to the Covenant of Jehovah.
> (98:40–5; E258)

A number of observations are relevant to a reading of nature and animality in this passage. First, as we saw in the previous chapter, many of the animals listed here (dove, serpent, eagle, lion) are the very ones who earlier chose, in the wake of the Polypus's creation on plate 66, to "build a habitation separate from Man" (66:70–3; E219). Since Blake has already depicted the "vast form of Nature" as "a serpent" (43:76, 80; E192–3), the serpent's fleeing at this point into "the four-fold wilderness" (66:71) – and away from a less than four-fold humanity – suggests that "nature" itself, far from sanctioning the creation of the Polypus, knows enough to abhor it as somehow un- or anti-natural. There is scant evidence, in short, that the Polypus is an authentic delegate or representative of non-human nature or of the material realm "as such." On the contrary, this horrific monster signifies what becomes of nature as a result of the way nature is conceptualized – indeed the way it discursively materializes – in contexts supporting human political strife and corporeal warfare. At the end of *Jerusalem*, the individual animals' return to humanity represents a necessary reconciliation between the poem's human and non-human spheres. Indeed, the return of nature itself as "the all wondrous Serpent clothed in gems & rich array" (98:44) recalls *Milton*'s reference to "this Vegetable World," which Blake figures as "a bright sandal formd immortal of precious stones & gold" (M 21:12–13; E115). As I argued in chapter 3, the binding on of this sandal enables the poet subsequently "to walk forward thro' Eternity" (21:14), just as the return of nature in *Jerusalem* is a necessary prerequisite to the apocalyptic restoration of eternal mutuality. The comedic reunion of Albion's human and non-human constituents emphasizes the ultimately non-divisive and egalitarian character of Blake's philosophy of human-nature relations. In the idealized non-hierarchical context of post-apocalyptic eternity, in which the tyrannical laws of "King & Priest" no longer exist, *both* humans and animals are united in their freedom from the authoritative discourses that had earlier sanctioned the violence and "Desolation" upon which "the Kingdoms of the World & all their glory ... grew" (J 98:51; E258).

While this emancipatory scenario is in many ways politically attractive, one major aspect of Blake's apocalypse remains to be considered. Given the violence that humans perpetrate upon the realm of nature throughout most of *Jerusalem*, how should we interpret Blake's proclamation that the returning animals and the Serpent of nature "Humanize / In the Forgiveness of Sins" upon their reconciliation with humanity? Despite the syntactical ambiguity of this passage, critics are virtually unanimous in concluding that Blake is speaking here of *nature's* transformation, that he is issuing nothing less than "a call for lion and tiger" – and even "tree, metal, earth, and stone" – to "assume human form" (Frosch 1974, 147–8).[6] Since all things in Blake's unfallen cosmos are integral particulars of Albion's organic body (the cosmic morphology that, as I have argued, provides the structural basis for Blake's particular poetic formulation of an environmental ethics), I do not exactly take issue with this thesis. I would like to conclude, however, by questioning its particular anthropocentric bias.

Arguably, when Blake says that animals "Humanize," he speaks not only of their transformations into human form but also of an activity they perform transitively upon others. Although these others are not explicitly identified in the sentence in which the verb appears, Blake's subsequent references to "Moral Virtues" and to the "Kingdoms of the World" (98:46–53; E258) suggest that the object of the transitive verb is a politicized human realm, which has heretofore been anything but humane in its treatment of either human or nonhuman entities. When the animals "Humanize / In the Forgiveness of Sins according to the Covenant of Jehovah," in other words, they are not simply the beneficiaries of a condescending human forgiveness (which implies a structure of hierarchy that eternity abhors). Rather, as Blake plainly states in his depiction of the reconciliation between Joseph and Mary on plate 61,[7] Jehovah's Covenant signifies an act of *mutual* forgiveness: "this is the Covenant / Of Jehovah: If you forgive one-another, so shall Jehovah Forgive You" (61:24–5; E212). In short, as all "the Living Creatures of the Earth" (98:54) witness the eradication of the institutions that throve upon Albion's "Desolation" (98:46–53), they "Humanize" each other *mutually* in a profound "ministry of reconciliation" (2 Corinthians 5:18), thus actualizing the cosmic covenant God establishes in Genesis between himself, humanity, and literally "every living creature" (J 9:10).[8] With this ongoing act of cosmic community, the "Fibres of love" that once

extended "from man to man thro Albions pleasant land" (4:8; E146)
– fibres whose severance at the beginning of *Jerusalem* marked
Albion's fall into catastrophic division – are at last reconnected, thus
affirming the mutuality, as well as the value and integrity, of *all*
entities inhabiting Blake's divine cosmos.

Notes

1 For a selection of explicit comments concerning the human right of "dominion" or "empire" over nature, see Genesis 1:26–8, Francis Bacon's *Novum Organum* (1860, 4:114), René Descartes' *Discourse on Method* (1955, 119), and Joseph Glanville's *Plus Ultra* (104–5). See also Donald Worster's *Nature's Economy*, chapter 2.

2 See Reiss 1982, 29.

3 According to eco-feminist Ariel Salleh, the rise of Baconian science must be considered in relation to "the corresponding elimination of one class of social actors, namely, the 6 million women who perished as witches for their scientific wisdom" (1995, 84). See also Carolyn Merchant (1980, 164–72).

4 See my discussion in chapter 3.

5 Foucault himself acknowledges the "banality" of discourse theory and its concomitant premise that philosophy must "keep watch over the excessive powers of political rationality." "Everybody is aware of such banal facts," he remarks. "But the fact that they're banal does not mean they don't exist. What we have to do with banal facts is to discover – or try to discover – which specific and perhaps original problem is connected with them" (1982, 210).

6 For a succinct discussion the difference between a "finished" and an "unfinished" production in Blake's *œuvre*, see Morton D. Paley's introduction to the Princeton edition of *Jerusalem* (1991, 9).

7 As historian R.S. Neale has pointed out (1976, 39–40), unscrupulous local physicians like Dr Oliver clearly capitalized on Bath's contemporary association with the magical healing arts. Indeed, Oliver went so far as to suggest that the unhealthy effects of sensual self-indulgence – which everyone knew could be had at Bath – could also be magically cured there.

8 For an astute theoretical discussion of Bacon's fetishization of nature's womb, see Stuart Peterfreund (1998, 153–4).

9 Even if we interpret the word "man" in this aphorism as a reference to humanity in general (rather than as an exclusive reference to members of the male sex), the aphorism arguably retains an element of sexism, since humanity becomes the privileged term in a binary equation locating a masculine-seeming activity or agency in the human subject and a curiously "feminine" passivity in nature or the natural object. Such a subject/object dynamic has long defined gender relations in the Western world. For a pointed discussion of subject/object dichotomies and their relationship to the domination of women and nature under patriarchy, see Karen J. Warren (1996, xi–xiii).

10 See ibid., xii.

11 I am indebted to Carolyn Merchant's discussion of Descartes and Glanville (1980, 188–9).

12 See Minna Doskow's brief discussion of the relationship between Blake and Adam Smith (1982b, 139–40n.13).

13 I am indebted here to J. Baird Callicott's theory of biosocial morality, which reminds us that Darwin's model of evolution involved more than simply a one-sided emphasis upon competitive and violent modes of biological survival in nature. As Callicott observes, Darwin also noted "the survival-reproduction advantages of social membership. Concern for others and self-restraint are necessary for social amalgamation and integration ... 'Ethical' behavior is, in effect, the dues an individual pays to join a social group; and the survival advantages of group membership to individuals more than compensate them for the personal sacrifices required by morality" (1992a, 254–5).

14 Such consensus is implicit in the psychology that atomistic epistemology entails. For John Locke, ideas "are produced in us ... by the operation of insensible particles on our senses" (quoted in Taylor 1989, 167). According to this "atomism of the mind," as Charles Taylor has called it, "a good part of the assembly of these [atomistic ideas] is accounted for by a quasi-mechanical process of association" (1989, 167). Locke's understanding of this associative process is, moreover, one in which the human mind is fundamentally passive, governed primarily, one might say, by the workings of external nature. In Blake's view, the notion of

such cognitive passivity is politically dangerous, providing a theoreti-
cal ground for the false political consensus or homogeneity that he
disdainfully criticizes in his discussion of the "Atom."

15 Mary Lynn Johnson reminds us that natural philosophers debated the
existence of the atom throughout the eighteenth and nineteenth centu-
ries, precisely because it could not be verified experimentally (1994,
121). Strictly speaking, this is still the case with the post-Einsteinian
atom, which, as Lyall Watson remarks, "nobody has actually ever
seen." Watson thus refers to the atom as a "metaphorm" – an *idea* that
"seem[s] to take on an existence in the real world" as a result of what
it is "*believed* to do" (1990, 44, 46; emphasis added).

16 As Errol E. Harris points out, "Infinity is a concept that has given cos-
mologists trouble ever since Newton, and one which physicists today
do all they can to eliminate from their calculations" (1991, 11–12).

CHAPTER ONE

1 Important exceptions are David Punter and, much more recently,
Mark S. Lussier. Punter's 1981 essay "Blake: 'Active Evil' and 'Passive
Good,'" sees Blake's philosophy of nature as emphasizing the episte-
mological dilemma inherent in the relationship between a knowing
subject and a nature that is "very possibly … forever unknowable."
For Punter, Blake's insistent focus on the relationship between ideol-
ogy and epistemology and his resultant hesitancy to valorize nature
and natural objects *as such* demonstrates that Blake held "a far more
sophisticated concept of nature than was common among the English
romantics" (12). Building upon Punter's insights in his 1996 essay
"Blake's Deep Ecology," Mark Lussier opposes the "persistent atti-
tude" that Blake detested nature by arguing that Blake's poetry enacts
an "ethics of otherness" in which a "dialogical imperative [is] opera-
tive between an individual, visioning subject and a sentient, vibrant
nature" (398, 402). I shall consider aspects of Blake's "environmental
ethics" in the final section of this chapter.

2 By the time Wordsworth published *The Excursion* in 1814, the *Lyrical
Ballads* had already gone into a fourth edition. Blake's contemporary
reading audience was so small, by contrast, that between 1810 and 1815
he produced the only four extant individual copies of *Milton*, one of his
self-professed masterworks.

3 An "ecotone" is a liminal space in which two relatively distinct eco-
systems meet, mingle, and differentiate themselves. I use the term here
to signify the meeting of the human urban metropolis and the less-
developed relatively "green" pastoral countryside.

4 See my discussion of the plough metaphor in the introduction.

5 White himself recognizes an alternative vision of human-nature relations in Christian tradition when he proposes St Francis of Assisi as "a patron saint for ecologists" (1996, 14).

6 That Blake was influenced by antinomian theology is widely accepted in Blake studies, although to differing degrees. A.L. Morton was the first critic to identify this influence, calling Blake, indeed, "the greatest English Antinomian" (1966, 37). More recently, Iain McCalman (1994, 29) and E.P. Thompson (1993, 65–105) have argued for Blake's rather close acquaintance with Muggletonians and their doctrines. Thompson argues that Blake's mother, Catherine Hermitage, may have come from a Muggletonian family, a circumstance that "would explain very satisfactorily the derivation of William Blake's antinomian vocabulary" (ibid., 104). Jon Mee cautions that antinomianism was alive and well in Blake's time "not ... as a sect but as a tendency." For Mee, Blake's own antinomian tendencies are the product not of direct influence but "of a dialogue with the complex nexus of popular enthusiasm" (1994, 45, 55). For my part, I am most comfortable with Mee's cautious approach to Blake's seeming antinomianism.

7 See Dennis Danielson's discussion of Milton's cosmogony and its biblical sources (1982, 26, 29).

8 See, for example, *Jerusalem* 60:36 (E210) and 62:27 (E213).

9 Cf. Psalm 150:6, "Let every thing that hath breath praise the Lord."

10 See Regina Schwartz (1988, 22).

11 I discuss some of the contradictions implicit in the doctrine of the *via negativa* in my essay "The Devil of the Stairs: Negotiating the Turn in T.S. Eliot's *Ash-Wednesday*" (1996, *passim*).

12 Cf. Wilkinson's complaint, written in 1839, that Blake "naturalized the spiritual, instead of spiritualizing the natural" (xvi).

13 John Adlard (1972, 70) points out that sand is a traditional biblical image for infinity. In Hosea 1:10, for example, we are told that "the number of the children of Israel shall be as the sand of the sea, which cannot be measured nor numbered." It is thus interesting to note that Blake, unlike Hosea, uses a single, minutely particular grain of sand (rather than an abstract expanse of the same substance) to invoke infinity.

14 According to *The Blake Concordance*, "life" is the forty-second most common word in Blake's poetic canon.

15 See, for example, Blake's Preface to *Milton*, E95.

16 "Hylozoism" derives from the Greek terms *hylē* and *zōos*, meaning, respectively, "matter" and "alive" or "living." Thus, "hylozoism," like "panvitalism," refers to the doctrine that all created things are alive or have life.

17 See, for example, Schorer (1959, 96) and Paley (1985, 28).
18 For a brief but tantalizing discussion of the possibility of conducting "a Gaian reading" of Blake's work, see Lussier (1996, 404).
19 I am indebted to Roderick Nash's discussion of Bentham's tentative claim for the validity of animal rights (1989, 23).
20 The objection may arise that Blake is speaking figuratively here – that he is not concerned with lions or oxen at all but with the logic of meta-phorical application. In chapter 2 I shall examine this aspect of Blake's animal symbolism in a close reading of the Eagle and Mole of "THEL'S Motto." It is my contention that Blake employs his animal symbols in a highly self-reflexive manner, so that despite their human metaphorical valence, they retain something of their non-human referentiality.
21 The association of the lion with monarchical power is, of course, a commonplace of popular discourse. On the relative nobility of the ox, see Elizabeth Barrett Browning's interpretation of Deuteronomy 22:10 (1993, 7:350–1).
22 On the concepts of "inherent worth" and "intrinsic value" in environ-mentalist discourse, see Eugene C. Hargrove (1992a, xvii; 1992b, 169) and Paul Taylor (1992, 99–100). For a trenchant if unsympathetic cri-tique of this aspect of "deep ecological" philosophy, see Luc Ferry (1995, 59–90).

CHAPTER TWO

1 Quoted in Bentley 1969, 170.
2 See my discussion of Lawrence in chapter 1.
3 Cf. Milton's *Paradise Lost*, 1992, 10.1031–36.
4 On the usage and validity of the concept of speciesism in environmen-talist discourse, see Mary Midgley 1992a, *passim*.
5 See Eaves, Essick, and Viscomi 1993a, 75.
6 While it is possible to argue that "dominion" in Genesis 1:28 properly refers to the notion of "stewardship," the term seems to have been interpreted in a less-responsible manner in mainstream Christian tradition. Roderick Nash points out that

Hebrew linguists have analyzed Genesis 1:28 and found two opera-tive verbs: *kabash*, translated as "subdue," and *radah*, rendered as "have dominion over" or "rule." Throughout the Old Testament *kabash* and *radah* are used to signify a violent assault or crushing. The image is that of a conqueror placing his foot on the neck of a defeated enemy, exerting absolute domination. Both Hebraic words are also used to identify the process of enslavement. It followed that the Christian tradition could understand Genesis 1:28 as a divine commandment to conquer every part of nature and make it humankind's slave. (1989, 90)

7 *The Economy of Vegetation* and *The Loves of the Plants* were published together in 1791 as Books 1 and 2 of *The Botanic Garden*.

8 Erasmus Darwin's writings render somewhat problematic J. Baird Callicott's assertion that holistic concepts of nature derive from the discipline of ecology proper. According to Callicott, before the "rather recent emergence of ecology as a science the landscape appeared to be, one might say, a collection of objects, some of them alive, some conscious, but all the same, an aggregate, a plurality of separate individuals" (1992b, 45). In contrast to Callicott's generalization, I would argue that conceptual invocations of "nature's economy" in such writers as Isaac Biberg and Erasmus Darwin suggest an earlier, eighteenth-century date for the emergence of a "holistic" vision of nature and natural process.

9 For a much more positive reading of Darwin's naturalism, see Anne K. Mellor (1988, 89–101). Mellor makes a distinction between "that scientific research which attempts to describe accurately the functionings of the physical universe and that which attempts to *control* or *change* the universe through human intervention," attributing the former science to Darwin and the latter to thinkers like Sir Humphry Davy and Luigi Galvani (90). While this distinction may hold true in a relative sense, my reading of Darwin's "Mechanic Genius" should make plain that Darwin is not above celebrating an interventionist manipulation of the natural environment for human profit.

10 Many of Blake's readers construct a pathologically regressive Thel by reading the Vales of Har as the same vales Blake depicts in the poem *Tiriel*, wherein the characters Har and Heva dwell in an unquestionably pathological state of arrested development (see, for example, Erdman's commentary on E896). Although it is certainly logical to read the published and engraved *Thel* in light of *Tiriel*, we do so at the peril of overlooking "the difference between an abandoned manuscript and a finished work" (Paley 1983, 280). In interpreting *Thel*, I would argue, we must bear in mind that Blake chose *not* to engrave or publish *Tiriel*. Because Blake's small contemporary reading public would not have read *Tiriel*, *Thel*'s "Vales of Har" would have retained a much more flexible signification in the late eighteenth century than readers tend to give it today.

11 Blake, whose father and brother were hosiers, would probably have been aware of the appalling consequences of Smith's influential doctrine of *laissez-faire* for weavers and other members of the English working class. As E.P. Thompson pointed out in a discussion of the weaving trade in eighteenth-century England, this orthodox view of

political economy led to the impoverishment of large numbers of weavers, who "did not 'share in the benefits' of economic progress but ... suffered a drastic decline" (1975a, 343). For social groups such as the weavers, *laissez-faire* was "a system designed by employers, legislators and ideologists to cheapen human labour in every way" (346). Blake would also likely have discussed the doctrine of "free trade" with his close friend George Cumberland, who published writings on the topic (see Bentley 1975, xxii, 71).

12 Although Blake is here referring to "Harmony" of colour in painting – "One Species of General *Hue*" – the concept also has a more general application in his thought. In *Jerusalem*, for example, he speaks of Harmony in terms of "Concords & Discords / Opposed to Melody," "Lights & Shades, opposed to Outline," and philosophical "Abstraction opposed to the Visions of Imagination" (74:24–6; E229).

13 The idea that humans should allow wild nature to exist on its "own" terms, free from human intervention, is common in present-day environmentalist discourse. See, for example, Hargrove's discussion of the policies of non-interference advocated by Peter Singer and Tom Regan (1992a, xi) and Callicott's potentially misanthropic proposal that each wild being "should be ... left alone to pursue its *modus vivendi* – even if its way of life causes harm to other beings" (1992a, 257).

14 As Thomas H. Birch argues, the naming and categorizing of wild creatures involves an exercise of power that often has adverse ecological ramifications. But such power remains subject to performative uncertainty and subversion, since "in attending to wilderness, one sees, or is likely to see, that the other is more than, other than, independent of, the definitions, models, and simulations that the imperium proposes as exhaustive of it" (1995, 151).

15 For insightful remarks on "the significance invested in [the hymen]," see Nelson Hilton (1983, 130–2).

16 Blake's readers often oppose Thel's behaviour to that of Oothoon in *Visions of the Daughters of Albion*. In their summary analysis of the important differences between these two characters, for example, Morris Eaves, Robert N. Essick, and Joseph Viscomi make the following case: "At the end of her poem, Thel flees from the body and its deadly associations. In contrast, Oothoon accepts the body and its potential for delights that overwhelm conventional distinctions between the physical and the spiritual, even in the face of continued sexual and cultural violence ... Thel preserves her virginity through an act of denial; Oothoon is raped and becomes a revolutionary" (1993b, 229). Such a reading of Thel and Oothoon is troubling, for it assumes that in Blake's view women's identity or coming-to-consciousness must be based on a masculinist violation of the female body, a violation Thel arguably refuses when she flees the "thousand fighting men" who are

prepared to "ambush" her near the end of her poem. While I do not wish entirely to deny the revolutionary aspect of Oothoon's critique of patriarchy in *Visions* (see my essay "Pastoral, Ideology, and Nature in William Blake's *Visions of the Daughters of Albion*," forthcoming, as I write, in *Interdisciplinary Studies in Literature and Environment*), I would argue that a dichotomous reading of Thel and Oothoon in terms of unsuccessful and successful revolutionary activity effaces the significant complexity of the sexual politics informing and constituting their actions. For a succinct discussion of the problems inherent in the view of Oothoon as a revolutionary, see David Aers (1981, 27–32).

17 In "Nietzsche, Genealogy, History," Foucault speaks of the study of *Herkunft*, or "descent" (1977a, 145), as an important aspect of "counter-memory" or "'Effective' history" (154). "Descent," in its Nietzschean usage, implies not the historical search for a unified racial or familial origin but the uncovering of "a profusion of lost events," including a plethora of historical "accidents," "minute deviations," and "complete reversals ... that gave birth to those things that continue to exist and have value for us" in the present (146). Crucially, "descent" is concerned not only with the social world but with the ways that world inscribes and produces the "body – and everything that touches it: diet, climate, and soil" (148). It is in this sense that Foucauldian genealogy (of which Nietzschean "descent" is an aspect) concerns itself with the relationship between the human social world and the non-human environment.

18 Analogues to the somewhat essentialist concept of biophilia can be found in the writings of authors from various fields of environmental inquiry. For example, under the rubric of the "call of the wild," environmental ethicist Eric Katz discusses "our *attraction to value* that exists in a natural world outside of human control" (1995, 164); animal liberationist writer Mary Midgley calls "the sense of unity with the rest of nature ... something which is probably necessary for our psychic health" (1992b, 33); and eco-theologian Seyyed Hossein Nasr speaks of "the need in the souls of human beings for the religious understanding of nature" (1996, 194–5).

19 In *The Rime of the Ancient Mariner* (1798), when the Mariner overcomes his earlier abhorrence of the slimy "water-snakes," he sees them for the first time as beautiful and worthy of spontaneous blessing (Coleridge 1967, lines 272–87). At this pivotal point in the poem, the Mariner's heart, formerly "as dry as dust" (247), produces a gushing "spring of love" (284). The Mariner's altered perception of these serpents, the poem suggests, is the catalyst that enables his own spiritual transformation (288–91).

20 See also Kiralis 1968, 13.

21 With its emphasis on relationality, the concept of "nature's economy" arguably prefigures twentieth-century cybernetic theory, a naturalistic paradigm in which causes and effects are so complexly interrelated that they cannot ultimately be differentiated. Indeed, for J.E. Lovelock, the question of the relationship between cause and effect "has no relevance" in cybernetics (1987, 52). Because of its atomistic logic, traditional physical science is ill equipped to understand the entities and relations constituting biological or ecological systems.

22 See Eaves et al. 1993a, 74–81.

CHAPTER THREE

1 1993, *Aurora Leigh* (3:193–4).

2 See Joseph Anthony Wittreich's discussion of Newton's prophetic stance (1973, 30–1).

3 I am indebted to Joseph Anthony Wittreich for my understanding that prophecy "involves a way of relating." I should point out, however, that Wittreich includes in the prophetic relationship only the writers of explicitly prophetic texts (1978, 77–8). But Blake, I would argue, potentially takes the idea of prophecy much further than Wittreich's argument suggests. Because all humans are potential prophets in Blake's eyes – and because Blake wishes to play a catalytic role in actualizing this innate potential – Blakean prophecy logically implies an ideal form of human relations *in general*.

4 For an Old Testament antecedent to this passage, see Zechariah, chapter 4.

5 Significantly, Muggleton makes this claim on the title page to his *True Interpretation of the Eleventh Chapter of the Revelation of St John* (1662), an exegetical study of the very chapter wherein St John refers to "the two olive trees."

6 For brief illuminating discussions of the Newton-Leibniz debate, see Henry 1988, 135, and Golinski 1988, 165–6.

7 For brief discussions of the empirical basis of ecology, see Paul Taylor 1992, 108–9, and Cooper 1992, 71.

8 For an astute revisionist reading of the relationship between Blake and Newton, see Greenberg 1983, *passim*. Henceforth I shall use the adjective "Newtonian" and the noun "Newtonianism" to differentiate Newton's discursive legacy from the work of Newton's own pen.

9 For examples of this view, see Damon 1988, 298–9, and Peterfreund 1990, *passim*. In this early version of "Blake and Anti-Newtonian Thought," Peterfreund argues that, in his response to Newton, Blake

wishes "to show matter for what it is: mere inessential 'dirt'" (1990, 151). In the revised version of the essay, however, Peterfreund changes Blake's definition of matter to "mere inessential 'din'" (1998, 49).

10 George H. Ford quotes Whipple in the *Atlantic Monthly* 39 (1877): 353.

11 Blake employs this colouring in Copy C, reproduced in the fully coloured Princeton edition of the poem, edited by Robert N. Essick and Joseph Viscomi (1993).

12 In the design to plate 32 (see Figure 14), Blake situates the east on the right-hand side of the plate and west on the left-hand side. One might also observe that the sun and moon appear to move across the Earth's ecliptic from east to west, following what Blake calls in *Jerusalem* "the current of / Creation" (77:4–5; E232).

13 Later in *Milton*, Blake speaks directly of "the Newtonian Voids between the Substances of Creation" (37:46; E138).

14 Cf. Newton, who argues, in plain contrast to the antinomian position, that the two basic commandments of the Decalogue "always have [been] and always will be the duty of all nations and the coming of Jesus Christ has made no alteration in them" (quoted in Brooke 1988, 182).

15 Maureen McNeil points out that while Blake depicts Newton "staring down at the ground, away from higher aspirations, [Newton's] figure is noble and not unsympathetically rendered" (1988, 226). Moreover, as Damon notes, Newton performs his geometrical calculations on a scroll, which in Blake's iconography tends to symbolize imaginative creation (1988, 299). For a fine full-colour reproduction of "Newton" see Klonsky (1977, 62).

16 The frontispiece to *Europe* (Figure 12) suggests something of Blake's disagreement with Milton's representation of Christ as circumscriber of chaos during the creation. In *Paradise Lost*, as Blake likely noted, Milton represents the Son's role in creation in terms suggesting his subordination to the Father. "[A]ll his father in him shone" (1992, 7:196), says Milton, as Christ prepares to leave heaven's gate on his journey into chaos. Christ rides out into this realm, furthermore, "in paternal glory" (7:219). Finally, after Christ measures and circumscribes the portion of chaos necessary for creation, Milton writes: "Thus *God* the heaven created, thus the earth" (7:232; emphasis added). Like the compasses he himself wields, the Son seems a mere instrument of God during Milton's scene of creation. Hence Blake represents not Christ but Urizen as the wielder of the "golden compasses" (7:225) in the frontispiece to *Europe*.

17 It is significant that Milton enters Blake's "tarsus," for although this term refers to "the flat of the foot" and "the seven small bones of the human ankle" (Oxford English Dictionary, 1st ed.), it also alludes to

St Paul, who was known as Saul of Tarsus prior to his Christian conversion. For an analysis of the relationship between the Blake-Milton convergence in *Milton* and Blake's critique of Pauline dualism, see Hutchings 1997, 284–8.

18 While Enitharmon's status as Los's Emanation suggests that Blake gives time generative priority over space (Peterfreund 1998, 28), *Milton*'s text indicates that this is not always the case. When Enitharmon creates "a New Space to protect Satan from punishment" in the wake of his usurping Palamabron's harrow, for example, the Eternal Assembly ratifies this "kind decision" and gives "a Time to the Space" (M 13:13, 16; E107), an act suggesting the possible precedence that space may have over time. For a brief discussion of some of the problems inhabiting Blake's gendering of time and space, see Lussier 1994, 277–9.

19 Youngquist refers here to plate 27 of *Jerusalem*, where, in his prose address "To the Jews," Blake declares that Albion "anciently containd in his mighty limbs all things in Heaven & Earth" (E171). As Youngquist observes, the problem of the fallen Albion's relation to eternity is usually solved in Blake criticism "by being ignored" (1993, 605).

20 According to Frye, Orc's problem in *Milton* involves not his static atemporality, as I am arguing, but his immersion in a temporal process Frye identifies as the "Orc Cycle" (1970, 207–35). For Frye, Orc's political activity in Blake's *œuvre* takes a cyclical form in which Orc inevitably internalizes and duplicates the governmental structures he originally sets out to oppose. Thus, the Orcian revolutionary unwittingly *becomes* the Urizenic oppressor, necessitating the rise of a new Orc, whose activities, unfortunately, are also co-opted by Urizenic structures (and so the violent process of revolution and conquest repeats itself in the mundane world, presumably *ad infinitum*). In Frye's reading, this pernicious cycle is not only related to but cognate with the processes of nature: "the rebirth of Orc, the reappearance of life in a new form … is the ordinary process of life" (322). With comments like this one, Frye in effect essentializes political cycles of revolution and conquest, thus leaving virtually no hope for an effective earthly emancipatory politics. For an alternative reading of the "Orc Cycle," see Hutchings 1997, *passim*, wherein I argue that the replication of governmental structures in *Milton* points to a problem not of natural process but of politics and revolutionary strategy.

21 See, for example, Frosch 1974, 177, 179, and Rose 1970, *passim*.

22 For additional critical remarks concerning Blake's ostensible belief in the need for humans to transcend nature's cyclical temporality, see Wittreich 1973, 44, and Curran 1973, 330. For readings of cyclical time

as potentially positive or redemptive in Blake's poetic mythology, see Fisher 1961, 33–5, and Lesnick 1970, 410.

23 As Karl Kroeber remarks, cyclical time is exceedingly more complex than traditional mechanistic discourse will allow, for "the temporal ordering of an ecosystem is necessarily constituted by a variety of intersecting rhythms and tempos" occurring within "an ever-self-transforming set of interlocking systems" (1994, 107, 142).

24 Satan's desire for absolute omnipotence in *Milton* suggests that his Mill properly symbolizes the sort of "pure" mechanism that, as I pointed out above, deists like John Hutchinson opposed to the mechanism of the Newtonian system. Since Newton's Water-wheels move "by compulsion *each other*," the "power" that drives them might be said to stem not from some external "Prime Mover" (as in Hutchinsonian mechanism) but from the "active principles" with which Newton's system imbues all bodies. Blake does not, however, consistently distinguish between these two forms of mechanism but tends instead to associate "Newton" with mechanism in general.

25 I am indebted to Edward Larrissy for suggesting similarities between Blake's and Frost's critiques of Newtonian cosmology (1994, 61).

26 Satan "incircles" Albion's body in a similarly predatorial manner at 39:16–21, E140.

27 Los hides Satan's murder of Thulloh from Enitharmon "lest she should die of grief" (8:41; E102), thus denying her the opportunity to understand the violence of Satan's character and activity.

28 To quote William Whiston's *A New Theory of the Earth* (1696), "'Tis very well known that an *Egg* was the solemn and remarkable symbol or Representation of the World among the most venerable Antiquity" (164).

29 One should note the parallel between the "moony shade" confining the "weak traveller" of the vortex passage and the "Space" that Enitharmon creates for Satan earlier in the poem; for, as we have seen, Enitharmon seals this Space with the "tender Moon" (8:43–4; E102) of atomistic or solipsistic enclosure.

Simply stated, the vortex allows one to escape such enclosure. Because it can be passed through like a window, the vortex is, as Lussier asserts, best conceived as spiral (rather than circular) in structure (1994, 285n.15). Indeed, this complex figure functions to expose the ultimate *lie* of the perfect circle as a description of natural process. Since the circle is a purely mathematical structure, it has for Blake the same status as the Newtonian fluxional atom: it is a conceptual fiction, "A Thing that does not Exist" (E783). In other words, if "*every* thing has its / Own Vortex" (M 15:21–2), then the seemingly "repetitive revolutions" of the circle can be "opposed to the spiral rotation of the vortex" (Lussier 1994, 285n.15) only in the way that falsehood is opposed to truth, since in Blake's poetics even those phenomena that appear to move in a purely circular manner actually have vortices enabling the transcendence of such mathematical determinism. Here, to a limited extent, Blake is actually in agreement with Francis Bacon, who argues in the *Novum Organum* that the "human understanding is of its own nature prone to suppose the existence of more order and regularity in the world than it finds. And though there may be many things in nature which are singular and unmatched, yet it devises for them parallels and conjugates and relatives which do not exist. Hence the fiction that all celestial bodies move in perfect circles; spirals and dragons being (except in name) utterly rejected" (1860, 4:55).

30 Arguably, with the passage through the vortex, the Earth becomes a *horizontal plane*, because according to the decentred model of the open system the verticality of hierarchy is subverted, so that even the most minuscule of entities or systems can suddenly be understood to exercise seemingly disproportionate influences on their much larger counterparts. See, for example, Conley 1997, 68–75.

31 Blake's "stormy seas" can be read as a direct reference to earthly seas. More accurately, perhaps, the figure might be read as referring to "the deep" of Genesis 1:2, the locus of the "dark materials" (1992, *Paradise Lost*, 2.916) out of which, according to the theology of Milton and – with crucial differences – that of antinomian divines Reeve and Muggleton (1760, 34), God originally fashioned heaven and Earth.

32 The notion that we "become what we behold" is a common theme in Blake's late epics. See, for example, *Milton* 3:29 and *Jerusalem* 30:50, 54; 32:9, 14–15, 19; 65:75, 79; and 66:36.

33 See Neil Everden's discussion of this passage (1985, 17–22).

34 One of the major thinkers of "catastrophism" was Thomas Burnet, whose *Sacred Theory of the Earth* (1697) attributed the sublime and terrifying aspects of earthly geography to a series of ancient cataclysmic upheavals involving such things as floods, earthquakes, conflagrations, tempests, urban devastations, etc. For Vincent de Luca, Blake's use of catastrophic settings and images is part of a discourse of sublimity designed to actualize in the reader "intimations of the infinite and the eternal" (1991, 80) by memorializing these ancient and terrifying events. Since *Milton*'s preface explicitly privileges Inspiration over Memory (E95), I would argue that the poem's catastrophic imagery must also be read in terms of a forward-looking prophetic warning that widespread environmental catastrophe will occur again if we do not change our minds and practices.

35 "Desertification" is a geographical term referring to the combination of natural processes and human activities contributing to the relentless advance of desert areas (Blake's "plains of burning sand") around the globe. For a succinct discussion of this climatological phenomenon, see Kemp 1990, 54–60. Ecological theologian Michael S. Northcott points out that, in the Old Testament, (e.g., Isaiah 5:8–10), the danger of desertification looms when land is "inequitably acquired for the commercial gain and greed of the rich" (1996, 192). For Blake, desertification follows as a consequence of similar appropriative acts, as Satan strives to transform "All Things" into "One Great Satan" (M 39:1; E140).

36 See Richard J. Clifford's analysis of this scriptural passage (1994, 23).

CHAPTER FOUR

1 See, for example, Northrop Frye (1970, 356), W.J.T. Mitchell (1978, 169), Edward J. Rose (1963, 51), and Joseph Anthony Wittreich (1973, 52).

2 In *The Supplement of Reading*, Tilottama Rajan observes that a critical emphasis on *Milton* and *Jerusalem* in Blake studies "has naturalized a hermeneutic reading of the earlier texts because it seems to be what Blake 'finally' wanted" (1990, 209). Among other things, the privileging of such a reading has profound ramifications for our understanding of Blake's philosophy of nature, since *Jerusalem*'s seemingly hostile judgment of nature thus becomes the philosophical standard against which critics measure *all* of Blake's earlier poetic utterances concerning human-nature relations.

3 For a pertinent analysis of the problem of masculinity in Blake's emanational theory, see David L. Clark (1994, 185–8).

4 In a discussion of animality in Heidegger's philosophy, Derrida explains how "a certain dominant logic of opposition" entails a denial of difference: "if you draw a single or two single lines, then you have homogenous sets of undifferentiated societies, or groups, or structures … [D]rawing an oppositional limit *itself* blurs the differences, the différance [Derrida's coinage] and the differences, not only between man and animal, but among animal societies – there are an infinite number of animal societies, and, within the animal societies and within human society itself, so many differences" (1987, 183–4). Far from advocating "the *blurring* of differences" (183), Derrida's deconstruction *multiplies* differences between and among entities, just as Blake's poetic philosophy attempts to do by continually privileging minute particulars over homogenizing generalities.

5 Here I follow Minna Doskow's reading of *Jerusalem*'s title page. Doskow interprets this design as depicting the process Blake describes in the opening lines of chapter 1 (4:1–2; E146): "Of the Sleep of Ulro!

and the passage through / Eternal Death! and of the awaking to Eternal Life" (4:1–2; E146). As Doskow remarks of the frontispiece design, "Jerusalem sleeps in Ulro at the bottom of the plate, passes through eternal death at the left, and finally floats in her fully awakened, winged form at the top" (1982b, 19).

6 All references to colour in my discussion of *Jerusalem's* designs refer to Copy E of the poem, which is beautifully reproduced in the Princeton edition.

7 According to Seyyed Hossein Nasr's eco-theological survey of mainstream world religions, the notion that the fall of humanity is coextensive with the loss of earthly paradise is "accepted in one form or another by religions ranging from Hinduism to Islam" (1996, 286).

8 Significantly, these are the same words Albion's fraternal valleys, hills, and rivers use to characterize his pathology at 36:11–12 (E182).

9 See chapter 3, note 32.

10 In his iconography, Blake opposes St Paul's to the living form symbolized by Westminster Abbey's gothic structure (Paley 1991, 181), the latter of which Blake appropriately situates in this design beside the naked Jerusalem and her female attendants.

11 I discuss this conflict in my introduction.

12 See, for example, S. Foster Damon (1988, 213), Harold Bloom (1963, 407); Brenda S. Webster (1983, 283), and Peter Otto (1991, 174). Each of these critics speaks primarily in terms of Joseph's forgiveness of Mary rather than of the need for their mutual forgiveness.

13 On the ecologically inclusive nature of God's covenant with humanity, see, for example, Clifford (1994, 8–9) and Northcott (1996, chapter 5).

14 For a trenchant corrective response to deep ecology's critique of ecofeminism, including the charge that ecofeminist discourse reinscribes traditional essentialist views concerning feminine identity, see Ariel Salleh (1995, *passim*).

15 See, for example, Minna Doskow (1982b, 61).

16 In *The Marriage of Heaven and Hell*, Blake formulates his famous argument that the Milton of *Paradise Lost*, who set out to justify the ways of God, was in fact "of the Devils party without knowing it" (plate 5; E35).

17 I am indebted to Nelson Hilton (1983, 87–8) for his references to the contemporary work of Sandys, Baker, and Darwin, and for his discussion of the relationship between the biological polypus and Blake's depiction of "the Great Selfhood / Satan" and his "Devouring Power" (J 29:17–24).

18 Although Milton speaks of the "embryon atoms" of chaos (1992, 2:900), his subsequent assertion that chaos comprises "neither sea, nor shore, nor air, nor fire" (2:912) supports the notion that this realm is

"pre-elemental," referring not to "the elements themselves, but rather to their component qualities" (Chambers 1963, 60–1). Being in a sense substance without form, Milton's chaos is, as Christopher Hill puts it, "nothing in itself" (326). In this sense, Miltonic atomism (which refers not to the created world but to its pre-created, proto-elementary materials) differs from the arguably more substantial atomism of mainstream Enlightenment materialism.

The notion that atomism was atheistical was a commonplace in Milton's time as well as in Blake's. Walter Charleton, physician to Charles I, called it an "execrable delusion," probably because the philosophy tended to posit chaotic "matter" (rather than God) as a first principle (quoted in Schwartz 1988, 25).

19 Strictly speaking, Blake's association of Newton's physics with Epicureanism is another aspect of his reductive reading of Newton (see my discussion in chapter 3, above), for Newton himself attacked Epicurean atomism in his commonplace book (Manuel 1974, 41).

20 As mentioned in chapter 1, the other fundamental and necessary trait of Blakean "Life" is "minute particularity."

21 See Paley's discussion of this design (1991, 158).

22 The other pre-Enlightenment "similitudes" Foucault discusses are *convenientia* or juxtaposition, *aemulatio* or emulation, and analogy (1994, 17–25).

23 For one of Naess's own discussions of the process of "Identification as a Source of Deep Ecological Attitudes," see his essay by that name (especially 1984, 261–5).

24 Cf. Evan Eisenberg's discussion of walls or boundaries in *The Ecology of Eden*: "Any organism is really a wall or system of walls. The wall defines a living thing; in a sense it defines life … All living systems need walls or boundaries of some kind. All require some degree of closure, as well as some degree of openness to the outside world" (1998, 102–3).

25 According to Robert N. Essick and Joseph Viscomi, the word "Throw" in this passage is likely an error for "Thro," which Blake often uses instead of "through" (1993, 167). My reading suggests, however, that Blake deliberately used the word that appears in the text. Indeed, "thro" would make little sense in this context, given the syntax of the sentence; for if Blake had intended to use this word he would likely have chosen "in" rather than "into" as the appropriate preposition for the sentence.

26 Quoting Matthew Baillie's *The Morbid Anatomy of Some of the Most Important Parts of the Body* (printed by one of Blake's publishers, Joseph Johnson, in 1793), Nelson Hilton reminds us that the term "polypus"

could refer in the eighteenth century to "a very common disease of the uterus" (1983, 89).

27 On the homogeneity of masculinity and the "multiplicity of female desire," see Luce Irigaray (1991, *passim*).

CODA

1 For a trenchant critique of misanthropic tendencies in environmentalist discourse, see Luc Ferry (1995, 70–6). For corrective responses to the all-too-common charge that environmentalism and animal rights activism are *necessarily* misanthropic, see Ariel Salleh (1995, 92) and Mary Midgley (1992b, 32).

2 I am indebted to Christopher Manes (1996, 16) for bringing Duerr's insight to my attention.

3 See Peter F. Fisher (1961, *passim*).

4 On human "parasitism," see Michel Serres (1992, 9–10). For a discussion of similar problems inherent in the deep ecological "sacralization of nature," see Luc Ferry (1995, 132–3). For a succinct summary of the ways naturally occurring forms of "violence" have been used to justify the aggressive policies of some extremist forms of ecological activism, see Roderick Nash (1989, 190–6).

5 The inappropriately named Pinery Provincial Park in Grand Bend, Ontario, contains within its narrow boundaries more than one-half of North America's remaining oak savanna. It is interesting to note that P. Burns and D. Reidy, the authors of *Cedar Trail: Oak Savanna Ecology*, one of the park's published trail guides, quote from Blake's *Auguries of Innocence* in their introductory remarks on the trail, assuring visitors to the park's rare oak habitat that they will "'see a world in a grain of sand / and a heaven in a wild flower'" (1996, 1). One wonders what Blake would have made of this most interesting public usage of his poetry (not to mention how he would have felt about the virtual extinction of so many of the world's great oak forests, the "Druid Temples" of old).

6 For diverse anthropocentric readings of nature's ultimate humanization in *Jerusalem*, see Bloom (1963, 433), Frosch (1974, 147–9), and Doskow (1982a, 239).

7 See my discussion of this event in chapter 4.

8 See chapter 4, note 13.

Bibliography

Ackroyd, Peter. 1995. *Blake*. London: Sinclair-Stevenson.

Adamson, J.H. 1971. "The Creation." *Bright Essence*. Ed. W.B. Hunter. Salt Lake City: University of Utah Press, 81–102.

Adlard, John. 1972. *The Sports of Cruelty: Fairies, Folk-songs, Charms and Other Country Matters in the Work of William Blake*. London: Woolf/Daedalus Press.

Aers, David. 1981. "Blake: Sex, Society and Ideology." *Romanticism and Ideology*. Ed. David Aers, Jonathan Cook, and David Punter. London, Boston, and Henley: Routledge and Kegan Paul, 27–43.

Ault, Donald. 1974. *Visionary Physics: Blake's Response to Newton*. Chicago and London: University of Chicago Press.

Bacon, Francis. 1860. *The Works of Francis Bacon*. 7 vols. Ed. James Spedding, Robert Leslie Ellis, and Douglas Denon Heath. London: Longman.

Bate, Jonathan. 1991. *Romantic Ecology: Wordsworth and the Environmental Tradition*. London and New York: Routledge.

Beer, John. 1968. *Blake's Humanism*. Manchester: Manchester University Press.

Bentham, Jeremy. 1948. *An Introduction to the Principles of Morals and Legislation*. 1789. New York: Hafner.

Bentley, G.E., Jr. 1975. *A Bibliography of George Cumberland (1754–1848)*. New York and London: Garland.

– *Blake Records*. 1969. Oxford: Clarendon Press.

Bewell, Alan. 1989. "'Jacobin Plants': Botany as Social Theory in the 1790s." *The Wordsworth Circle* 20, no. 3: 132–9.

Biberg, Isaac J. 1759. "The Oeconomy of Nature." 1749. *Miscellaneous Tracts Relating to Natural History, Husbandry, and Physick*. Trans. Benjamin Stillingfleet. London.

Biehl, Janet. 1991. *Finding Our Way: Rethinking Ecofeminist Politics.* Montreal and New York: Black Rose Books.

Birch, Thomas H. 1995. "The Incarceration of Wildness: Wilderness Areas as Prisons." *Postmodern Environmental Ethics.* Ed. Max Oelschlaeger. Albany, NY: State University of New York Press, 137–61.

Black, Joel. 1990. "Introduction: Newtonian Mechanics and the Romantic Rebellion." *Beyond the Two Cultures: Essays on Science, Technology, and Literature.* Ed. Joseph W. Slade and Judith Yaross Lee. Ames, IA: Iowa State University Press, 131–9.

Blake, William. 1988. *The Complete Poetry and Prose of William Blake.* Ed. David V. Erdman. Rev. ed. New York and London: Doubleday.

– 1991. [c. 1804–20] *Jerusalem: The Emanation of the Giant Albion.* Ed. Morton D. Paley. Princeton, NJ: William Blake Trust/Princeton University Press.

– 1993a. [c. 1789–90] *The Book of Thel. William Blake: The Early Illuminated Books.* Ed. Morris Eaves, Robert N. Essick, and Joseph Viscomi. Princeton, NJ: William Blake Trust/Princeton University Press.

– 1993b. [c. 1804–18] *Milton a Poem.* Ed. Robert N. Essick and Joseph Viscomi. Princeton, NJ: William Blake Trust/Princeton University Press.

– 1993c. [1793] *Visions of the Daughters of Albion. William Blake: The Early Illuminated Books.* Ed. Morris Eaves, Robert N. Essick, and Joseph Viscomi. Princeton: Princeton University Press.

– 1995. [1794] *Europe: A Prophecy. William Blake: The Continental Prophecies.* Ed. D.W. Dörrbecker. Princeton, NJ: William Blake Trust/Princeton University Press.

Bloom, Harold. 1963. *Blake's Apocalypse: A Study in Poetic Argument.* Ithaca, NY: Cornell University Press.

Bové, Paul A. 1990. "Discourse." *Critical Terms for Literary Study.* Ed. Frank Lentricchia and Thomas McLaughlin. Chicago and London: University of Chicago Press, 50–65.

Bracher, Mark. 1985. *Being Form'd: Thinking Through Blake's "Milton."* Barrytown, NY: Station Hill Press.

Briggs, John. 1992. *Fractals, the Patterns of Chaos: Discovering a New Aesthetic of Art, Science, and Nature.* New York: Simon and Schuster.

Bronowski, J. 1947. *William Blake: A Man without a Mask.* London: Secker and Warburg.

– 1960. *The Common Sense of Science.* New York: Vintage.

Brooke, John. 1988. "The God of Isaac Newton." *Let Newton Be!* Ed. John Fauvel et al. Oxford, New York, and Tokyo: Oxford University Press, 169–83.

Browne, Sir Thomas. 1968. *Sir Thomas Browne's Works, Including His Life and Correspondence.* Vol. 3. New York: AMS Press.

Browning, Elizabeth Barrett. 1993. *Aurora Leigh.* 1856. Oxford and New York: Oxford University Press.

Bruder, Helen. 1994. "The Sins of the Fathers: Patriarchal Criticism and *The Book of Thel.*" *Historicizing Blake.* Ed. Steve Clark and David Worrall. London: St Martin's Press, 147–58.

Buell, Lawrence. 1995. *The Environmental Imagination: Thoreau, Nature Writing, and the Formation of American Culture.* Cambridge, MA, and London: Harvard University Press.

Burns, P., and D. Reidy. 1996. *Cedar Trail: Oak Savanna Ecology.* Grand Bend, ON: Ontario Parks/The Friends of Pinery Park.

Butler, Judith. 1997. *The Psychic Life of Power: Theories in Subjection.* Stanford, CA: Stanford University Press.

Butlin, Martin. 1981. *The Paintings and Drawings of William Blake [Text].* New Haven and London: Yale University Press.

Callicott, J. Baird. 1992a. "Animal Liberation and Environmental Ethics: Back Together Again." *The Animal Rights/Environmental Ethics Debate: The Environmental Perspective.* Ed. Eugene C. Hargrove. Albany, NY: State University of New York Press, 249–61.

– 1992b. "Animal Liberation: A Triangular Affair." *The Animal Rights/ Environmental Ethics Debate: The Environmental Perspective.* Ed. Eugene C. Hargrove. Albany, NY: State University of New York Press, 37–69.

Campbell, Sueellen. 1996. "The Land and Language of Desire: Where Deep Ecology and Poststructuralism Meet." *The Ecocriticism Reader: Landmarks in Literary Ecology.* Ed. Cheryl Glotfelty and Harold Fromm. Athens, GA, and London: University of Georgia Press, 124–36.

Cantor, Geoffrey. 1988. "Anti-Newton." *Let Newton Be!* Ed. John Fauvel et al. Oxford, New York, and Tokyo: Oxford University Press, 203–21.

Chambers, A.B. 1963. "Chaos in *Paradise Lost.*" *Journal of the History of Ideas* 24: 55–84.

Clark, David L. 1994. "Against Theological Technology: Blake's 'Equivocal Worlds.'" *New Romanticisms: Theory and Critical Practice.* Ed. David L. Clark and Donald C. Goellnicht. Toronto, Buffalo, and London: University of Toronto Press, 164–222.

– 1997. "On Being 'The Last Kantian in Nazi Germany': Dwelling with Animals after Levinas." *Animal Acts: Configuring the Human in Western History.* Ed. Jennifer Ham and Matthew Senior. New York and London: Routledge, 165–98.

Clark, Lorraine. 1991. *Blake, Kierkegaard, and the Spectre of Dialectic.* Cambridge: Cambridge University Press.

Clark, Steve, and David Worrall. 1994. Introduction. *Historicizing Blake.* Ed. Steve Clark and David Worrall. New York: St Martin's Press, 1–23.

Clifford, Richard J. 1994. "The Bible and the Environment." *Preserving the Creation: Environmental Theology and Ethics.* Ed. Kevin W. Irwin and Edmund D. Pellegrino. Washington, DC: Georgetown University Press, 1–26.

Coleridge, Samuel Taylor. 1967. "The Rime of the Ancient Mariner." 1798. *English Romantic Writers.* Ed. David Perkins. San Diego: Harcourt, 404–13.

Conley, Verena Andermatt. 1997. *Ecopolitics: The Environment in Poststructuralist Thought.* London and New York: Routledge.

Cooper, David E. 1992. "The Idea of Environment." *The Environment in Question: Ethics and Global Issues.* Ed. David E. Cooper and Joy A. Palmer. London and New York: Routledge, 165–80.

Crehan, Stewart. 1984. *Blake in Context.* Goldenbridge, Dublin: Gill and MacMillan/Humanities Press.

Curran, Stuart. 1973. "The Structures of *Jerusalem*." *Blake's Sublime Allegory: Essays on "The Four Zoas," "Milton," "Jerusalem".* Ed. Stuart Curran and Joseph Anthony Wittreich. Madison, WI: University of Wisconsin Press, 329–46.

– 1986a. "Blake and the Gnostic Hyle: A Double Negative." *Essential Articles for the Study of William Blake, 1970–1984.* Ed. Nelson Hilton. Hamden, CT: Archon Books, 15–32.

– 1986b. *Poetic Form and British Romanticism.* New York and Oxford: Oxford University Press.

Curry, Walter C. 1947. "Milton's Chaos and Old Night." *Journal of English and Germanic Philology* 46: 38–52.

Damon, S. Foster. 1988. *A Blake Dictionary: The Ideas and Symbols of William Blake.* Rev. ed. Hanover and London: University Press of New England.

Danielson, Dennis Richard. 1982. *Milton's Good God: A Study in Literary Theodicy.* Cambridge: Cambridge University Press.

Darwin, Erasmus. 1803. *Zoonomia; or, The Laws of Organic Life.* Vol. 1. 2d American ed. Boston: D. Carlisle.

– 1973a. *The Botanic Garden.* 1791. Menston, Yorkshire, England: Scolar Press.

– 1973b. *The Temple of Nature; or, The Origin of Society.* 1803. Menston, Yorkshire, and London: Scolar Press.

De Luca, Vincent Arthur. 1991. *Words of Eternity: Blake and the Poetics of the Sublime.* Princeton: Princeton University Press.

Deen, Leonard W. 1983. *Conversing in Paradise: Poetic Genius and Identity-as-Community in Blake's Los.* Columbia and London: University of Missouri Press.

Den Otter, A.G. 1991. "The Question and *The Book of Thel*." *Studies in Romanticism* 30, no. 4: 633–55.

Derrida, Jacques. 1991. "At This Very Moment in This Work Here I Am." Trans. Ruben Berezdivin. *Re-Reading Levinas.* Ed. Robert Bernasconi and Simon Critchley. Bloomington and Indianapolis: Indiana University Press, 11–48.

– 1987. "On Reading Heidegger: An Outline of Remarks to the Essex Colloquium." *Research in Phenomenology* 17: 171–85.

– 1994. *Specters of Marx*. Trans. P. Kamuf. London and New York: Routledge.

Descartes, René. 1955. "Discourse on the Method of Rightly Conducting the Reason and Seeking for Truth in the Sciences." 1637. *The Philosophical Works of Descartes*. Vol. 1. Ed. and Trans. Elizabeth S. Haldane and G.R.T. Ross. New York: Dover, 81–130.

Dollimore, Jonathan. 1991. *Sexual Dissidence: Augustine to Wilde, Freud to Foucault*. Oxford: Clarendon Press.

Doskow, Minna. 1982a. "The Humanized Universe of Blake and Marx." *William Blake and the Moderns*. Ed. Robert J. Bertholf and Annette S. Levitt. Albany: State University of New York Press, 225–40.

– 1982b. *William Blake's "Jerusalem": Structure and Meaning in Poetry and Picture*. London and Toronto: Associated University Presses.

Dreyfus, Hubert L., and Paul Rabinow. 1982. *Michel Foucault: Beyond Structuralism and Hermeneutics*. Chicago: University of Chicago Press.

Dryzek, John S. 1995. "Green Reason: Communicative Ethics for the Biosphere." *Postmodern Environmental Ethics*. Ed. Max Oelschlaeger. Albany, NY: State University of New York Press, 101–18.

Duerr, Hans Peter. 1985. *Dreamtime: Concerning the Boundary Between Wilderness and Civilization*. Oxford: Blackwell.

Eaves, Morris, Robert N. Essick, and Joseph Viscomi. 1993a. Introduction. *The Book of Thel. William Blake: The Early Illuminated Books*. By William Blake. Ed. Morris Eaves, Robert N. Essick, and Joseph Viscomi. Princeton, NJ: Princeton University Press, 71–86.

– 1993b. Introduction. *Visions of the Daughters of Albion. William Blake: The Early Illuminated Books*. By William Blake. Ed. Morris Eaves, Robert N. Essick, and Joseph Viscomi. Princeton, NJ: Princeton University Press, 1993, 225–42.

Eisenberg, Evan. 1998. *The Ecology of Eden*. Toronto: Random House.

Erdman, David V. 1961. "Blake: The Historical Approach." *Discussions of William Blake*. Ed. John E. Grant. Boston: Heath, 17–27.

– 1969. *Blake, Prophet against Empire: A Poet's Interpretation of the History of His Own Times*. 1954. Rev. ed. Princeton: Princeton University Press.

– 1974. *The Illuminated Blake: William Blake's Complete Illuminated Works with a Plate-by-Plate Commentary*. New York: Dover.

Essick, Robert N. 1989. *William Blake and the Language of Adam*. Oxford: Clarendon Press.

Essick, Robert N., and Joseph Viscomi. 1993. Introduction and Notes. William Blake. *Milton a Poem*. Ed. Robert N. Essick and Joseph Viscomi. Princeton, NJ: William Blake Trust/Princeton University Press.

Evelyn, John. 1664. *Sylva, or A Discourse of Forest-Trees, and the Propagation of Timber in His Majesties Dominions*. London: Royal Society.

Evernden, Neil. 1985. *The Natural Alien*. Toronto, Buffalo, and London: University of Toronto Press.

– 1992. *The Social Creation of Nature*. Baltimore and London: Johns Hopkins University Press.

Fauvel, John, Raymond Flood, Robin J. Wilson, and Michael Shortland. 1988. Introduction. *Let Newton Be!* Ed. John Fauvel et al. Oxford, New York, and Tokyo: Oxford University Press, 1–21.

Ferry, Luc. 1995. *The New Ecological Order*. Trans. Carol Volk. Chicago and London: University of Chicago Press.

Fisher, Peter F. 1961. "Blake and the Druids." *Discussions of William Blake*. Ed. John E. Grant. Boston: Heath, 28–43.

Ford, George H. 1965. *Dickens and His Readers: Aspects of Novel Criticism Since 1836*. New York: Norton.

Foucault, Michel. 1972. *The Discourse on Language*. Trans. Rupert Swyer. *The Order of Things: An Archaeology of the Human Sciences*. New York: Vintage, 215–37.

– 1977a. "Nietzsche, Genealogy, History." Trans. Donald F. Bouchard and Sherry Simon. *Language, Counter-Memory, Practice*. Ithaca, NY: Cornell University Press, 139–64.

– 1977b. "What Is an Author?" Trans. Donald F. Bouchard and Sherry Simon. *Language, Counter-Memory, Practice*. Ithaca, NY: Cornell University Press, 113–38.

– 1980. *The History of Sexuality*. Trans. Robert Hurley. New York: Vintage.

– 1982. "Afterword: The Subject and Power." *Michel Foucault: Beyond Structuralism and Hermeneutics*. Ed. Hubert L. Dreyfus and Paul Rabinow. Chicago: University of Chicago Press, 208–26.

– 1988. "Politics and Reason." Trans. Alan Sheridan. *Michel Foucault: Politics, Philosophy, Culture: Interviews and Other Writings*. Ed. Lawrence D. Kritzman. New York and London: Routledge, 57–85.

– 1991. "Politics and the Study of Discourse." Trans. Colin Gordon. *The Foucault Effect: Studies in Governmentality*. Ed. Graham Burchell, Colin Gordon, and Peter Miller. Chicago: University of Chicago Press, 53–72.

– 1994. *The Order of Things: An Archaeology of the Human Sciences*. New York: Vintage.

– 1995. *Discipline and Punish: The Birth of the Prison*. 2d ed. Trans. Alan Sheridan. New York: Vintage.

Frosch, Thomas R. 1974. *The Awakening of Albion: The Renovation of the Body in the Poetry of William Blake*. Ithaca and London: Cornell University Press.

Frost, Isaac. 1846. *Two Systems of Astronomy: First, The Newtonian System, … Second, The System in Accordance with the Holy Scriptures*. London: Simpkin, Marshall.

Frye, Northrop. 1970. *Fearful Symmetry: A Study of William Blake*. 1947. Reprint. Princeton, NJ: Princeton University Press.

Galileo. 1967. "The Assayer: A Letter to the Illustrious and Very Reverend Don Virginio Cesarini." 1623. *Discoveries and Opinions of Galileo*. Trans. Stillman Drake. Garden City, NY: Doubleday, 231–80.

Gjertsen, Derek. 1988. "Newton's Success." *Let Newton Be!* Ed. John Fauvel et al. Oxford, New York, and Tokyo: Oxford University Press, 23–41.

Glanville, Joseph. 1668. *Plus Ultra; or, the Progress and Advancement of Knowledge Since the Days of Aristotle*. London: James Collins.

Gleckner, Robert F. 1959. *The Piper and the Bard: A Study of William Blake*. Detroit: Wayne State University Press.

– 1960. "Blake's *Thel* and the Bible." *Bulletin of the New York Public Library* 64: 573–80.

Golinski, Jan. 1988. "The Secret Life of an Alchemist." *Let Newton Be!* Ed. John Fauvel et al. Oxford, New York, and Tokyo: Oxford University Press, 147–67.

Greenberg, Mark L. 1983. "Blake's 'Science.'" *Studies in Eighteenth-Century Culture*. 12: 115–30.

Hagstrum, Jean H. 1966. "William Blake Rejects the Enlightenment." *Blake: A Collection of Critical Essays*. Ed. Northrop Frye. Englewood Cliffs, NJ: Prentice-Hall, 142–55.

– 1973. "Babylon Revisited, or the Story of Luvah and Vala." *Blake's Sublime Allegory: Essays on "The Four Zoas," "Milton," "Jerusalem"*. Ed. Stuart Curran and Joseph Anthony Wittreich. Madison, WI: University of Wisconsin Press, 101–18.

Hargrove, Eugene C. 1992a. "Animal Welfare Ethics 'versus' Environmental Ethics: The Problem of Sentient Life." *The Animal Rights/Environmental Ethics Debate: The Environmental Perspective*. Ed. Eugene C. Hargrove. Albany, NY: State University of New York Press, ix–xxvi.

– 1992b. "Foundations of Wildlife Protection Attitudes." *The Animal Rights/ Environmental Ethics Debate: The Environmental Perspective*. Ed. Eugene C. Hargrove. Albany, NY: State University of New York Press, 151–83.

Harris, Errol E. 1991. *Cosmos and Anthropos: A Philosophical Interpretation of the Anthropic Cosmological Principle*. New Jersey and London: Humanities Press.

Harrison, Robert Pogue. 1992. *Forests: The Shadow of Civilization*. Chicago and London: University of Chicago Press.

Hassler, Donald M. 1973. *Erasmus Darwin*. New York: Twayne.

Hayley, William. 1782. *An Essay on Epic Poetry*. London: J. Dodsley.

Henry, John. 1988. "Newton, Matter, and Magic." *Let Newton Be!* Ed. John Fauvel et al. Oxford, New York, and Tokyo: Oxford University Press. 127–45.

Hill, Christopher. 1977. *Milton and the English Revolution*. London: Faber and Faber.

Hilton, Nelson. 1981. "The Spectre of Darwin." *Blake: An Illustrated Quarterly* 15, no. 1: 36–48.

– 1983. *Literal Imagination: Blake's Vision of Words*. Berkeley, Los Angeles, and London: University of California Press.

Hirst, Desirée. 1964. *Hidden Riches: Traditional Symbolism from the Renaissance to Blake*. New York: Barnes and Noble.

Houghton, Walter E. 1957. *The Victorian Frame of Mind, 1830–1870*. London: Oxford University Press.

Howarth, William. 1996. "Some Principles of Ecocriticism." *The Ecocriticism Reader: Landmarks in Literary Ecology*. Ed. Cheryl Glotfelty and Harold Fromm. Athens, GA, and London: University of Georgia Press, 69–91.

Hutchings, Kevin. 1996. "The Devil of the Stairs: Negotiating the Turn in T.S. Eliot's *Ash-Wednesday*." *Yeats Eliot Review* 14, no. 2: 26–35.

– 1997. "Locating the Satanic: Blake's *Milton* and the Poetics of Self-Examination." *European Romantic Review* 8, no. 3: 274–97.

Irigaray, Luce. 1991. "This Sex Which Is Not One." 1981. Trans. Claudia Reeder. *Feminisms: An Anthology of Literary Theory and Criticism*. Ed. Robyn R. Warhol and Diane Price Herndl. New Brunswick, NJ: Rutgers University Press, 350–56.

John, Brian. 1974. *Supreme Fictions: Studies in the Work of William Blake, Thomas Carlyle, W.B. Yeats, and D.H. Lawrence*. Montreal and London: McGill-Queen's University Press.

Johnson, Mary Lynn. 1970. "Beulah, 'Mne Seraphim,' and Blake's *Thel*." *Journal of English and Germanic Philology* 69: 258–77.

– 1994. "Blake, Democritus, and the "Fluxions of the Atom': Some Contexts for Materialist Critiques." *Historicizing Blake*. Ed. Steve Clark and David Worrall. London: St Martin's Press, 105–24.

Jonas, Hans. 1968. *The Phenomenon of Life*. 1966. Reprint. New York: Dell.

Jones, W.P. 1937. "The Vogue of Natural History in England, 1750–1770." *Annals of Science: A Quarterly Review of the History of Science Since the Renaissance* 2: 345–56.

Katz, Eric. 1995. "The Call of the Wild: The Struggle against Domination and the Technological Fix of Nature." *Postmodern Environmental Ethics*. Ed. Max Oelschlaeger. Albany, NY: State University of New York Press, 163–72.

Kauver, Elaine. 1976–77. "Los's Messenger to Eden: Blake's Wild Thyme." *Blake Newsletter* 10: 82–4.

Keats, John. 1988. *John Keats: The Complete Poems*. 3d ed. London: Penguin.

Kemp, David D. 1990. *Global Environmental Issues*. London and New York: Routledge.

King, James. 1991. *William Blake: His Life*. London: Weidenfeld and Nicolson.

King-Hele, Desmond. 1986. *Erasmus Darwin and the Romantic Poets*. London: MacMillan.

Kiralis, Karl. 1961. "Intellectual Symbolism in Blake's Later Prophetic Writings." *Discussions of William Blake*. Ed. John E. Grant. Boston: Heath, 102–14.

– 1968. "'London' in the Light of *Jerusalem*." *Blake Studies* 1, no. 1: 5–15.

Klonsky, Milton. 1977. *William Blake: The Seer and His Visions*. New York: Harmony Books.

Krell, David Farrell. 1992. *Daimon Life: Heidegger and Life-Philosophy*. Bloomington and Indianapolis: Indiana University Press.

Kroeber, Karl. 1994. *Ecological Literary Criticism: Romantic Imagining and the Biology of Mind*. New York: Columbia University Press.

Larrissy, Edward. 1994. "'Self-Imposition', Alchemy, and the Fate of the 'Bound' in Later Blake." *Historicizing Blake*. Ed. Steve Clark and David Worrall. New York: St Martin's Press, 59–72.

Lawrence, John. 1796. *A Philosophical and Practical Treatise on Horses, and on the Moral Duties of Man towards the Brute Creation*. Vol. 1. London.

Lee, Dennis. 1977. *Savage Fields: An Essay in Literature and Cosmology*. Toronto: Anansi Press.

Leonard, David Charles. 1978. "Erasmus Darwin and William Blake." *Eighteenth-Century Life* 4.3: 79–81.

Lesnick, Henry. 1970. "Narrative Structure and the Antithetical Vision of *Jerusalem*." *Blake's Visionary Forms Dramatic*. Ed. David V. Erdman and John E. Grant. Princeton: Princeton University Press, 391–412.

Levinson, Marjorie. 1980. "'The Book of Thel' by William Blake: A Critical Reading." *ELH* 47: 287–303.

Liu, Alan. 1989. *Wordsworth: The Sense of History*. Stanford: Stanford University Press.

Lovejoy, Arthur O. 1953. *The Great Chain of Being: A Study of the History of an Idea*. Cambridge, MA: Harvard University Press.

Lovelock, J.E. 1987. *Gaia: A New Look at Life on Earth*. Rev. ed. Oxford and New York: Oxford University Press.

Lussier, Mark S. 1994. "Blake's Vortex: The Quantum Tunnel in *Milton*." *Nineteenth-Century Contexts* 18: 263–91.

– 1996. "Blake's Deep Ecology." *Studies in Romanticism* 35, no. 3: 393–408.

Malkin, Benjamin Heath. 1806. *A Father's Memoirs of His Child*. London: T. Bensley.

Manes, Christopher. 1996. "Nature and Silence." *The Ecocriticism Reader: Landmarks in Literary Ecology*. Ed. Cheryl Glotfelty and Harold Fromm. Athens, GA, and London: University of Georgia Press, 15–29.

Manuel, Frank E. 1974. *The Religion of Isaac Newton*. Oxford: Clarendon P.

– 1980. *A Portrait of Isaac Newton*. London: Frederick Muller.

Mayr, Ernst. 1992. "The Idea of Teleology." *Journal of the History of Ideas* 53, no. 1: 117–35.

Mazel, David. 1996. "American Literary Environmentalism as Domestic Orientalism." *The Ecocriticism Reader: Landmarks in Literary Ecology.* Ed. Cheryl Glotfelty and Harold Fromm. Athens, GA, and London: University of Georgia Press, 137–46.

McCalman, Iain. 1994. "The Infidel as Prophet: William Reid and Blakean Radicalism." *Historicizing Blake.* Ed. Steve Clark and David Worrall. New York: St Martin's Press, 24–42.

McKusick, James C. 1996. "Coleridge and the Economy of Nature." *Studies in Romanticism* 35, no. 3: 375–92.

McNeil, Maureen. 1988. "Newton as National Hero." *Let Newton Be!* Ed. John Fauvel et al. Oxford, New York, and Tokyo: Oxford University Press, 223–39.

Mee, Jon. 1992. *Dangerous Enthusiasm: William Blake and the Culture of Radicalism in the 1790s.* Oxford: Clarendon Press.

– 1994. "Is There an Antinomian in the House? William Blake and the After-Life of a Heresy." *Historicizing Blake.* Ed. Steve Clark and David Worrall. New York: St Martin's Press, 43–58.

Mellor, Anne Kostelanetz. 1974. *Blake's Human Form Divine.* Berkeley, Los Angeles, and London: University of California Press.

– 1988. *Mary Shelley: Her Life, Her Fictions, Her Monsters.* New York and London: Methuen.

Merchant, Carolyn. 1980. *The Death of Nature: Women, Ecology, and the Scientific Revolution.* San Francisco: Harper.

Midgley, Mary. 1992a. "The Significance of Species." *The Animal Rights/Environmental Ethics Debate: The Environmental Perspective.* Ed. Eugene C. Hargrove. Albany, NY: State University of New York Press, 121–36.

– 1992b. "Towards a More Humane View of the Beasts?" *The Environment in Question: Ethics and Global Issues.* Ed. David E. Cooper and Joy A. Palmer. London and New York: Routledge, 28–36.

Milton, John. 1992. *John Milton.* New York: Oxford University Press.

Miner, Paul. 1960. "The Polyp as a Symbol in the Poetry of William Blake." *Texas Studies in Literature and Language* 2: 198–205.

Mitchell, W.J.T. 1970. "Blake's Composite Art." *Blake's Visionary Forms Dramatic.* Ed. David V. Erdman and John E. Grant. Princeton, NJ: Princeton University Press, 57–81.

– 1978. *Blake's Composite Art.* Princeton, NJ: Princeton University Press.

Morton, A.L. 1966. *The Everlasting Gospel: A Study in the Sources of William Blake.* 1958. Reprint. New York: Haskell House.

Muggleton, Lodowick. 1662. *A True Interpretation of the Eleventh Chapter of the Revelation of St John.* British Library, Muggletonian Archive, MS 60250. N.p.

Munby, A.N.L., ed. 1971. "A Catalogue of the Very Valuable and Extensive Library of the Late William Hayley, Esq." *Sale Catalogues of Libraries of Eminent Persons.* Vol. 2. *Poets and Men of Letters.* London: Parke-Bernet, 83–171.

Naess, Arne. 1984. "Identification as a Source of Deep Ecological Attitudes." *Deep Ecology*. Ed. Michael Tobias. San Diego: Avant Books, 256–70.

Nash, Roderick. 1989. *The Rights of Nature: A History of Environmental Ethics*. Madison, WI: University of Wisconsin Press.

Nasr, Seyyed Hossein. 1996. *Religion and the Order of Nature*. New York: Oxford University Press.

Neale, R.S. 1976. "Bath: Ideology and Utopia, 1700–1760." *Studies in the Eighteenth Century*. Vol. 3. Ed. R.F. Brissenden and J.C. Eade. Toronto and Buffalo: University of Toronto Press, 37–54.

Newton, Isaac. 1733. *Observations Upon the Prophecies of Daniel, and the Apocalypse of St John*. London.

– 1962. *Philosophiae Naturalis Principia Mathematica*. Vol. 1. 1729. Trans. Andrew Motte. Trans. revised by Florian Cajori. Berkeley, Los Angeles, and London: University of California Press.

Nietzsche, Friedrich. 1982. *The Portable Nietzsche*. Trans. Walter Kaufmann. Reprint. New York: Penguin.

Northcott, Michael S. 1996. *The Environment and Christian Ethics*. Cambridge: Cambridge University Press.

Norvig, Gerda S. 1995. "Female Subjectivity and the Desire of Reading In(to) Blake's *Book of Thel*." *Studies in Romanticism* 34, no. 2: 255–71.

Oelschlaeger, Max. 1991. *The Idea of Wilderness from Prehistory to the Age of Ecology*. New Haven and London: Yale University Press.

Otto, Peter. 1991. *Constructive Vision and Visionary Deconstruction: Los, Eternity, and the Productions of Time in the Later Poetry of William Blake*. Oxford: Clarendon Press.

Paley, Morton D. 1983. *The Continuing City: William Blake's "Jerusalem."* Oxford: Clarendon Press.

– 1985. "'A New Heaven Is Begun': Blake and Swedenborgianism." *Blake and Swedenborg: Opposition Is True Friendship*. Ed. Harvey F. Bellin and Darrell Ruhl. New York: Swedenborg Foundation, 15–34.

– 1991. Introduction and Notes. *Jerusalem, The Emanation of the Giant Albion*. By William Blake. Ed. Morton D. Paley. Princeton, NJ: Princeton University Press.

Parker, Kelly A. 1996. "Pragmatism and Environmental Thought." *Environmental Pragmatism*. Ed. Andrew Light and Eric Katz. London and New York: Routledge, 21–37.

Pearce, Donald R. 1978. "Natural Religion and the Plight of Thel." *Blake Studies* 8, no. 1: 23–35.

Perkins, David, ed. 1967. *English Romantic Writers*. San Diego: Harcourt.

Peterfreund, Stuart. 1990. "Blake and Anti-Newtonian Thought." *Beyond the Two Cultures: Essays on Science, Technology, and Literature*. Ed. Joseph W. Slade and Judith Yaross Lee. Ames, IA: Iowa State University Press, 141–60.

– 1998. *William Blake in a Newtonian World: Essays on Literature as Art and Science*. Norman, OK: University of Oklahoma Press.

Pite, Ralph. 1996. "How Green Were the Romantics?" *Studies in Romanticism* 35, no. 3: 357–73.

Plant, Judith. 1997. "Learning to Live with Differences: The Challenge of Ecofeminist Community." *Ecofeminism: Women, Culture, Nature*. Ed. Karen J. Warren. Bloomington and Indianapolis: Indiana University Press, 120–39.

Pope, Alexander. 1733. *An Essay on Man*. Dublin.

Prigogine, Ilya, and Isabelle Stengers. 1984. *Order out of Chaos: Man's New Dialogue with Nature*. Boulder and London: New Science Library.

Prior, Moody E. 1964. "Bacon's Man of Science." *The Rise of Science in Relation to Society*. Ed. Leonard M. Marsak. New York and London: Macmillan, 41–54.

Punter, David. 1981. "Blake: 'Active Evil' and 'Passive Good.'" *Romanticism and Ideology*. Ed. David Aers, Jonathan Cook and David Punter. London, Boston, and Henley: Routledge and Kegan Paul, 7–26.

– 1997. "Blake: His Shadowy Animals." *Studies in Romanticism* 36, no. 2: 227–38.

Quigley, Peter. 1995. "Rethinking Resistance: Environmentalism, Literature, and Poststructural Theory." *Postmodern Environmental Ethics*. Ed. Max Oelschlaeger. Albany, NY: State University of New York Press, 173–91.

Raine, Kathleen. 1985. "The Swedenborgian Songs." *Blake and Swedenborg: Opposition Is True Friendship*. Ed. Harvey F. Bellin and Darrell Ruhl. New York: Swedenborg Foundation, 69–85.

Rajan, Tilottama. 1990. *The Supplement of Reading: Figures of Understanding in Romantic Theory and Practice*. Ithaca, NY, and London: Cornell University Press.

Reeve, John. 1652. *A Transcendent Spiritual Treatise*. British Library, Muggletonian Archive, MS 60246. N.p.

Reeve, John, and Lodowick Muggleton. 1760. *A Divine Looking-Glass*. 1656. 4th ed. British Library, Muggletonian Archive, MS 60252. N.p.

Reiss, Timothy J. 1982. *The Discourse of Modernism*. Ithaca, NY, and London: Cornell University Press.

Riede, David. 1978. *Swinburne: A Study of Romantic Mythmaking*. Charlottesville: University Press of Virginia.

– 1987. "Blake's *Milton*: on Membership in the Church Paul." *Re-membering Milton: Essays on the Texts and Traditions*. Ed. Mary Nyquist and Margaret W. Ferguson. New York and London: Methuen, 257–77.

Rose, Edward J. 1970. "'Forms Eternal Exist Forever': The Covenant of the Harvest in Blake's Prophetic Poems." *Blake's Visionary Forms Dramatic*. Ed. David V. Erdman and John E. Grant. Princeton, NJ: Princeton University Press, 443–62.

Rousseau, G.S. 1976. "Nerves, Spirits, and Fibres: Towards Defining the Origins of Sensibility." *Studies in the Eighteenth Century.* Vol. 3. Ed. R.F. Brissenden and J.C. Eade. Toronto and Buffalo: University of Toronto Press, 137–57.

Rousseau, Jean-Jacques. 1993. *Émile.* 1762. Trans. Barbara Foxley. London: Everyman.

Said, Edward W. 1979. *Orientalism.* New York: Vintage.

Salleh, Ariel. 1995. "Class, Race and Gender Discourse in the Ecofeminism/ Deep Ecology Debate." *Postmodern Environmental Ethics.* Ed. Max Oelschlaeger. Albany, NY: State University of New York Press, 79–100.

Schama, Simon. 1996. *Landscape and Memory.* Toronto: Vintage.

Schorer, Mark. 1959. *William Blake: The Politics of Vision.* 1946. Reprint. New York: Vintage.

Schwartz, Regina. 1988. *Remembering and Repeating Biblical Creation in "Paradise Lost."* Cambridge and New York: Cambridge University Press.

Serres, Michel. 1992. "The Natural Contract." Trans. Felicia McCarren. *Critical Inquiry* 19: 1–21.

Shakespeare, William. 1969. *William Shakespeare: The Complete Works.* Ed. Alfred Harbage. London and New York: Penguin.

Sherover, Charles M. 1975. *The Human Experience of Time: The Development of Its Philosophic Meaning.* New York: New York University Press.

Smith, Adam. 1937. *The Wealth of Nations.* 1776. New York: Modern Library.

Soper, Kate. *What Is Nature?* Oxford and Cambridge, MA: Blackwell, 1995.

Swedenborg, Emanuel. 1781. *True Christian Religion; Containing the Universal Theology of the New Church.* 2 vols. London.

Tarr, Rodger L. 1971. "'The Eagle' Versus 'the Mole': The Wisdom of Virginity in *Comus* and *The Book of Thel*." *Blake Studies* 3, no. 2: 187–94.

Taylor, Charles. 1975. *Hegel.* Cambridge: Cambridge University Press.

– 1989. *Sources of the Self: The Making of the Modern Identity.* Cambridge, MA: Harvard University Press.

Taylor, Paul W. 1992. "The Ethics of Respect for Nature." *The Animal Rights/ Environmental Ethics Debate: The Environmental Perspective.* Ed. Eugene C. Hargrove. Albany, NY: State University of New York Press, 95–120.

Taylor, Thomas. 1792. *A Vindication of the Rights of Brutes.* London.

Thompson, E.P. 1975a. *The Making of the English Working Class.* 1963. Reprint. Harmondsworth: Penguin.

– 1975b. *Whigs and Hunters: The Origin of the Black Act.* London: Penguin.

– 1993. *Witness against the Beast: William Blake and the Moral Law.* New York: New Press.

Tillich, Paul. 1967. *A History of Christian Thought from Its Judaic and Hellenistic Origins to Existentialism.* New York: Simon and Schuster.

Toffler, Alvin. 1984. "Science and Change." *Order Out of Chaos: Man's New Dialogue with Nature.* By Ilya Prigogine and Isabelle Stengers. Boulder and London: New Science Library, xi–xxvi.

Tomkinson, Thomas. 1724. *Truth's Triumph: or, A Witness to the Two Witnesses, Part VII*. British Library, Muggletonian Archive, MS 60255A. N.p.

Vogt, Anton. 1982. "Environmental Ethics in Fourfold Time." *Sparks of Fire: Blake in a New Age*. Ed. James Bogan and Fred Goss. Richmond, CA: North Atlantic Books, 407–19.

Warburton, William. 1742. *The Divine Legation of Moses Demonstrated on the Principles of a Religious Deist*. Vol. 2. London.

Warren, Karen J. 1996. "Ecological Feminist Philosophies: An Overview of the Issues." *Ecological Feminist Philosophies*. Ed. Karen J. Warren. Bloomington and Indianapolis: Indiana University Press, ix–xxvi.

Warren, Mary Anne. 1992. "The Rights of the Nonhuman World." *The Animal Rights/Environmental Ethics Debate: The Environmental Perspective*. Ed. Eugene C. Hargrove. Albany, NY: State University of New York Press, 185–210.

Watson, Lyall. 1990. *The Nature of Things: The Secret Life of Inanimate Objects*. London: Hodder and Stoughton.

Webster, Brenda S. 1983. *Blake's Prophetic Psychology*. London and Basingstoke: MacMillan Press.

Whiston, William. 1696. *A New Theory of the Earth, from Its Original, to the Consummation of All Things*. London.

White, Lynn, Jr. 1996. "The Historic Roots of our Ecologic Crisis." *The Ecocriticism Reader: Landmarks in Literary Ecology*. Ed. Cheryl Glotfelty and Harold Fromm. Athens, GA, and London: University of Georgia Press, 3–14.

Wicksteed, Joseph H. 1971. *Blake's Vision of the Book of Job with Reproductions of the Illustrations*. 1910. Reprint. New York: Haskell House.

Wilkie, Brian. 1990. *Blake's Thel and Oothoon*. Victoria, BC: English Literary Studies Monograph Series. Vol. 48.

Wilkinson, J.J. Garth. 1839. Preface. *Songs of Innocence and of Experience*. By William Blake. Ed. J.J. Garth Wilkinson. London.

Williams, Raymond. 1973. *The Country and the City*. New York: Oxford University Press.

Wilson, Alexander. 1992. *Culture and Nature: North American Landscape from Disney to the Exxon Valdez*. Oxford: Blackwell.

Wilson, Edward O. 1992. *The Diversity of Life*. New York and London: Norton.

Wilson, Luke. 1987. "William Harvey's *Prelectiones*: The Performance of the Body in the Renaissance Theater of Anatomy." *Representations* 17: 62–95.

Wittreich, Joseph Anthony, Jr. 1972. "Domes of Mental Pleasure: Blake's Epics and Hayley's Epic Theory." *Studies in Philology* 69: 101–29.

– 1973. "Opening the Seals: Blake's Epics and the Milton Tradition." *Blake's Sublime Allegory: Essays on "The Four Zoas," "Milton," "Jerusalem."* Ed. Stuart Curran and Joseph Anthony Wittreich. Madison, WI, and London: University of Wisconsin Press, 23–58.

– 1978. "Blake's Milton: 'To Immortals ... A Mighty Angel.'" *Milton Studies* 11: 51–82.

Wollstonecraft, Mary. 1982. *A Vindication of the Rights of Woman: With Strictures on Political and Moral Subjects*. 1792. Edited by Ulrich H. Hardt. Troy, NY: Whitson.

Wordsworth, William. 1967. "The Tables Turned." 1798. *English Romantic Writers*. Ed. David Perkins. San Diego: Harcourt, 209.

Worrall, David. 1975. "William Blake and Erasmus Darwin's *Botanic Garden*." *Bulletin of the New York Public Library* 78, no. 4: 397–417.

Worster, Donald. 1995. *Nature's Economy: A History of Ecological Ideas*. 1977. 2d ed. Cambridge: Cambridge University Press.

Youngquist, Paul. 1993. "Reading the Apocalypse: The Narrativity of Blake's *Jerusalem*." *Studies in Romanticism* 32, no. 4: 601–25.

Index